~~I Understand~~

What the Hell was I Thinking?

by Christine Harris

EPI

Andover, MN

ISBN 13: 978-1-931045-37-0
ISBN 10: 1-931945-37-3

Library of Congress Catalog Number: 2005932626

Printed in the United States of America

First Printing: October 2005

Andover,
MN

Expert Publishing, Inc.
14314 Thrush Street NW
Andover, MN 55304-3330
1-877-755-4966
www.ExpertPublishingInc.com

DEDICATION

---■---

To: Lueck and Katherine,
     the cornerstones of my life.

I would have never made it this far without the two of you. You have given me reasons not only to survive life, but to live life.

I will love you always, and I like you too.
Mom

CONTENTS

ACKNOWLEDGEMENTS

I could not have written this book without the support of so many people. I would like to thank all my friends who encouraged me to write. I will not forget you. Thank you to those who read and critiqued my writing before it was published. Luann and Linda, I thank you for caring about me and not caring for me. That showed you believed in me enough that I could handle my problems.

I thank Expert Publishing, for all the knowledge they have about publishing books and to Doug Dybsetter and Jerri Morris who designed the covers of the book.

I am so thankful for my mom and dad who gave me a solid foundation in life. And thank you to my current friends who are always there for me. Life is good.

INTRODUCTION

This story of my life is written to help anyone who has been in an abusive relationship where family and friends are telling you to get out. I want you to know that I understand how you feel. I understand when you say you still love a person even though they abuse you mentally and/or physically. I understand why you stay in the marriage even though you know you should leave. I understand when you want to take your children and kill them along with yourself. I have been there. But I am not there any longer. Looking back at my marriage, I see how wrong I was to stay in a place that was not safe for my family. I can't go back and change anything. I feel I did the best I could at the time. I can't change the past, but I can learn from it. And I can share my experience with you.

As I wrote my story and I relived many of the feelings I tried so hard to hide for so many years. At the beginning of most chapters, and sometimes in between chapters, I captured how I was feeling as I was writing this book. I want to share those thoughts and feelings with you. It was my healing journey. Once a situation is over, it doesn't mean everything instantly becomes okay. The wounds are there and they take many years to heal. They do heal.

CHAPTER 1

THE CALL

Just as I was hanging up the phone I heard the loud noise. Was it a gunshot or a door banging? I held the phone to my ear in stunned silence when I heard the same sickening noise again. I hung up with panic overtaking my whole body and called 911. I cried, while trying to control my voice, that I thought my husband just shot himself. I wasn't sure; it could have just been a door slamming. He could just be playing games with me. I asked them to please do a welfare check on him to make sure he was okay. As the five or six police cars rushed past my house to the apartment where my husband was living, I pleaded with the 911 operator to please have the police turn the sirens off. I told the dispatcher that if Phil had not shot himself he would be so mad at me for calling the police. He was mad at me already, and I couldn't handle any more of his anger. I begged again to please turn off the lights and sirens and just check on him quietly.

I didn't remember Phil's address since he had just moved in there the previous month. It was a small town and I knew how to get to his place. I told the dispatcher how to get there and what apartment he was in. I could not remember the number of his room, but it was on the third floor farthest away from the road. Once the police found and entered the apartment the operator told me to stand by my phone and she hung up. I knew it was not good news when she would no longer talk to me.

I didn't know who to call. I had to talk to someone. I was so scared. I had a nephew Dan who lived a mile from me. I didn't want to call him because I didn't want him judging Phil or worrying about me any more than he did already. I didn't call my sister Luann who lived one hour from me for the same reasons. I figured I got myself in this mess and I had to figure a way out. I used the cell phone and called our counselor, Gwen, who both Phil and I were seeing on a weekly basis. Gwen talked to me and told me she really didn't think Phil would kill himself. She had just seen him the previous day and he was doing okay. But I knew in my heart she was wrong.

While Gwen and I were talking, the dreaded knock on the door came. I ended our call, and Gwen drove the three blocks to my house. There they stood, bigger than life, two policemen asking me if I was Chris Harris. I felt like I was in a movie. This was not real life. I knew. I knew he was dead. I don't remember what the police said, except that they were sorry.

Anger overtook my body. I looked at the police officers and wanted them to know how angry I was at Phil for shooting himself. My small hundred-year-old house was not large enough for my anger. I turned and walked from my small living room into my dining room where my aunt's square antique table sat with four empty chairs. From there I walked into my kitchen where the defected floor slanted towards the middle of house. The entire time I was pacing from one room to the next, I was pounding my fist on the painted paneled walls. I could hear the old plasterboard falling from the slates behind the paneling. How dare he do this to me. I was angry and yelling at Phil. "Damn you, Phil. Damn you, Phil. Damn you, Phil. DAMN YOU, PHIL! How could you do this? How could you do this? I stayed with you for twenty-four miserable years just so you could be a dad and the kids would have a father, and you took that all away from them. Damn you, Phil."

I felt that dads are very important to their children, and Phil took their dad away from our children. He did it to get even with me for leaving him. I hated that he did not think of his children's future. He didn't think that some days his children would need his advice and his hugs. He didn't think about his future grandchildren and how much they will need him too. I felt he thought only about was how much he hated me and what he could do to get even with me for leaving him.

Gwen arrived and I started to pull myself together enough to make phone calls. I was so tired and I just wanted to go to bed. I didn't want to think anymore. I wanted to go to bed so I could wake up from this nightmare. But my nightmare was real life. I first called my thirty-five-year-old nephew Dan, who came over right way to see if I needed anything. He called his mom, my sister Luann. This was real. This was really happening.

■ That is just how I feel when writing this. I feel all the pain all over again. Tears are trying to wash away the pain, but there is so much pain that I feel I might drown in the tears before they stop flowing from my eyes.

Once Dan saw Gwen was with me, he headed over to Phil's apartment building to see if he had to do anything there. The police told him he did not have to go into the apartment. I don't believe he did.

I had to call our children. I didn't want to call our children. What would I tell them?

I called Phil's Uncle Norm in Portland, Oregon, who lived near Lueck, our nineteen-year-old son. I told Norm what had happened and asked if he would go and tell Lueck that Phil just died. I also asked him to call Donna and Jim, Phil's parents, and let them know the bloody news too.

I thought of Kati, our eighteen-year-old daughter. Where was she and how was I going to tell her that her father just shot himself and is now dead? She was daddy's little girl who tried so hard to make him happy.

■   I have to take a break from writing now and refresh my soul with a few laughs by watching my grandnephew Josh play flag football and then head over to watch my daughter, Kati, play college soccer. You should do that too. Go find something that will make you laugh. Laughing is good for the soul. It heals lots of wounds. Live life while you can.

CHAPTER 2

MY EARLY YEARS

My sisters say I was born an only child. As I see it, they were right. My dad, Harold, was forty; my mom, Vivian, was thirty-four; Luann was eleven; and Linda was eight when I came into this world.

My parents bought a small grocery store in Lafayette, Minnesota, when I was three or four years old. It was a magical small grocery store in a little town of five hundred people where everyone knew everyone. The outside of the store was painted red, with two large square windows showing spray painted signs telling of the weekly specials. The two large Kasota steps led to the inset screen door which, in turn, led to the red painted wood door which, in turn, led into the store. I spent many hours sitting, watching people come and go into our tiny grocery store. Above the outside of the store was a painted metal sign that read "Harold's Grocery." At each end of the sign was the 7 Up logo.

In 1961, Lafayette was a booming town. It had three grocery stores, two gas stations, three restaurants, besides hardware, drug, and liquor stores, and a chicken hatchery. My friends and I hung out many days in the hardware store and the chicken hatchery because their parents owned those stores.

I am glad I experienced Harold's Grocery. The old wooden floor was home to a four-foot by four-foot metal heat grate that warmed old farmers' cold feet on cold winter days as they caught up on the latest news. In the winter a large cardboard box of salted-in-the-shell peanuts stood next to the floor grate. Without much thought of having to pay for them, visiting customers munched on peanuts. My parents valued their customers and felt "what was one peanut, or maybe two, or twenty among friends?" I don't remember either of my parents ever saying anything to their customers about paying for the peanuts they ate. There were two rows of shelves, maybe fifteen to twenty feet long, in the middle of the store. One side of the shelf held the breads and cookies and faced the counter where mom and dad stood adding up the total of groceries that were sold as they talked to customers as friends, because they were. My parents used a brown adding machine with a paper tape and a handle on the right side. I can still hear the clicking of the keys on the adding machine as my parents' caring hands added each item. When I was just a tot I was allowed to bag the groceries in brown paper bags. Sometimes we would give Green or Gold stamps customers could use to buy a variety of things from catalogs.

As a small child, I slept on the lowest bread shelf while waiting for Dad and Mom, who had already worked fifteen hours, to close the store so we could go home and eat ice cream. Spending many hours in the grocery store was like living in a storybook with all the strange and wonderful characters. I learned to love the people and respect each person for who they were and what they had or didn't have. I learned to have patience.

To the right of Harold's Grocery was the yellow hatchery built with the same style storefront as Harold's. That is where I met my first friend, John. He was the same age as me, about four, and also had chosen to spend the day with his dad on the main drag of Lafayette. It was so great having a friend my age to talk to, so when he asked to ride my red tricycle one day, of course I shared it. I remember wanting to ask for it back so I could have a turn, but I could not get myself to ask

John. No one asked for anything in my family. My parents were very giving people, and I was learning to do the same.

My family was also very loving. I don't remember any fights or name-calling or any abuse of any kind. My parents went to all my activities as I advanced in life without ever telling me to do better. They just loved me for who I was. When I was on stage modeling my flop of a dress that I had sewn for 4-H, my dad commented that I was the prettiest one there, even though I won nothing. My mom stood by my side as I made mistakes, never putting me down with words or actions.

My sister Linda and I fought like normal sisters. I figured out at a young age that if I didn't do dishes quick enough for her, she would yell at me and tell me to get out of the kitchen. That was an easy way to get out of dishes. I once told Linda to shut up and she gave me the riot act. I felt as if I told her to die or something. I never told her to shut up again.

Luann was married when I was in first grade. I became an aunt to Dan when I was in second grade. Linda left for college when I was beginning fourth grade and that made me an only child with older parents who loved me very much. The truth was, I was a very spoiled child, but not a brat. I had a lot of clothes, went out with my friends, got the car most times I asked for it, but when I was told no, I usually didn't argue. I already knew material things did not make me happy. Sharing is what made me happy, but then again, maybe I needed to make other people happy so I could feel good about myself. I loved to work so I could buy Christmas presents for the family. I was born a giver and a feeler and a caretaker. As a tot I took turns sleeping with my stuffed animals so they would not get their feelings hurt if I slept with one more than the others. I cried watching the cartoon "Popeye the Sailor Man." At night, after saying my prayers, I would shout down the hall to my parents, "Goodnight Mom. Goodnight Dad. I love you, Dad. I love you, Mom." If I said one name first, I would make sure I said the other name first for the "I love you." At that point in my life there was nothing I could think of that would make me be so sensitive to other people's feelings or my desire to give of myself except for my parents' caring examples.

Across the street from Harold's, which had no running water and a dirt floor in the basement, was the liquor store. My parents were not drinkers, but there were children in the area who were not as lucky as I was. I remember one hot summer afternoon a dad came to town with three young worn children and left them in the car for hours while he drank his way through the day. These children were left without a place to go to the bathroom and without water and food. My dad went out to those children and gave them all ice cream. He never made a big deal about doing those little things that were so important.

My nephews and nieces, along with my cousins, always seemed to have a good time with my dad too. His grandchildren knew they could go behind the counter of the store to the candy shelf to fill a small brown paper bag full of candy before they headed for home. When I was with my cousins and I asked for money, Dad would open up his coin holder and offer my cousins money also.

My dad was also a good listener. He talked a good friend of his out of killing himself after his wife died. Dad also once talked a customer out of committing suicide after the customer had consumed too much booze. Mom and Dad would hold the town character's silver dollar until he had paper money to get it back. They never cheated anyone. They were a team. They had compassion.

Mom was also a giving person. Mom always had little children's books in her purse and she let children read them when we were in church or other places that children got bored. Mom was also the one that would work in their grocery store so Dad could take me to the high school basketball games. She cut people's hair when they could not afford to go to a beauty shop. They paid her perhaps a dollar per cut, if anything. She baked and shared with the neighbors or elderly people.

There were a few old men that would enter the store with filthy bodies and matching minds. Mom and I would go and hide in the back of the store until they left. Dad was always polite to these guys, but we knew they were not always polite in return. One of those dirty old drunken men was our neighbor and my Sunday school teacher, Emery. He tried to kiss us with his stale boozing cigarette thunder breath.

I am not sure how old I was, but I figure I was about eleven or twelve when Emery was teaching my Sunday school class of four young adults. Class was over and the other students left the room. I was by the bookshelf putting away the Sunday school books when Emery came over to me and placed his dirty, filthy, truck driving fingers between my legs. I was wearing a short spring green plaid dress and his Bible holding hands touched my panties. As he held his hand on my crotch, I just stood there in shock. I moved away from him acting as if nothing happen. I was silent. I left the room, not saying anything to anyone. I figured it must have been my fault. I knew Emery should not be trusted and I left myself alone with him. He had not been drinking, so I thought it would be okay. He was teaching us about God, so he must have been okay. I was wrong. He was not okay and it was not okay and I was not okay. I never told anyone about that day until I had kids of my own. It was just something that happened and not much thought was given to it. It was just Emery, and everyone knew he was a drunken perverted, truck driver that taught Sunday school. He was a lot worse than he was ever good.

I went to the grade school in Lafayette, Minnesota. We were basically the same twenty-four children throughout the seven years we attended the two-story brick building. They were good years—lots of birthday parties, friends, and great lunches. I was not the most popular girl in the class, but I had plenty of friends. I did have a crush on one of the boys from sixth to twelfth grade. I will save face and not mention his name because he never did ask me out. I dated a lot in high school. There were a few weekends that I would go out with three different guys from three different towns three nights in a row. They were all friends of mine and knew about each other. I went out for a fun time of talking, partying, and dancing. I did not allow much touching. I did not want to be talked about. I wanted the guys to like me for who I was, not what I put out. I was very serious about saving myself for the special guy I would marry. I wanted him to have a whole me and not just leftovers.

New Ulm, Minnesota, was where I went to junior and senior high school. There were about three hundred students in my grade. That was a huge difference from twenty-four classmates. Once again, I was not in the popular crowd in school. I didn't have the self-esteem to join their ranks. I couldn't be cruel to friends just to get what I wanted. I lived twelve miles from New Ulm and could not make the trip there anytime I pleased. My friends were still the Lafayette group, but I didn't always fit in with them either. My parents were not drinkers and most of theirs were. My parents didn't go to the lake on weekends, nor have a cabin, and most of theirs did.

I did not have brothers or sisters my age to hang around when I was lonely. I was perfectly fine staying in my house with my parents. I painted, played games, listened to music, and talked on the phone. I hardly ever cleaned, did dishes, or cooked. I never was grounded. I wanted to be grounded like the rest of the kids. I wanted brothers and sisters my age to talk to. I wanted chores I had to do. My mom did not want to spend her time disciplining me. She said she hardly saw me, so the little time we had together at home was not going to be spent fighting. She felt guilty leaving me alone or with my grandparents while she worked so many hours in the store.

Harold's Grocery was sold at auction when I was sixteen. It was a sad day as I sat across the street watching people bid on boxes of my life as I had known it. I had made so many friends, and I knew I would not see them as often as I liked. Kermit was a friendly older farmer who stood by the grocery counter on Saturday nights and played many games of tic-tac-toe with me. Then there was Tom, the city street worker who came in and barked orders to me. I learned to give him the same treatment back and we became friends. Benny Johnson, a little bent-over man, always gave me a penny when he saw me. I loved those days in the store. Not all men were bad.

Dad had gotten the job as janitor at the grade school in Lafayette. I still didn't have to work around the house because now Mom was home and she had the time to do those things that had to be done. Dad thought he had died and gone to heaven, only having to work forty hours a week instead of ninety hours and even getting paid vacation days. And then he did die. Dad was fifty-eight years old when he died. I was a senior in high school.

My mom was lost without my dad. Many mornings I found Mom in my bed with me crying, and I had to comfort her. I didn't know how to comfort a parent.

In one year, my life changed in almost every way possible. I turned eighteen in February, my dad died in March, I graduated in May, left home for the air force in September, met Phil in October, married him five weeks later, then moved with him to California in January.

CHAPTER 3

THE MARRIAGE

---■---

It was a Sunday evening in October and my mom and Luann and her family had just left after visiting me for the weekend at Chanute Air Force Base, in Illinois, to go back home to Minnesota. I was attending a technical school for three months as a jet engine mechanic. After my family left that evening I went to the laundry room to wash clothes and study for an upcoming test. I was sitting near the washer when I saw this handsome guy sitting in the corner of the room next to the dryer. He, too, was studying for a test. He had a dark tan all over his medium framed muscular body. Even with his military haircut I could see that he had dark curly hair. His blues eyes sang sad sexy songs. On his right arm there was a new tattoo of an eagle with wings pointing to the sky. It was red around the edges and I went up to this stud of an air force man and asked him about his tattoo. He spoke with confidence as he told me about his new inked eagle. He had an air about him I had not seen in anyone before. He seemed so sure about himself. He was covered with charisma from head to toe, and I became mesmerized by Philip Mark Harris. We sat and flirted with each other in the laundry room until our clothes were dried. He then asked me out for dinner, so we headed to the chow hall where we each had our own meal cards. Neither of us had a car and it was getting very cold in Illinois.

After only one of week of spending as much time together as we possibly could, he asked me if I wanted to come to California with him. I went back to my dorm and told my two roommates that I think Phil just asked me to marry him and I think I said yes. I was confused and happy and wondering what I had just done. I hadn't ever even gone steady with anyone and now I was going to marry someone I hardly knew. Oh, but Phil, he was so handsome and so sad and so different and he picked me to marry him.

Phil and I talked a lot during that first week and we were both hurting. Phil had a high school girlfriend Jill who died in March of the same year my dad died—only eight months before we met. We saw that their deaths, being only a few days apart, were a sign from God that we were to spend the rest of our lives together. Phil and I felt our paths had crossed for a reason. This was the basis of our relationship. We had nothing else in common except we were both in the air force as jet engine mechanics. Phil was honest with me and told me he had tried twice to kill himself after Jill died. I believe Jill was only sixteen and Phil was seventeen when she died of a brain hemorrhage while Phil was holding her. Phil knew Jill was sick for a short period of time before she died. They had plans on getting married after Jill thought she was pregnant. I know she never had a baby, but I am not sure if she was ever really pregnant or not. All I knew was that I thought I could make this sad person happy. I felt this was my calling in life. I could take Phil's pain and make his life wonderful. All Phil needed was someone to care for him and love him and he would be okay. I was that someone.

By this time I had orders to Shaw Air Force Base in South Carolina, and Phil had orders to Castle Air Force Base in California. If we were not married in the next month our orders could not be changed, and we would probably never see each other again. We planned our wedding date to be in four weeks, December 10, 1976, after only knowing each other seven days.

I called my family and told them I was getting married. This was only one week after they had been down to see me, and I didn't even mention having a boyfriend because I didn't know Phil at the time. My mom's first response was, "No, you're not," and then she asked if he was Catholic. (I was brought up Lutheran and Lutherans were not supposed to marry Catholics.) My sister Luann's question was, "Is he black?" Linda's first question was, "Are you pregnant?" He wasn't any of those things. He was just this handsome young man that was hurting so bad.

After the phone calls to our families, I was sitting on Phil's knee in the hall of our dorm when the first sergeant walked by and called us in his office. We were in trouble for PDA (public display of affection). I had to wash floors in the day room while Phil had to stand door guard duty. We were not allowed on each other's floors in the dorm, let alone in each other's rooms. Not even after we were married.

We also had to make a few more phone calls and write letters. I had to write to Gary, Ron, and Rick and tell them I was getting married. These guys had become my friends during high school, and we kept in touch during basic training. Phil had to call Cheryl, the girl with whom he was going steady, and let her know he was getting married and wanted his class ring back. (Looking back I should have seen this as a sign of trouble, along with a lot of other signs. Phil had planned on marrying Jill when she died of a brain hemorrhage less then eight months earlier, and he was already going steady with another girl. He could not stand to be alone, and that was why he needed me.)

Phil was the romantic person. He always knew the right things to say. He could talk me into anything with his charisma. He wanted to have premarital sex, but there I stood my ground. I had waited this long and was not about to blow it now with our wedding only four weeks away. He did have me rub his genital any chance he could. I had never even touched this male body part before except though clothing. I placed my hand in Phil's pants, rubbing a soft handful of cylinder muscle, making it grow and become stiff. This happened wherever the urge overtook Phil. Sometimes it would be in the music room in one of the buildings on base or at the movie theater. Sometimes it would even be in a group of our fellow dorm mates as we sat around studying for our tests. I am sure they had to know what was going on even though Phil would have a coat over his lap. I was naive. I was stupid. He had some power over me that I could not tell him no. If I did say no, he would get mad at me, and I wasn't used to people being angry with me.

It must have been something I was doing wrong. I remember the first time Phil was really angry with me. We were walking down the sidewalk on the base, just talking as we often did, and all of a sudden he was angry with me and turned around and headed the other direction. I stood in the middle of the sidewalk in total confusion, looking at him with tears in my eyes wondering what I had said or done. I couldn't understand this sort of behavior. "What did I do? What I am getting myself into?" I wondered. I asked him later that afternoon what I had done to make him so mad, and his answer was, "You should know." No, I didn't know what I did or said to set him off and he was not going to tell me. I tried to think of everything I had said to him that afternoon, and I couldn't think of anything that deserved that type of reaction. I was so confused. I was starting to doubt myself. I was starting to doubt us.

In the wee morning hours, and weather permitting, we marched the six or seven blocks to class. It was dark and snowy on those early morning marches. Each morning Phil checked both his and my flashlights to see which one was brighter. The brighter light would be his for the day. It became a joke between us and we often laughed about it. "Mine" was often a word Phil used, and I just shrugged it off and we laughed. If having the brighter light was that important to him, then I would let him use it. It wasn't worth a fight. It wasn't funny, but ignoring the red flags was becoming a way of life for me already.

The wedding day was a couple days away, December 10, and we had planned a very small wedding. We were going to get married after class on Friday. None of our parents were going to be there. With my dad's death only nine months earlier, I felt having my mom there would be too sad for both of us. I knew I would be sad that my dad was not there for me. I wanted him to walk me down the aisle and give me a little kiss and tell me things were going to be okay. I wanted my dad to like Phil and Phil to like my dad. If my dad couldn't be there, I didn't want my mom to be there either. I didn't want my mom crying for me. I didn't want my mom telling me I shouldn't be getting married. I am not sure why Phil's parents didn't come. Most likely they did not have the money to do so.

We had gone through a few hours of marriage counseling with the base chaplain and thought we were ready to be together forever. I don't remember the questions we were asked. I think I answered them like a test. I answered the question with the answer they were looking for, but not the answer in my heart.

I was getting frozen feet. I had never gone steady with anyone. I never dated anyone more than a year, and even at that, we both dated other people during that year. I loved to date new people. I had just left home for the first time to be on my own. I was not ready for marriage, to give myself to one person for the rest of my life. I was not ready to belong to someone. I talked to Phil and told him this. There we stood, in the middle of an empty road under a street light with snow gently falling around us. I tried to make my words as gentle as the snow, but Phil would not listen. He said he needed me and he loved me. He would make my life wonderful. I could not back out of the marriage when he was already so sad after losing Jill. I gave in. Two days later we were married in front of ten of our technical school friends. My sister Linda and her husband, Doug, came down from Minnesota by train to be in the wedding. Doug walked me down the aisle and Linda was at my side. My instructor,

Sergeant Brown, was Phil's best man. It was a very simple wedding and our words were spoken with feelings. If I was getting married, I was going to give my all. After our wedding, Phil and I went to the Holiday Inn Senior in Rantoul, Illinois, three miles from Chanute Air Force Base. We had dinner with Linda and Doug, and then headed to our room for the evening.

Scared does not describe how I felt. I was not ready for this marriage stuff. I was on the pill, and I was a virgin. I quickly learned that sex was not what people made it out to be. Phil was gentle, but what did I have to compare him to? After he hit his peak, I was expecting fireworks and a wonderful feeling, but I felt nothing but pain and confusion. I asked him, "Is that it?" That wasn't a very good way to start out a marriage. Later, when I went to the bathroom all I passed was blood. I did not like this. I didn't think looking at a man's private was that sexy. I didn't think having a penis inside of me with some guy bouncing up and down to make himself feel good was anything I wanted to do on a daily basis. I wanted someone to hug me and hold me and talk to me. I wanted a friend that would not get mad at me if I messed up.

Linda and Doug left early the next morning on the train. We did not see them off, but stayed in our room. I don't remember if we did the sex thing or not, but I am sure we tried.

Two days later we were back in our separate rooms in the dorm and ready for school. We were planning our trip to Minnesota for Christmas so everyone could meet my new husband. I had written to my friend Wendy, and she was shocked I was married. She and my other friends had a wonderful going away party for me when I left for the air force four months before, and now she was planning a bridal shower for me.

In the meantime, Phil had gotten an award pasted on his dorm room door by his fellow classmates and dorm mates. He had won a grouch award that was especially made for him. Phil was a very moody person.

It was not only me who noticed his nonsocial personality. He was not Minnesota nice, but was California grumpy. I just called him my "California Creep," my "Buddy Ol', Pal Ol', Friend Of Mine." He was this cocky guy with a stride of a walk that could turn any woman's head. Phil stood five-feet six-inches, but with the air of assurance he had about himself, he stood over seven-feet tall. No one was going to mess with him. He was a California stud.

On weekends we would proceed to the Holiday Inn Junior that was in walking distance from the base. Neither of us had a vehicle. After romping in the bed, Phil's legs often cramped up from the muscles he had from playing soccer in high school. I massaged his legs and he massaged my stomach since I was often so tense. Some of our favorite things to do on base were bowling, dancing, and the movies. Bowling was one of the more relaxing things we did. Dances caused many fights after Phil inhaled a few beers. Phil was a very jealous person and would see guys looking at me. His words would hurt as he flung them at me, accusing me of looking at the other airmen. I am not sure why we continued going to the dances. I guess it was just something to do besides have sex in the motel on weekends.

The movies were not any better than the dances. At the beginning of the movies we had to stand at attention while the national anthem was being played. Again Phil would get angry with me and would go and sit somewhere else. I stood there with noiseless tears lurking down my cheeks, not knowing where I should go. "Now what had I done that was so horrible? Do I go and follow him or do I stay where I am? Will he get up and leave again if I go by him? Will he cause a scene and shout at me in public if I go near him? Will he come back to me if I just stay where I am? Should I go to my dorm?" were all thoughts that raced through my confused mind. I must have done something really bad, but what? I wasn't going to leave him. I knew he would come and tell me what I had done, and then he would realize that I had just made a silly mistake and didn't mean anything by what I must have said or done. Wrong. We never talked about what was wrong. I was supposed to know what I had done to make him so angry. If I didn't know, then I was to think about it until I figured it out. I didn't understand this type of behavior. I must have been really stupid not to understand what I did.

It was Christmas time and I was bringing my new military-issue husband home. We rode with an airman to Minneapolis, where Linda and Doug picked us up. I was very nervous at the bridal shower my friends and family had for me. They asked many questions about Phil, since no one had ever met him. We received many wonderful gifts, and once again I was home with people that loved and understood me. I was home where no one put friends down, where no one got angry over little things, where no one left me because I did something wrong. While staying at my mom's house, Phil came down with strep throat and became extremely ill. My mom was a good mom and took great care of her new son-in-law, bringing him hot soup, hot water bottles, and lots of attention. Phil loved all the attention. He was treated with so much respect. He was my husband and my family would treat him nice no matter how he treated me.

After Phil felt better, we stayed up one night just talking in my bed in my old bedroom. We talked about our pasts, our present, and our future. It was a wonderful talk. We started to become friends that night. We were caring about each other. It felt good to talk in bed and not just have sex. It was precious sharing thoughts and dreams. The next day Phil met all my sixteen cousins on my mom's side. It was a warm family day, even through it was negative twenty degrees outside.

After our short trip to Minnesota, it was time to get back to technical school. We took the train from Minneapolis to Rantoul, Illinois. The train was packed, and Phil pushed our way to a seat. In Chicago we almost missed the train because of snow, and Phil plowed through everyone so we could get on the train. He was sure that if we did not get back to the base on time, we would be in trouble. I thought for sure that our commanders would understand if we were a day late because of the weather. I knew for sure someone had common sense and would understand if something unexpected came up.

■ I want to stop my story here. The next twenty-four years are more than I want to think about. I want to forget about the past and just live for today. But it is the past the makes me who I am today.

Back on Chanute Air Force Base we got ready for our move to Castle Air Force Base near Atwater, California. We took Phil's orders to Castle instead of my orders to Shaw Air Force Base in South Carolina. Phil wanted to be near his family and, as far as Phil was concerned, there was no other state besides California that was worth living in.

We flew to Fresno to surprise Donna and Jim Harris, Phil's parents. I was their first and only daughter-in-law at the time. We stayed with his parents, and Phil introduced me to the few friends he had from high school. Donna had a wedding reception for us to meet the rest of the family. It was quite a crew. Laugh and drink are what most of them did best. Phil had informed me that Jim, his dad, was an alcoholic but had not had a drink in years. I had my share of wine that night too. Phil and I had a fight about something, one of the many to come. Phil enjoyed his booze, but the booze did not like him. He only ever had "two," but it always seemed like more.

The next week we went out and looked for a truck. Phil found a brand new beautiful black 1977 Ford step-side pickup. He said his parents had given him a thousand dollars, and he was going to use it for a down payment. Other than this money, Phil had nothing from his childhood to help start a household. He didn't have a bike, a radio, a stereo, a car, nor a saving or checking account. He had nothing but a gun that I can remember. It was years later that I found out the money Phil used as a down payment to buy his expensive truck was our wedding present from his parents. It was not money Phil's parents owed him as he told me.

We found a furnished two-bedroom apartment sixty miles away from his parents. It was only three miles from the base and something we could afford. We rented the place and started our married life together at last. The tears, they just kept flowing.

"What had I done? Why was he drinking so much? Why was he always mad at me? Did we have to have sex every day? Why would I want to have sex when I was compared to a log? Now why was he mad again? He was sleeping on the couch, why? I thought I'd better go and sleep on the floor near him so he would know I really loved him. He must have known I really loved him and whatever I had done I didn't mean to. Sex again? Drinking again? It was okay. It was only "two beers." Oh, he loved me. He could see that I was sad. He bought me ice cream cones to dry up my tears. He bought me balloons for my birthday. He knew I loved balloons. He must have loved me. He was mad again. Now he was sick and throwing up. It had nothing to do with the "two beers" he just drank. It was the V8 juice he had just drunk that was no good. I said these things over and over again in my mind.

Balloons meant freedom to me. They just floated in the air, relaxed, taking in the sites. Seeing what life had to offer is what balloons did best. When they were held down, they only saw what was next to them instead of seeing the whole world and being all that they could be. My balloons were being held down. The strings were being stepped on. They were starting to shrivel up before they had a chance to see the world.

CHAPTER 4

BEACHWOOD

■ This is really hard to go back and try to remember. I have worked hard to forget so I could be happy. I tried to ignore all the bad things that were happening around me so I could live in my rainbow world where balloons filled the skies.

Phil thought we should look for a house to buy, and I thought that sounded like a good idea. We looked at houses all over the area and most of them we could not afford since we were both only airmen in the air force and nineteen years old. We found a house on Beachwood Drive in between Merced and Atwater. It was only $22,000.00 and needed a little work. Structurally it was fine, but paint-wise, it needed some help. The living room was painted orange with gold shag carpet covering the floor. Our furniture was olive green soft fake fur with big round arms. The colors of the furniture and the walls made a mess together just like Phil's and my life would end up. Alone they were fine, but together they worked against each other. The kitchen was yellow, while the bathroom was bright green, one bedroom bright baby blue, the other bedroom jump-out pink, and the last was just as bold and obnoxious as the rest. In other words, I don't remember the color, but it was bright. I started painting in the living room while Phil started fixing things in the kitchen. He was very handy when it came to fixing things. The house turned out pretty cute when we were all done. We laid wooden floor tiles in the kitchen and left the rest of the floors alone. Our own little sweet home was supposed to be our haven, but it was just the start of my hell.

I was still naïve. I trusted the world. I thought everyone was like me and wouldn't hurt anyone. Everyone took turns sleeping with their stuffed animals so the animals would not feel left out. Every little town was like Lafayette, where you could leave your doors unlocked and money laying on the table for the milkman when he walked in your home to leave milk in the refrigerator. I was wrong, and it took me many years to believe it. I wanted to believe in mankind.

The first thing I did when we moved into our new house was greet our neighbors that lived next to us. When looking out our front door this neighbor's house was to the left of our house. In their little house, with most of the paint faded off, lived Eddy, Eddy's girlfriend, their son, and Eddy's mother. I talked to Eddy's girlfriend and invited her and another lady in for coffee and cookies, because that is what you do in Minnesota. They turned out to be some interesting neighbors, along with other neighbors that lived on the other side of us and the neighbors that lived across the street.

The neighbors to the right of our house had a pet goat they raised in their backyard. They also had an old claw-foot bathtub they used to water the goat. It was the same claw-foot bathtub they used to roast the goat and then have a feast of goat meat.

The neighbors across the street from our house were Ralph and Carol and their three boys, two of which had learning problems. Ralph and Carol knew how to eat and how to borrow. They would call at 7:00 a.m. asking to borrow a Pepsi or toilet paper or scissors or anything else they didn't have at the time. Both Ralph and Carol each weighed at least two-hundred-fifty pounds and stood close to five-feet seven-inches in height. Ralph was rarely seen with a shirt on. Even on the colder days, sweat streamed off the rolls of his body. Not a pretty sight.

But they were nice, and in Minnesota you always treated your neighbors neighborly.

Eddy and his crew turned out to be the most interesting to live next to. We didn't need a TV to be entertained. It was around 3:00 a.m. on a dark spring morning that I drove Phil to Merced, the neighboring town, so he could go fishing with his supervisor, Ron. After returning home in the dark, I was starting to crawl back in my bed when I heard Eddy shouting. I crouched as I looked out the window and saw Eddy standing across the street, facing his house while shouting to his girlfriend to get the hell out of the house before he blew it full of holes. He screamed at her and held a gun in his short thick fingers. I was so scared. I didn't know if I should call the police or not. This kind of thing didn't happen in my secure world. If I didn't call the police and something happened I would have to live with it the rest of my life. I called.

I stayed down on the side of the bed, looking out the window so no one could see me. By the time the police arrived, Eddy had calmed down and was walking down the street to a friend's house. The police stopped Eddy and asked him if he was the one who called them. Okay, so now Eddy knew that someone called the cops on him, and since I was the new person in the neighborhood, I was sure he would know it was me who called. That whole next day I was afraid to go out because I did not know what he would do to me. Would he come over and yell at me? Would he hurt me physically? Nothing happened because I became a prisoner in my own small house.

The Beachwood neighborhood was a learning experience for me. I knew when it was welfare payday by all the traffic that flowed in and out of Eddy's house. That is when the semi-truck full of hay would pull in front of their house. I probably should say "grass" that was hidden in the bales of hay. Their yard looked like a junkyard with cars that did not run. Instead of a bed and breakfast, they ran a car and grass hotel. In the morning there were strange straggly faces creeping up over the seats of the dysfunctional cars. They literally kept six months worth of garbage by their back door until they had a backhoe come and dig a hole. No, they did not bury the garbage; they just dug a hole to have someplace to throw the garbage.

One California cold winter night, Phil's parents came to see us in our little humble home. When they went out to their car to get their suitcases they noticed bloody handprints on the trunk of their white car. We found out later that they were from Eddie. He had gotten into a fight and was struggling to his house when he leaned against their car.

It was while living at this house that I learned how to drive a stick shift. We bought me a small royal blue Toyota Corolla, and Phil taught me to drive it. I should have had wipers on my eyes as well as the car. Phil would yell at me, "You can't be that stupid. You can't be that uncoordinated," as we jerked down the back road behind our house. I am not sure how I ever learned, but I did. I was just glad Phil was not with me when I came home from work going forty-five miles per hour and shifted into first gear to make the turn without slowing down first. The car revved to its max without coming apart.

More parties, more drinking, more name calling, more tears, more sex in the hall by the heater, only two beers, always only "two" beers, my fault. Phil's high school friends had a party for him in Fresno, and I was invited. We were to stay at his parents' house that night. His Uncle Phil and Aunt Marge would be at his parents' house also to visit with us after the party. At the party his old girlfriend Cheryl was there. Phil and Cheryl were going steady until I came into the picture. She had Phil's class ring, but had since returned it to his mom. There sat Phil in a corner, with beer in hand and Cheryl strutting over to Phil and placing her fingers ever so gently over Phil's tattoo while asking, "Is that new?" I talked to a few of his friends, but pretty much stayed to his side. Phil was jealous and it didn't take much to set him off. We decided that a walk would be good since he was drunk. As we were walking the streets, once again Phil was mad at me and called me a bitch. It was first time anyone ever called me a bitch to my face. My own husband, whom I loved, called me a bitch. I was not griping at him, but something was my fault. He only had two beers, so, of course, it was not that he was drunk. Phil decided we had to drive back the sixty miles to Atwater that night instead of heading a few miles to his parents' house. I drove his black step-side truck home, stopping once in awhile so he could throw-up from the flu, cause he only had two beers. I called his parents from somewhere and made up an excuse why we were not coming over.

Back home again in our little house. Phil got busy fixing it, painting it, and building a mailbox cover for the boxes in front of our home. I wallpapered the dining room and calmed down the remainder of the rooms with light cool colors.

We would be the perfect couple. People would tell us we go together like peanut butter and jelly. My mask was wonderful. I wanted my marriage to be everything a little girl dreams of living. I wanted my husband to understand and love me.

It was soon Thanksgiving time and my mom and her new husband, Harvey, were coming to spend some time with us. Phil's family were going to be with us for Thanksgiving Day also. I planned to cook the perfect turkey and both of our opposite families would get to know one another. My mom was a keeper of everything, a junk collector, a food collector, and a very thrifty person. My dad was a very even-tempered man with a dry sense of humor who always put his children first. Phil's mom was a throw-it-away person. She would buy clothes, take them home, wash them, and then try them on. If the clothes did not fit, or if she did not like them, in the Salvation Army box they would go. Phil's dad was a dry drunk who only thought about himself. If he went to the store to get six apple turnovers, he thought nothing of eating three of them even though there were four of us at the house. Phil came from Fresno where he didn't know most of his neighbors or care to know them. I came from a town of five hundred where I knew everyone and everyone knew me. The first time Phil came with me to my home church he was in total amazement when everyone called me by my name.

Getting back to the turkey, both families were at our small home in the middle of our ghetto trying their best to be nice to each other. My mom helped me cut the turkey when Phil stepped into the picture and wanted the whole drumstick. My mom, being the thrifty person she was, thought that was way too much meat for any one person to eat by himself. Phil being the "this is my house and I don't care what you think" kind of guy, did not agree with his mother-in-law. I can't remember who won that one, but it set the stage for tension and a power play whenever they were together. We did make it through the rest of the day with many fake smiles and much artificial politeness.

In the summer of 1978, Phil and I drove to Minnesota to see my family. While my mom was out of the house at an appointment, her phone rang. It was Ralph, our California neighbor who was watching our house while we were gone. He told Phil that someone had broken into our house and took most of our things. Being young and foolish, we barely waited for my mom to get back home until we drove off in our little car to race back to California. We drove almost straight through, only stopping once for a quick nap. Once at home we saw that they pried open the back bedroom window to enter the house. They took three cameras, jewelry, a TV, and a stereo. They used one of our pillowcases to carry all the things they stole from us. The police came over and we all knew it was Eddy and his hoodlums that broke into our house, but we had no way to prove it. The only way someone could get into our backyard was to come over Eddy's fence, and they had a malicious pit bull for a pet. Eddie was also seen breaking the streetlight in front of our house a few nights before they robbed us.

About four days after we got back from Minnesota, Phil had to leave for Florida on a temporary duty assignment (TDY). I slept on the couch so I could hear what was going on outside as well as inside the house. I had a loaded rifle, a knife, and a flashlight on the coffee table next to the coach. I slept great.

While in Florida, Phil bought himself some new cowboy boots and other expensive things. While he was gone I painted a room and bought Phil an Avon brush and comb set. It wasn't so much that he bought himself things, but I felt he didn't think of me. I didn't want material things. I wanted to know that he was thinking of me while he was gone and maybe saved his money so we could do something together when he got home. Or, at least, he could have bought me something he knew I liked. I didn't want something given to me without much thought or feeling.

At our house, it was still the same old thing. Phil did not drink every night, but when he did, he changed from a halfway normal person to someone who hated me. More tears, more sex, more yelling, more tears. "When will this stop? Why does he hate me so much?" were questions that scared me. He was always sorry the next day. He bought me flowers because he was mad at me. My balloons were getting smaller. I wanted to be happy. Maybe if I acted happy I would be happy. "Okay, smile, Chris. Phil must love you," is what I would tell myself. He said he was sorry. Oh, he was drinking again. "Please stop. I wanted to go home. A marriage is not supposed to be like this," are cries that echoed through my head. I had made a promise to God, for better or worse. Phil must have seen how much he was hurting me. If I said something to him about him hurting me, he would tell me how much "I" was hurting "him." If I mentioned something about his drinking, he snapped back, "Well, you do it." I was not a drinker. I did not like to feel sick. I did not want to act stupid because of booze. I didn't want something else controlling how I felt or acted.

We still went to Fresno almost every weekend to see Phil's parents and play games with the cousins. We really did have a good time. No one had much money and we played bingo for prizes we all brought to the house. Other times Phil and I would go driving around Fresno, just like he did when he was in high school.

One night, while cruising Blackstone Avenue in the new black stepside pickup someone shouted, "That's Phil Harris," with the excitement of seeing a movie star. I ducked down on the seat feeling so embarrassed. I think I lacked self-confidence, and I didn't want anyone to see me with this cool guy I was married to. I was just a hick from a small town in Minnesota, and Phil was this stud of a guy that all the girls drooled over. Phil drove me up to the mountains that night to talk about us and then we drove back down to spend the night with his folks.

Sex was what I called it, because I was not feeling loved. I felt used. I hated the silent treatment. If it was not the silent treatment being stuffed in my face, then it was calling me names such as "a log." A log with no feelings was pretty much how I felt. I would lay there and hope he got done quickly. He always tried to make me feel good too, but a log without feelings can be stubborn when it comes to sex. His truck wasn't even sex free. We could hardly drive to Fresno without Phil taking his penis out of his pants and wanting me to rub it while he drove down the highway. He reached his fingers over to my empty body and tried to please me also. I hated it. I just wanted to sleep and let time pass. I wanted to get to our destination as quickly as possible. He especially liked my denim shorts that were three-sizes too large. He could easily slip his hands into the legs of my shorts and into the leg of my panties where his fingers would search for the spot that would make me wiggle. I hated to go anywhere with Phil. This continued even after we had children, and they would be asleep in the back seat or too young to know what was going on.

Phil and I started square dancing lessons one night a week with another couple from base. This was a good time because we were getting to know other people. It was non-drinking fun, and we did something together we both enjoyed. After the dance practices, we often went out to eat with our new friends. We passed the lessons and then quit going.

On the base Phil worked in a small shop fixing fighter engines. Many days they cleaned up early so they could play pinochle and drink beer. They had a bar right in their shop, as most military shops did. Phil's supervisor, Ron, loved drinking with Phil, and many times they would take off early and go to the base bar or the bowling alley to play pinball and get drunk. Their shop picnics were at Merced Lake where the families would get together, drink, and water ski and drink some more. But, of course, Phil only had two beers.

While at Castle, I worked phase docks on the B-52s and the KC-135s at the far end of the flight line. Phil figured since he never really worked, I must not be working either. If I wasn't working, what was I doing all day in a little trailer at the end of the flight line with four or five other guys, was Phil's question. Phil would get angry with me for looking at his supervisor or any of his other co-workers. He was sly enough that no one else usually saw the evil looks I received or the silent treatment he powerfully dished out. Usually I had no idea why he was not speaking to me. When I asked him why, I again was told I should know. Peanut butter and jelly we were not. It was more like sauerkraut and chocolate. Both are fine alone, but together they could make you sick.

I was transferred to the engine shop where I tore down and built up the J57 engine, updated engine records, and received and returned engine parts. It was the same building Phil worked in, only I was in SAC (Strategic Air Command) and Phil was in TAC (Technical Air Command). I was working in the office on engine records when I received my military orders to Iceland. I called Phil on the phone and told him the news. Phil's icy reply was "bye."

CHAPTER 5

ICELAND

———————————■———————————

Where in the hell is Iceland? We got a map and found a small dot east of Greenland. Yep, that was Iceland, a small island in the middle of nowhere. After all the hard time Phil gave me about my orders to Iceland, he did apply, after all, for joint-spouse. Joint-spouse is when the military gives married couples orders to the same military base. Just because a military member is married to another military member, it doesn't automatically mean they will both get orders to the same base. Phil was granted joint-spouse so we could go to the barren land together.

We tried to sell our house. It was on the market before I had my orders because we had been looking at buying a home in a nicer neighborhood in Atwater, the neighboring town. The realtor would take care of the renting out of our house for us. Phil was left to take care of the packers and movers. The air force shipped our necessary things first, like sheets, pots and pans, and uniforms. The rest of our things went by boat and got to Iceland a couple months after we did.

Phil and I planned to meet in New Jersey and fly to Iceland together. We had a two-year tour planned for Iceland, otherwise known as "The Rock."

Before we left for Iceland, I had to go to a few weeks of training at Shaw Air Force Base in South Carolina for the engine on the F4, while Phil had to go to only a week of training in New Mexico. I first flew to Minnesota to see my family. Linda drove me to the airport in Minneapolis so I could leave for Shaw Air Force Base. Linda and I shared many tears that morning. She felt like she was seeing me off for the last time. I had to go. I had a commitment to both the air force and to Phil.

We flew on canvas seats that ran along the cargo section of the plane. We were issued earplugs and box lunches on the five-hour flight across the Atlantic Ocean to Iceland. The air force didn't want their passengers too comfortable. It was one very long, cold, hard flight, and I was relieved when we landed. Arriving in Iceland at the beginning of September was quite a change from September in California. It was cold and windy with snow blowing across the flight line. There was nothing to stop the blowing snow from racing from one end of the country to the next. No trees, not much grass, and a lot of wind is what Iceland was. Our plane parked out in the middle of nowhere on the godforsaken flight line, and we were loaded onto a shuttle bus and driven to the base air terminal.

After arriving at the terminal and getting checked in, Phil and I were loaded onto another shuttle bus and headed off to our dorms. They did not have base housing for us, so we stayed in separate dorms until base housing became available. Phil was moved onto the second floor of an all male dorm, and I was on the third floor of the neighboring dorm. I don't remember what was on the first floor of my dorm. The second floor of the dorm is where the male unaccompanied (without their spouses) and single master sergeants and chief master sergeants lived. There were not as many women on the base as there were men, so a dorm solely of women was not available. My new roommate was Katie and Phil's roommate was Katie's husband. After a few weeks, we swapped roommates. Phil moved onto the female floor with me and Katie moved into the male dorm with her husband. Our supervisor knew about our living arrangements and okayed it for us to be together unless someone complained. He also said we did not hear that he gave us the okay from him.

The female floor had a small kitchen, which about eighty women shared. My room was directly across from the kitchen, and women from all over the U.S. cooked wonderful meals in it. My room was about twenty feet by twenty feet, with a small bookshelf dividing the sink from the rest of the room. The small room had two single beds that could be arranged as bunk beds. There were two built-in closets against one wall and a large picture window overlooking the overgrown grass lot that led to the commissary. We were allowed to paint our room any color we wanted because of the low moral on the base due to the lack of light in the winter.

In Iceland the sun does not show its warmth in the winter and doesn't allow any darkness in the summer months. The Fourth of July fireworks were displayed at noon because the sun never goes down so, it wasn't any darker at midnight than it was at noon. Icelandic people did not celebrate our Fourth of July, but we were stationed on a U.S. military base.

It didn't take long with those cold dark nights before I became pregnant. It was November and I had missed a couple of my periods, so I went to the hospital for the pregnancy test. Phil was beyond excitement. He so wanted to be a dad. Phil was very kind to me. How did I feel? I was scared and excited. I had so many questions. By this time we found out the two-year tour could be cut to one-year if we stayed in the dorms for the year. We could not get base housing for a year anyway, and by that time our tour could be up if we stayed in the dorms. I would not have to extend my military career. I had a new issue to deal with. The baby was due in July, and we could not raise him/her in our dorms. We also weren't going to get base housing. I wasn't sure where we would have this baby. But, I knew something would work out. It always did.

Katie and her husband left for their new base assignment in December. Phil moved back to the male dorm, and I got a new roommate. Phil's new bunk partner was Macky, a big guy who loved to eat and put model planes together. Macky was a crew chief on the F4, had a family back in the states, and was very easy going. I liked having Macky around because he refused to allow Phil to put me down when he was around. Macky was almost fifteen years older than Phil, and Phil looked up to him.

One afternoon, Phil and I were in the female dorm kitchen talking with the other women when one of them told us she just had a miscarriage. I had a strange feeling and wanted to tell her I was going to miscarry the child growing inside me too. I knew that would sound weird, so I didn't say anything, but I listened to her story. I had many worries about this baby that both Phil and I wanted. If I had to leave the Rock before Phil, where would I live? My mom wanted me to live with her, my sisters with them, and Phil's mom with her. I was going to have to hurt someone's feelings. Someone was going to be upset with me. I wanted my husband at my side when his child was born. Being with Phil was very unlikely, since we didn't have a lot of money and the air force wouldn't pay for Phil's flight to the states and back. Also, Phil could only take a couple weeks of leave and expecting the baby to come into the world during those two weeks was unrealistic. Many days the tears would slide down my cheeks, as if to be just like me, not knowing where to go.

In January, I started bleeding just a little and called the military hospital. They reassured me this was normal for the first trimester of a pregnancy, and I should not worry. I believed them, because I had no one else to ask. I was thousands of miles from my family. I didn't know any married women on the base that had children. I had to trust someone and that someone was the person on the other end of the phone. Without any examination, I was told I was okay.

The air force was playing war games, and I was called to work one evening. I chose to walk the mile instead of riding the shuttle bus. It was not very cold that night as I walked across the quiet base to the engine shop. I remember the northern lights putting on a show that would stay dancing in my mind for years after. Once at the shop, I did my work, then rode back to the dorms on the shuttle bus.

Phil stayed in my room that evening. I awoke in the middle of the night to wet pants. I mean really wet. No, I did not pee my pants. I woke Phil, and he called the base hospital. They asked me if I lost control of my bladder. NO! I did not lose control of my bladder. I knew the difference between peeing in my pants and what had just happened. My water broke. My little baby wanted to come in this world at only three months since conception. I headed for the dorm bathroom all the women in the dorm shared. Only one dim light was working and the bathroom was very dark and lonely. Sitting on the toilet, I felt the tears stream out of my eyes as fast as body fluids escaped into the toilet. Oh no! I sat alone in the bathroom when I passed my child into the mucky bowl of waste. It was too dark to see anything. I flushed. I flushed my baby down the toilet. The bleeding would not stop. My baby is gone, flushed down the toilet. I walked out of the bathroom and down a few feet to the phone booth where Phil was waiting for me.

My clothes were soaked with tears and blood as I stood by the phone booth in the hall of the dorm. I had a towel folded in the middle of my underwear soaking up the blood running from my body. Phil stood next to me talking on the phone trying to tell the hospital I did not lose control of my bladder, but just passed our baby into the toilet. The hospital finally told us to come in, but we had no way of getting there. Neither of us had a car, and there was not a taxi on base to call. They said they would send an ambulance in the morning when the hospital opened. Four hours later, waiting with a towel soaked in blood straddled between my legs, the ambulance showed up for me. I had to slowly walk down the three flights of stairs, crawl into the square vehicle that was just as cold inside as the weather was on the outside. I don't remember any caring words coming from the ambulance staff.

Once in the hospital, I was placed on a bed in the hall until the hospital staff was ready to see me. You know where they put me when they finally put me in a room? They put me in the maternity ward next to the crying newborn babies. There was at least one smart person at the hospital who realized this wasn't very caring, and after minutes went by, I was moved into a different room so they could do a physical on me. I didn't need a D and C because my body discharged everything when it threw my baby away.

Phil called my work to let them know what had happened, and Macky brought me flowers. I could not get in touch with my family to let them know about the miscarriage. I sent my sisters a free short letter through the United Service Organization. The letters were read by Ham radio operators to someone in the states, and from there were written out and mailed to the family. [Anyway, that is how I remember it.]

Life went on and so did the air force. I no longer had to decide where to live when I became a mom. I spent my last seven months in the air force on the tree barren island of Iceland.

Macky loved to eat, and I enjoyed cooking new foods. Phil and I invited Macky and Mary, a women that lived in my dorm, over for chili after work. I put the dry beans in the crock-pot to cook while I was at work. I ended up working overtime and by the time I got back to my room, the beans were burnt. That should have been my first clue not to cook that day. I was a little thickheaded and didn't catch on.

I threw on my winter garb and headed out to purchase kidney beans. I was pushed faster than my feet wanted to go across the grass field by the mighty wind. At the commissary (military grocery store) I purchased canned beans and headed back to the dorms. I was offered a ride back to the dorm by a co-worker in a military pick-up. As I stepped out of the truck the wind caught my door before I could and blew the door back farther than it normally went, springing the door. That should have been clue number two. No, I still didn't catch on that we should have gone to the chow hall to eat.

I proceeded to the dorm kitchen to make chili. As I was putting the ingredients together I had this brilliant idea of putting baking soda in the chili to cut down on the gas from the beans. I heard someplace that baking soda worked, but I could not remember how much to add to the beans. I thought a quarter of a cup of baking soda would be good. Wrong, again.

When Phil and Macky came up to the kitchen to taste my wonderful chili they didn't say much. I told them what I had done because I could see on their faces that the taste was not very good. But Phil and Macky, being the kind of guys that they were, helped me doctor the chili up. They poured in a whole bottle of chili powder to hide the taste. The worst part of the whole thing was that Phil, Macky, and Mary didn't want to hurt my feelings, so they ate the chili and told me it really wasn't that bad. They were even nice enough to have seconds. True friends were hard to find, and that day they were true friends.

I was young and cute back in those days so Phil's older male friends let me practice cutting their hair. They loved it when I blew the hair off from around their ears. Phil didn't act jealous when we were around other people. He would share his anger with me later, when we were alone. Phil wanted to look like a good sport among his peers. I didn't like touching any of the guys because living with Phil's anger was not something I looked forward to. I was nervous cutting their hair for two reasons. I was always worried about what Phil would say, and I was not good at cutting their hair. Most of the time my haircuts were so bad that the guys would have to go to the base barber to get the haircut up to military standards. I got a lot of teasing because of this, which I handled very well.

Phil didn't only have a temper with me, but with others also. For some reason, which I can't figure out to this day, Phil never got in trouble when he did something stupid. I had heard, but do not know for sure if it was true, that Phil hit a military officer while working on the flight line. He did not get in trouble for this because, of course, the officer knew he had it coming, according to Phil. But Phil had a way about lying. I never knew if he was telling the truth or not. I don't think he knew if he was telling the truth or not. Phil had a way of manipulating people with lies and bullsh*t so they would apologize to him for something he did wrong. He could turn any disagreement around to make the other person wrong. He always came out looking like the hero.

Iceland was good for me. I didn't have to depend on Phil for conversation. This time that Phil was away from his family he saw there was a world besides California. Also, without family near, everyone around us became our family. We got together on holidays in the recreation rooms of the dorms and played games and shared food and drinks. If I was lonely, I could sit in the kitchen or in my room with the door open and someone would eventually stop and chat. Everyone was lonely and needed a friend to share their thoughts.

This was also one of the best years of my marriage. Phil was usually kind to me when we were around other people, and because we were living in the dorms, we were always around people. I liked having friends around for this reason. I did not know when Phil was drinking or not because he was spending most of the nights in his room with Macky. I, too, had a roommate, which made it harder for Phil to spend the night in my room. I did not experience as much of the verbal abuse since Phil worked the flight line and I worked in the engine shop.

Still, not everything was great. Phil worked many hours to better his career, but if I worked overtime, Phil thought they were taking advantage of me. I was so proud being in the air force. I loved wearing the uniform, standing retreat, and being part of a team. I joined the air force so I could travel and see the world. I wanted to go Japan where I spent five weeks when I was sixteen. I knew that joining the military was the only way for me to get there. It was now time for me to give up my dreams and live in Phil's dreams of being an air force career person.

My four years of enlistment had flown by and it was my time to get out of the air force. I was once again pregnant, and I did not want a stranger raising my child. I wanted the child to have my values. It also wasn't working for me to be in a male career field with a husband that was jealous. I would never be able to advance my career if I didn't have the support of my spouse. So, if I wanted my marriage to work and to have a real family, I had to give up my dream of the military to fulfill the commitment of my marriage vows.

I left Iceland three days before Phil, and I was discharged from the air force in Delaware. Phil caught up with me in Delaware on the third day, and we flew to Minnesota to visit my family. Phil had reenlisted and once again we headed to California to be near his parents. We were going back to Castle Air Force Base. Back to the same stuff again, only this time with a child due to come into this world in six months.

CHAPTER 6

BACK TO CALIFORNIA

---■---

■ Another chapter. It is funny how writing about life all of a sudden equals a chapter of my life. I am going to have to work really hard on trying to remember so many things that I worked so hard to forget. The only thing that kept me going was that God was at my side and my dad was watching over his shoulder. I guess I best get on with the next part. I can't put it off forever.

I knew in my heart that Phil would be happy now that he was going to be a dad and was living back in his wonderful state of California. I knew Phil would quit drinking because he didn't like that his dad drank when he was a child. He always wanted to be a father, and now he could be that father he always his dad to be. Whatever Phil "always" wanted, Phil "always" got.

We both decided we would not move back into the house on Beachwood that we had rented out while living in Iceland. It was no place to raise a family with all the strange neighbors that sold pot and smoked goats. The house sold within a couple of months of our return. We moved into an unfurnished apartment in Atwater for about four months. We found a rambler style house on Clinton Avenue in Atwater, three miles from Castle Air Force Base, to purchase. It was in perfect shape to store our belongings and start our new life as parents.

Phil was back in his old squadron at Castle Air Force Base. He was back in the Technical Air Command working on fighters and trainers. He was back with his old drinking buddies.

■   Oh, the memories are coming back and I don't like this. I want to quit writing now. I want to go back to my non-thinking safe place. I have to keep writing. I have to put this down on paper so I can see and feel that it really did happen. Once it is down on paper I don't have to think about it anymore.

I got a job in the Merced Mall working in Hickory Farms as extra Christmas help. I worked the day we moved into our house. Phil and his mom moved our things into the house and put everything away. We did not have a lot of things, but enough. Most of our belongings had been in storage for a year and the air force delivered them to our new home. The rest of our things we sold with our old house. I arrived home from work with everything in place and neighbors at our door to greet me. I had a real neighborhood with neighbors that became our friends and didn't rip us off when we weren't home. This felt more like Minnesota, where neighbors knew each other and helped each other if needed.

During my seventh month of pregnancy I developed a dislike for riding in the front seat of a car. Phil picked me up from work on Saturday, the day before Christmas, and we took off for Fresno. About twenty miles from town I started to feel sick. My stomach was getting really oozy, my body was getting clammy, and my eyes were rolling back. I passed out. Phil pulled over, and I started to come around a little. Phil saw there were police ahead that had pulled someone over and he drove up to them to see if they could help. They couldn't do anything, so Phil turned around and headed back to Castle Air Force Base to the hospital. I was examined and told I would be just fine. I was told that it wouldn't hurt me any if I passed out. It was just my estrogen or hormones or something out of control because of the pregnancy. We got back in the car and headed back to Fresno. I only passed out a few times on the sixty-mile drive there. Other than passing out, I never did get sick.

We celebrated Christmas with Phil's family. They were excited about becoming grandparents soon. Next Christmas would be so different with a new little body and big eyes of excitement.

I was Phil's parents' first and special daughter they had never had before. My mother-in-law, Donna, confided in me things she would never have told anyone else. Jim, her husband, was so demanding. He was often sick from working in a sawmill and smoking two to three packs of cigarettes a day. Donna hated taking care of him. They gave each other the "finger," slammed doors, and just threw tantrums.

Donna was somewhere in the middle of twelve brothers and sisters, and her dad left the family when she was in her teens. She got pregnant when she was in her late teens by a married man. Jim knew she was pregnant when he asked her to marry him, and he knew the child was not his. When Rick was born, his stepdad, Jim, treated him like dirt. Phil told me that for the longest time he thought his oldest brother's name was "Bastard" because that he what his dad always called him.

Jim had two sisters and, I believe, two brothers. One, if not both of his brothers, has committed suicide. Jim has been a dry alcoholic ever since I have known him. Donna left him at least once when he was still drinking and the kids were small. Donna and her boys moved back in with her mom during that time. While they were separated, Jim sold their bedroom set and burned all the negatives of their family pictures. Donna never seemed to forgive him for this. At least once, Jim tried to kill himself by cutting himself with a butcher knife in front of the boys when they were little. He also had a temper, whether he was drinking or not drinking. Donna took him back after he promised he would never drink again. He stopped cold turkey without any group help. Often he was just a hateful dry drunk who thought the world owed him something. He always treated me very kindly because I was his new daughter and soon the mother of his first grandchild.

Phil said his parents beat all three of the boys as they were growing up. Phil said his dad would hit him when he came home from work without knowing if Phil had done something wrong or not. His dad just knew that Phil must have done something wrong during the day. Phil was just as afraid of his mom. She often hit harder than his dad and would use a tree branch instead of the belt. Donna was just a small woman, no more then five-feet two-inches and, when the boys were young, weighed less than one hundred pounds. She was beautiful with a lot of spunk. When the boys were little, she always kept the house immaculate, washing walls weekly, scrubbing floors, and doing the rest of the general cleaning. The boys grew up neat and spick-and-span clean on the outside, but the insides of the boys were starting to grow mold and fungus as they were trying to get the positive attention they cried for.

Donna had to take care of so many people. Jimmy, her middle child, had been in a wheelchair since he was seventeen. Jimmy was driving the car when he served to miss another car. His passenger friend died in the accident that day. Jimmy had a hard dealing with the facts of his friend dying and that he would never walk again. The first few years that I knew Jimmy, he was trying to kill himself by slicing his legs to get rid of the mental pain he was feeling. If he couldn't kill the pain, he tried to make it numb with booze. He was an alcoholic and had a wicked temper when he drank. Jimmy thought everyone should know he had a temper and should leave him alone when he drank. His temper wasn't "his" problem—everyone else had the problem.

When I met Phil, Rick had been in the marines but was getting discharged early because of problems. He did get an honorable discharge because he used the GI Bill to go to school later on in life. Rick liked his drugs. He would steal money from his mom or steal blank checks if there was no cash. Donna never did anything about this. If she told Jim, it would only cause more hate between Jim and Rick. Rick once sold a camera to his brother, Jimmy, then borrowed the camera back and sold it to someone else. Jim and Donna bought Rick a truck and a motorcycle so he could go back to school and get a job. The school didn't work out, and he had to pay the government back thousands of dollars for the GI Bill. Work didn't pan out either. He was always getting fired for some reason, but according to Donna, it was never Rick's fault. Other people would be taking money out of the cash register and Rick, being the sweet guy he was, would take the blame. Rick was very good looking with a smile and personality that matched. He started stripping in a dance club and did very well for himself.

Phil and I went to the Lamaze class to get ready for our child that was about to come into the world. We learned how to breathe as well as what to generally expect about the birth. We also were given a tour of the hospital. We were ready for this new life to pop into the world. Two weeks after the due date I had a few gas pains when I went to bed about ten that evening.

I slept till midnight and then awoke with more gas pains. I went to the bathroom and passed some type of white mucus along with my other bodily functions. I waited until one in the morning, then woke Phil. We timed the gas pains and they were coming at a regular interval, so we decided to drive the two miles to Castle Air Force Base to see what the doctors thought.

The doctors thought it was time for me to stay and have our baby. I was scared. The pain was too intense, and I wanted to go home and try this again tomorrow when I wasn't so tired. I had a very low tolerance for pain, but I did not want to take anything to stop it. The lady next to me was screaming with pain, but I just laid on the bed knowing that with each pain I was getting a little closer to knowing who that little person was that kept kicking me.

I closed my eyes and tried to breathe as Phil was coaching me. Phil liked to do everything by the book and kept telling me to open my eyes and focus. I was getting angry. Leave me alone. "I just want to close my eyes and let this pain go away," I said through gritted teeth. He insisted I open my eyes, but I did not want to look at anything.

They broke my water, and in less then two hours after we entered the hospital, our little Lueck James Harris was born.

Lueck was born with nature's best smelling white cream all over him. He was alert and ready for life except for his feet. His feet were almost upside down and backwards. They were very limber so at only eight hours old the sweet little guy had cold heavy casts wrapped around his deformed little feet and legs. This problem with Lueck's feet did not bother Phil or me. It was just his feet and we were thankful he was a healthy eight-pound, six-ounce cute little life that God trusted us to care for.

I was nervous being a mom for the first time. Lueck did not like sucking on my breast, so the nurses gave me a bottle nipple to place over my nipple for him to suck on. This was a lot easier on my sore breast, but it was like my son sensed my nervousness and did not want to get too close. The little guy didn't have enough struggles in his life, so we thought we would have him circumcised and bring him home to our dysfunctional family. The same day Lueck and I came home the new Grandpa and Grandma Harris came to visit. I have never been good around sick people, and Grandpa Harris was just released that day from the hospital after major surgery, and was literally coughing up blood. This did not help me to relax after just having a child.

I rocked Lueck and read to him. He rolled over when he was just a couple days old by raising his cast-wrapped feet into the air and then putting them down to his side. Lueck's Grandpa Harris had made him a beautiful wooden cradle that sat on the ground. I could hear Lueck during the night as he lifted his feet and hit the side of the boards with his plaster legs.

Lueck was only a few days old when we noticed he was full of what looked like fleas bites. I called the base doctor around 4:00 p.m. and cried that I did not know what to do. The base doctors at Castle really cared about their people and let us come in right away. Both Phil and I went, carrying Lueck in to see the doctor who asked us several questions while looking at Lueck's bites. They weren't bites, but a rash he contracted because of us being so nervous. The doctor put Lueck on a milk formula, showed us how to wrap him so tight in his blanket that he could not move, and, honestly, wrote down in Lueck's records that the problem was "new parents syndrome." We took Lueck home feeling much better about being parents.

Lueck must have liked the feeling of being wrapped tight because of his legs being so heavy. We laid Lueck at an angle in the middle of a baby blanket, then, taking one of corners to his side, wrapped the blanket tightly under his body. We then took the bottom and placed that on top of Lueck, then took the other corner and wrapped him in like a burrito so he couldn't fall out. He loved being wrapped so snug. I gave him sponge baths because his cast couldn't get wet. He loved the water and loved to pee while lying naked on the towel.

Appointments were set up for us to see Dr. London at the Oakland Naval Hospital. He was a very caring doctor. Lueck's first surgery was when he was three months old. They cut the tendons and muscles in one foot and put a pin in the foot to hold it in the correct place. Three months later they did surgery again and took the pin out of the first foot and cut the other foot. We made many trips back to hospitals to replace casts Lueck kicked off.

After Lueck's surgery on his feet, the doctors had him wear the metal bar in between his shoes. Lueck learn to crawl with those shoes. There was nothing that stopped that little guy, and we never made a big deal about his feet. People who saw Lueck's feet after his surgery thought his feet looked deformed. We thought they looked good compared to what they did before. I spent many hours reading and singing to Lueck. I knew I had to sing to my children when they were little, before they knew the difference between good singing and making strange noises.

Phil began drinking again. It was okay cause he only had "one" beer. Ron, Phil's drinking buddy from the first time we were at Castle, was back in the picture. The two of them would go out fishing for catfish until the wee hours of the morning. They went to the coast to go fishing on their days off or on weekends. Phil thought he did okay with one beer, so now he decided to try two. He could stop after two, so he decided he could have three. He was mad. What had I done now? What had I said? It was okay cause he only had three, and, of course, it wasn't the beers that made him so ugly. Of course it was the beers, and I knew that.

I didn't want to have sex, but I did because it was my duty as a wife. But he was drunk, and he was calling me names. I hated being called names. I hated being stupid and being asked, "What's the matter with you?" I hated the dirty looks that put fear all through my body. I would do just about anything to avoid those looks, including having sex when I didn't feel loved or beautiful. I felt dirty and ugly and stupid. Once he grabbed my thigh in his hand and squeezed it together to show me how fat and awful it looked.

It would have been easy to leave Phil if he had been a jerk all the time. He was like living with two different people. Each day I waited to see if he came home on time. If he was late, then I would get an uneasy feeling in the pit of my stomach. I would expect the evil Phil to enter the door. I would be prepared for the Phil that hated the world and hated me. I wanted to take Lueck and hide in a closet, a safe quite place where no one yelled at us and called us names.

Then there was the Phil who was kind and gentle. I just didn't know whom I was dealing with day to day. It was my five-year class reunion and either Phil did not want to go or could not go. I don't remember which it was. It was much closer for Lueck and me to fly out of Fresno, but I procrastinated too long and could only get a flight out of San Francisco. Phil had no problem driving us 120 miles to San Francisco instead of the sixty miles to Fresno. That day I felt equal to him. He did not get angry with me for inconveniencing him by my mistake. I did fly back into Fresno on the return trip.

This memory shouldn't have been something special in my life. This should have been an everyday feeling. It should have been the exception not to feel safe or equal in the marriage, but on the contrary.

THE NEIGHBORS

Across the street from our house lived Donna and Ed, a couple in their late fifties. Donna worked at a school, and Ed worked for a car dealership. They had children, but they were grown and had children of their own. To the left of us, as you faced our house, lived Urma and Ed. Several years before, Ed had been an auto mechanic in his own shop when a car fell on his leg and he had to have it removed above the knee. Urma worked at the school in the cafeteria. She also sewed for people. Ed was in his seventies and Urma in her late sixties. We adopted Ed and Urma as our parents and as Lueck's grandparents. Urma watched Lueck when I needed her to.

Around the corner, on the next block, lived Army and Bev. They were a retired military couple that had kids a little younger than Phil and I. God placed Bev in my life, and she became my mentor. She would listen to me and never judge why I stayed with Phil. Army was also an alcoholic that had a keg of beer in their garage refrigerator at all times. I never saw the man drunk. I never saw the man without a beer in his hand. Maybe it was that I never saw the man sober? Don and Wini, who were in their early seventies, lived only a few houses down the street from Bev and Army. They also were a retired military couple who took us in as family.

It was near Christmas and Lueck was nearly nine months old, when the Ed from across the street, told his wife I was pregnant. He told her I had a glow about me. Christmas Eve day, 1981, the doctors confirmed

Ed's observations. Phil and I were going to have another little person running around sometime in August. It was a great Christmas present telling Phil's folks they were going to be grandparents again. This would be the eighth grandchild for my mom.

I knew this marriage couldn't be right. Every day was the same. Every day I wondered whom I was living with. Every day wondered if he would be drinking again and how much. Two beers, again, only two beers was the answer. Anger, again, anger, for what? I had no idea. Maybe if I had another child I could leave the children with Phil and he would be happy. I knew that if I left him, he wouldn't physically or mentally make it. My mother-in-law had been through so much already, and I felt it wouldn't be fair to her if I left her son. She couldn't take much more pain in her life. I didn't know how I was going to get out of this marriage. If I had a dog that I kicked and yelled at every time I drank and came home, I would either have to get rid of the dog or quit drinking. Why couldn't Phil tell the dog (me) to leave? Why did he hate me so bad? I knew he would lie down and die if I took the kids and left. The kids deserved a dad. I missed my dad so badly. My dad was special to me, and I didn't want to take that special person, called dad, away from my children. They deserved a family with both parents.

No one on my side of the family had ever been divorced. What would my family think of me if I left him? If I left him, I wouldn't take much with me. I only needed to get myself back. If I were to leave I would have taken the kitchen table that had been in my family for years, the little cupboard that my grandpa made me, my son, and my unborn child, and that was it. No, I couldn't leave Phil just then. Things would get better. He would see how much I really cared about him, and he would quit drinking. He would see how a family was supposed to be if I only had more patience. I had to rationalize all these thoughts. I had to find a way to get out of the marriage, but kept finding excuses to stay.

It wasn't safe for Lueck to be around his dad either. Lueck was just a little tot, maybe two, when he had a doctor's appointment on base. I had to cancel the appointment because of the handprint that Phil had left on Lueck's bottom the night before.

Lueck did not like sleeping in his own bed and would wake up several times a night and come to our room. At night when I put Lueck to bed, I sang to him until he fell asleep. I did this for a couple of reasons: it got me out of the room where Phil was watching TV, and I didn't have to worry about what wrong words came out of my mouth to make Phil angry. If I could get Lueck to sleep without any crying, then Phil would not be angry with him. Phil was not always angry. I just never knew when he would be. It was like living with a live bomb. Sometimes that bomb would be a dud and was just harmless, and other times it would create an explosion that could be felt for years.

I was starting to see a pattern to Phil's drinking and his explosive personality. It was always worse around February and March. This is the time of the year his high school sweetheart Jill died. It was April this time that Phil lit his fuse, I was due to give birth in only four months.

Phil had been to a squadron party with Ron and had Lueck with him. Phil came home late, drunk and nasty, and I was upset that he had Lueck with him in the car. I was trying to feed Lueck as he was sitting in the highchair in our kitchen, when Phil and I got into a fight. Phil felt he could take his son whenever he wanted and did not have to answer to me. I felt he could let me know when he was going to be home and that he should not be driving around drunk with our little guy in the car. Phil grabbed me and held tightly on to my upper arms. I yelled. Phil yelled. I yelled, "I hope someone hears me and calls the police." I hit Phil on the chest and told him to let go of me. Lueck was crying. I was shouting. Phil was shouting. I was crying. I was mad. Phil was crazy and drunk. But how could he be drunk when he only had "two" beers?

I finally left the house and Phil screamed at me that I was not to take Lueck with me. I went over to Ed and Urma's sobbing and telling them what was going on. They wanted to know if they should call the police. I told them no because it would only make Phil more angry. Urma went over to my house with me to get Lueck just when Phil was about to leave and take Lueck with him. He was going to Fresno to see his buddy Coy. It was already late at night. Urma talked the drunken man into giving her the baby. I stood there shaking with anger and fear, watching the two of them talk in our backyard. Phil took off, peeling out of the driveway leaving tire marks behind. Urma made sure Lueck and I were going to be okay, then left for her own hell.

I laid on the couch that night praying Phil would not come back. I think I called his parents to let them know he might be on his way there. I can't remember if he had his shotgun with him or not. I cried. I was so scared, and I didn't want to live scared anymore. I just wanted this pain to stop. Oh darn, he came back. It was near three in the morning, and for some reason, he came back home. How could someone that was so drunk drive and not have an accident? How could he not be stopped? I called his parents to let them know he was back home. They came the next day, which was Saturday, to see us. Phil's dad talked to him and told him to straighten up. They saw the black and blue handprint Phil left on my right upper arm from where he grabbed me. I don't remember what was said about it. They cared about me, but this only caused more problems for Phil. He wanted their love. "God, why did you send him back to me?"

Back to the honeymoon stage. Life was good for awhile. I knew Phil had learned a lesson and wouldn't hurt our children or me again. He felt sorry for what he had done. Phil worked around the house and got things ready for the new life that was about to join us. We started going to church. I knew things would be different this time. I decided to go to college to get a degree. I still had the old GI Bill and that would pay all my college plus extra money to help make household bills. I started out taking one class—and pregnant.

I loved hanging clothes out to dry. They always smelled so good. One sunny day I took in the clothes and threw them in a spare bedroom until I had a chance to fold them. Walking past the room later that day, I noticed a bat hanging from the ceiling. I carefully closed the door and put a rolled-up rug at the bottom of the door so the bat could not get out. I called Phil at work and asked if he could come home and get the creature, but he was busy and could not get away at that time. I called the California conservation department to see if they could come and help, thinking they might want to see the bat. Yes, they did want to see the bat, but only after we caught it.

I went outside to get a few things done, and when I saw my neighbors, I told them about the bat in the bedroom.

Phil did get out of his meeting early and came home to save his wife from the bat hanging from the ceiling. He put on the big insulated gloves he had in the garage, picked up an empty coffee can and the broom, and headed to the bedroom ready to get the bat. He stood up on a chair and Lueck and I waited down the hall in the living room when I heard Phil yelling, "Christine Katherine Harris, don't you know the difference between a bat and a butterfly?" It seems it was a brown wood moth that decided to take a nap while hanging from our ceiling.

Phil had a good laugh and went back to work to share the story with his co-workers that he had to come home and save his wife from a butterfly. I had to call the conservation department and let them know not to expect a bat from us and then told the neighbors my story. We laughed about this for years. This was a good memory.

Phil was good at his job in the air force and was promoted several times ahead of schedule. He was not good at testing, so when it came to that part of his career, his promotions slowed down. He always looked good in his uniform, even his fatigues. He always looked good in whatever he was wearing. He was not a sloppy dresser, but he was not fanatic about his clothes either. He took pride in whatever he did. The yard was beautiful. One of the many arguments we had was that I would not let him spend more money on the yard. The cars were always clean. The oil was changed on a regular basis. He always picked up his clothes and put his dishes in the sink. He cleaned the house if needed. He could fix anything, except for himself.

SHE'S HERE!

It was 8:00 p.m. and I trimmed the hedge in front of our house that afternoon when I started getting some small pains. They weren't very strong, but they came on a regular basis. Those little pains were starting to get close together, so I told Phil we should go to the doctor and see what was up. We asked Urma to watch Lueck and drove the couple miles to the base. Shortly after I arrived at the hospital the doctor broke my water. I asked if I could go to the bathroom, and they allowed me to go and from there I walked into the delivery room. I was ready to have this baby, but the doctors were not ready for me. They told me not to push because there was a physician assistant coming to watch the birth. Yeah, right, like I was going to wait for some guy to come and watch me give birth. I had better things to do with my life, like seeing who was so anxious to come into this world. I pushed quietly while the doctor washed up. He turned in time to catch a beautiful little girl. In less than one hour after we had left the house, a new little person had become part of our lives.

Katherine Lee Harris weighed six-pounds, eight-ounces. She was covered with nature's cream and smelled like heaven. She was alert and prefect. I lie in bed that night with a contented smile, smelling the cream that was on my gown and thinking of the wonderful little girl in our life. This would surely make Phil happy now. We were now a perfect family. One boy, one girl, and both parents were all that it would take to make a perfect family.

Kati, as we called her, was a good baby. She hardly ever cried. Phil fell in love with her, and Kati could do no wrong in the eyes of her dad. If Lueck accidentally hurt his sister, he would be punished with demeaning words or a hand across his body.

No one was immune to Phil's switchblade words, including his own mom. Lueck was about two years old when we were spending another weekend in Fresno. Grandma Harris allowed Lueck to carry a porcelain cat around the inside of the house. As Lueck was rounding the corner of the living room with the cat in hand, he fell and cut his little finger. After we got the bleeding stopped, we took Lueck to the Children's Hospital in Fresno. The little guy was put on a small wooden board and held down with straps as the doctors looked at his little finger. They did surgery on his finger that afternoon. It seemed he had cut a nerve, an artery, and a ligament, and they were going to reconnect them. Phil was angry with his mom and told her it was all her fault because she should never have let him carry that cat around. In Phil's mind someone always had to be at fault. Accidents never happen. I stayed with Lueck that night in the hospital.

I knew it. Phil did love me. He was seeing how much his temper was hurting me. The first time I noticed Phil was beginning to calm down was when he tried to move a bed into a room and it didn't fit through the door. Usually Phil would become angry, cuss, and blame me for something, but this time Phil stayed calm. I was standing by his side waiting for him to blow, but it never came. It felt so good to see him this way. I now knew things would be different. I knew that he saw how much his temper was frightening the kids and me, and he was changing.

Ron, the old drinking buddy, had been gone for two years on a military assignment, but he was back in town. He had retired, and his wife had left him. Ron was alone and needed a fishing and drinking partner again, so he picked an easy target, Phil. It didn't take much, and Phil was drinking again.

At first, Phil handled one beer fine, so now he could handle two. Two was good, so now it was three or more. The flu in the bottle was back. Puking in the toilet. Phil felt so bad. He was always so sorry and would say he would never do it again. I wanted to believe him. I wanted a happy marriage. I wanted a normal family. I ended up feeling sorry for him because he felt so bad. I knew he meant it this time for sure. Why would he want to go and drink himself sick again? He said he was sorry, and I was sure he was, until the next time.

Phil's brother Rick came to spend the weekend with us. Phil, the kids, and I had someplace to go and left Rick at our home alone. When we returned I saw that my radio was gone, the brand new wine bottle was missing out of the refrigerator, and I could not find Rick. I just knew that he hocked the radio. As we went to bed that night, I lie there fuming. It was late when Rick returned, walking with lead shoes through the house. I listened to every step he took, wondering what he was going to do next. I didn't trust him.

I woke the next morning after little sleep with a knot in the pit of my stomach the size of a rotten grapefruit. I was not going to let Rick take our things and worry me sick about what he might do to our children if he was drunk. I had to live with one drunken jackass, and I was not going to have another one in the house too. I looked in the telephone book for numbers of the local Alcoholics Anonymous and a halfway house where I thought Rick might get some help.

I walked into the room where he was sleeping and woke his sorry butt to confront him about taking our things. This was not a pretty scene. I was shaking with anger and my voice was quivering when I told Rick that I felt he needed help, then put the numbers in his wallet. I asked him where my radio was. He could tell I was angry and hurt—but not nearly as hurt as Rick was when I got done with the one-way conversation. Rick had left the radio out in his truck and just forgot to bring it in that night. He got up, dressed, and left the house not to be seen at our house for several years.

It was the same day as Jim and Donna came over for some celebration. Donna was more than upset that I accused Rick of stealing. She could not control her tears, and they left after only being at the house an hour or so.

That evening I found an envelope lying on the entertainment center addressed with my name. I opened it and read a beautiful thank you card that Phil had given me for standing up to his brother. He felt the same way I did, but could not, or would not, say anything to him. I felt as if Phil really loved me that night. He had not gotten angry with me for standing up for our family the way I thought he would.

Bev Armstrong, whom I had spent much time with talking about my marriage, got very sick. She had cancer throughout her body and her bones were becoming very brittle. She died within a month of finding out about her cancer. I was devastated. I had not been to a funeral since my dad's death. I had just lost my best friend. Who would be my mentor now?

Phil bought an old huge GMC Jimmy and loved to go four-wheeling. There was an old gravel pit a few miles from our house. One evening while I was in college, Phil had been drinking, put both kids in their car seats and headed for the pit. It was getting dark and cold and he got stuck. Kati was still in diapers and was soaked to the bone. The people that lived across the street from the pit pulled Phil out of the mud and took the kids to their house to clean them up. Phil told me about it that evening when I returned from school. Of course he did not mention the being drunk part. The next day I baked cookies and brought them to the strangers that had helped my family, as suggested by Phil. It was another negative event in my life that I ignored. If I pretended it didn't happen, then it didn't happen. Right?

Phil spent a lot of time with the kids when he was home. He loved jumping in their little blowup swimming pool after work on hot California days. We grilled often and had friends over for dinner and games. Phil was full of stories, and I never knew what was true or not. He was always acting up, and I didn't know if he was serious or not. Being a dad that loved to play with his kids, he would throw Lueck up in the air and catch him.

I think he had "a" beer that day when he threw Lueck up and missed him. Lueck came down and hit Phil on the nose, which I did not see. I looked over from grilling and saw Phil lying on the ground. I thought he was just faking it, so I told him to get up and knock it off. Come to find out that Phil's nose was bleeding a little and that it was also broken. Phil gave me a hard time about this for years, but in a good way. I don't remember what happened to Lueck. I don't remember Lueck crying or hitting the ground.

The summer that Kati was going to turn one year old, my sisters, their families, Phil, our kids, and I planned to meet in Montana to camp near Yellowstone. I was washing clothes and getting everything ready for the trip when I bent over and my back snapped. I was in pain and every movement hurt, but things still needed to be done. Kati needed attention, so I went to pick her up because she was crying. My back snapped again, and I could hardly move at all. I went and sat on the couch and Urma came over. I was in so much pain that I felt sick to my stomach. Phil came home and took me to the hospital where they prescribed a muscle relaxer. Back home I lie on the Lueck's bed with hot and cold packs. Each day I could feel the muscles letting go and stretching back out to their normal length. A couple of days of resting and I was feeling pretty good. We were ready to leave on the camping trip, and I was going to try to take it easy.

I was in charge of finding a campsite for all of us. Looking at the pictures in campground books I picked a site that looked fun, along the side of a hill. After we all arrived and got settled, we did a little site seeing. The campground was not exactly like the picture in the book, and Phil informed me that I did a rotten job of picking a campsite. He continued by giving me the "I can't believe you're so stupid and worthless" look. My sisters and their husbands enjoyed having a beer now and then and offered Phil one too. I have never figured out what was in beer that turned Phil from a halfway decent guy to a mean ol' evil-word-slinging hateful human. He put me down with words that, if each word were a pail of dirt, I would have been buried alive under ten feet of dirt. Oh, wait, I was being buried alive. Parts of me were dying every day. I was no longer thinking about what I felt, but what Phil felt. He would not talk about his feelings, so I was spending all my energy trying to figure out what he was thinking so I could avoid the silent treatment or the stabbing words that came my way when he got angry.

After a few days it was time for all of us to go our separate ways. I went to the top of a hill and just stood there looking over the world, thinking that I didn't want to go back home. I knew I had to go with Phil because we were a family. I never complained about Phil to my family because I did not want them to know what was really going on. I wanted to be "that happy family" so bad, that if I pretended we were, then maybe we would be. As I was standing there alone, my sister Linda came up behind me. We just stood there not saying anything, but she saw the tears sneaking down my face. She knew. She heard the words Phil said to me during our stay together. The only thing Linda said to me standing alone on the hill was "I am sorry." No explanation was needed.

We took the next summer vacation to see family in Minnesota. This time we drove up with both kids. They were pretty good car riders. Near the end of the journey Lueck had a stomachache, so we stopped often for him to try to use the bathroom. Phil was relaxed and did not complain when we stopped every hour or so for Lueck. The first couple of nights we stayed at Luann's home with her and her family. They were having a party with a keg of beer for their friends. All of my nephew's friends were there, along with my niece Cammie who was fifteen or sixteen at the time. Phil was having his share of the beer, and he started teasing my niece by chasing her. The next thing I remember is that Cammie was lying on the kitchen floor with her Uncle Phil sitting on top of her holding her down, then Cammie getting really angry. She got up and ran to the bathroom crying and would not come out. I don't know if Phil went to the bathroom door.

It was Kati's second or third birthday, and we had tickets to the Shrine circus. Phil's parents and Phil's brother Jimmy and his family, as well as Lueck, Kati, and I all had a good time at the circus. Donna bought the kids toys to remember the evening. Phil did not go. He chose to go hunting instead.

I was getting smarter the longer I was in the marriage. I no longer would go and lie on the floor if Phil was mad and slept on the couch. If friends invited us out and he was drunk and said he was not going because he was mad at me for something, I sometimes went without him. I was getting tired of all the mind games, but still I would not leave him because I would hurt too many people. I didn't want to think about how this was hurting my children or me. I should have put my children first, if I couldn't put myself first. It seemed that I felt everyone was more important than me. It was my job to make everyone else happy. I had to think about how other people would feel. I knew I was going to make it in life, but the other people might not if I didn't help them.

There were still a few times that I would search for Phil when he was late from work. I wanted to crawl in a closet with the kids when he was late. I knew the anger would follow him in the door like a stink follows sardines. I knew all of the bar phone numbers where he hung out.

Money was never an issue with drinking because Ron paid for most, if not all, the beers. Ron needed a drinking buddy.

I wasn't totally smart yet. I was still married, right? I remember one day it was Phil's brother's birthday, and we were all invited to go to Madeira, California, north of Fresno, for his party. Phil was not at home, and I knew he was out drinking. The kids and I were waiting at home for him so we could go to the party. It was past time to leave and my patience was running thin. I jumped in my car and drove to the club on base and there I found him with Ron. Surprise? I told him we needed to get going, and he followed me back home where we all got in his truck and rode with the drunk for forty-five miles to a party. I was not smart enough yet to leave him at the bar and go on without him.

Another trying time was when Ron stopped by our house after he had been drinking and would not go home. The kids had a program at church, and I thought if I invited Ron to go with us he would surely go home. I was wrong. He said "sure" and came with us to church. I was sitting in the back seat of the truck with my kids when Ron reached behind his seat and placed his hand on my knee. I wanted to vomit right there on his slimy five-finger beer holder.

The last time I remember seeing Ron was when both Phil and Ron came to our house drunk. I was sitting on the couch switching from being really angry and being really scared. They must have been able to see my feelings just by looking at me when they walked in the door. Ron knew he was part of the trouble that Phil and I were having with our relationship. Both of the irresponsible persons with dicks told me that if "I" didn't want them to hang out together anymore, they would abide by my wish. I would not give them the satisfaction of me telling them what to do. I figured they were both grown males and if they couldn't see for themselves what they doing to our marriage and our lives, I was not going to tell them. I knew it would come back and haunt me if I said anything. I could hear Phil telling me later, "you even tell me who I can have for friends." I had learned whatever I said would be turned around to hurt me at some time in the future. Ron followed me into the bedroom where I went to let my tears flow as I ironed clothes. He came and put his arms around me from behind. He told me he would never do anything to hurt me and all I had to say was that I did not want him hanging around anymore. I told him that was between Phil and him, and I was not going to tell Phil who could be his friends. I wasn't Phil's parent, and I didn't want to be.

Phil was having a little problem at work too. His commanding officer was accusing him of drinking on the job. Phil could lie his way out of any situation and told the officer it was the Shasta cola that was making his breath smell like booze. Phil could make anyone that questioned him about his lies look foolish and feel awful for not believing him. The Shasta cola breath thing worked on me too.

Phil, the kids, and I were going camping for the weekend. I noticed the booze breath on Phil and could also detect the mood change. I am not sure where he was getting the booze from because I did not see it around the house. I asked Phil if he had been drinking because he was driving to the mountains with us. Of course he denied it and said it was the Shasta he had been drinking. I knew better, but I also knew better than to question him any further. I did not want a huge fight in the car with the kids in the back seat. One of us would have ended up walking back home, and I am sure it wouldn't have been Phil. I learned to keep quiet. Even my tears rolled down my cheeks without sound. No stifling, no bawling, no nose blowing, just silent tears reaching out for freedom.

When the children were little, we used to ride bikes with them sitting on the back in child seats. This was something we could do together and have a good time, most of the time. We stopped in downtown Atwater for some parts, and, as Phil got off his bike, he didn't lift his leg high enough and hit four-year old Lueck on the head with his foot. Lueck started to cry, and Phil yelled at Lueck for not ducking. Phil had a hard time being at fault for anything he did. I don't remember him telling any of us he was really sorry for anything except when he had been drinking.

One weekend the kids and I went to Fresno, and Phil stayed home for some reason. When we returned, Phil had been drinking again. He must have been really lonely that weekend because by some coincidence he told me that four of his high school friends had called and talked to him. Only one of his friends had stayed in contact with him, and that was Coy, so I believed him on that one. But the other three were a little hard to believe. One was supposed to be Rod; the other, Nena; both were old high school friends; and then the last was Jill's dad or mom. I don't remember for sure which one it was, but I just remember it was another thing I was not to question.

I thought I had things bad but then I realized other people had it worse. One day an Avon lady stopped by, and I invited her in so she could show me what was on sale. We got talking and she told me her husband made her change the sheets in their bed every day. After hearing a story like that and other stories, I did not think I had a reason to complain about Phil. Someone always had a tougher life than I did. After all, my husband was a good provider, a neat person, helped around the house, and went to church.

I don't know what other people thought of me, or what they saw when they looked at me. Two women within just a few months told me basically the same thing. One lady was near my age or a little older and was over for a party we were having. She looked at me and said, "You really are smart." I am not sure what she meant by that or why she said it. I know at times, I acted naive because it was one of my coping skills. If people thought I was dumb, or didn't understand something I was usually safer that way. That way when I really didn't understand something people couldn't tell if I was joking or not. I am not sure if Phil told someone I was dumb, or stupid, and this woman realized I wasn't. Or maybe Phil told his friends I was smart, and they saw it was true. Maybe the women thought I was really dumb for other reasons and then realized I wasn't. I don't remember who the other women were who told me that I was smart either.

Phil and I had another big fight about his drinking. I no longer called his parents when things got out of control. I no longer felt much of anything. I would tell myself, "Only thirteen more years and I can leave." This helped me get through many fights because I could see a soft light at the end of the hellhole. I had learned to detach myself from my body when it came to having sex. I learned it was just a body, and if I was not in the body, my feelings could not be hurt. I figured I could be raped and it would not be any worse than having sex with someone who smelled like a keg of stale beer, and gave me no choice unless I wanted the silent treatment for days. I no longer cared much about myself. I didn't have much to care about. I knew in my heart what I was doing was wrong, but didn't know how to fix it.

Again I wanted to leave Phil, but I knew he would not make it if I took the kids and left. I knew that if I told Phil I wanted out, he would just say, "Well then leave, but you are not taking the kids." Phil was just crazy enough to do something that would hurt the kids. Not knowing what he would do was another reason I stayed in the abusive marriage. Also, I did not want to stay in California, and I didn't know how I was going to get started in a new life. Yet, another reason was that I couldn't handle the depressed look Phil gave me when he didn't get his way. I thought about killing the kids and myself—that way we would not be subjected to Phil's brutal words and his destroying hands. I was not seeing any other way out of the hell I was living. I didn't do this because I really couldn't kill my children or myself. I looked forward to the day Kati graduated and I could leave. But I still hoped Phil would quit drinking and we could have the happy marriage we pretended we had. I wanted so badly to have a husband I could count on, that would support my dreams, build me up, and not just tear me down. I put a fleece in front of God, and told him that if Phil quit drinking I would stay in the marriage. God please!

Phil often bragged what a good person I was to other people, but to my face he told me how hopeless and lazy I was. After eight years of marriage, he still compared our sex life to "making love to a log." Why would I want to have sex with someone that didn't give me much choice in the matter? He made me feel ugly and I could never live up to the love Jill had for him. It was hard to live up to a saint, like Jill, who was dead.

On one of our other trips to Minnesota we brought along the children's bikes so they would have something to do while visiting relatives. On one of the rare times I was driving while Phil was in the car, a police car with its sirens on came racing up behind me and I pulled over. Phil was sleeping at the time and the first thing he said when he heard the siren was, "Now what did you do?" I hadn't done anything and the police were headed to some accident. Another time Phil was sleeping in the car and I noticed we were low on gas. I didn't know if I should stop and get gas and wake Phil or just keep driving. He had just fallen asleep and, if I woke him up, he might just get mad and put us all in a rotten mood. I decided to just keep driving. We were in the middle of Nevada and there were not many gas stations on the back highways. He woke and I don't remember if he starting driving or not, but we almost ran out of gas, and I was chastised for being so dumb and not stopping to get gas. I never knew what to do. I felt I would have been chastised for stopping and getting gas when Phil had just fallen asleep too. He would have accused me of never wanting him to sleep. There was no winning, only constant thinking of what results my actions would bring.

Back to California and back to fighting. Phil had been drinking and we had another fight. I didn't know where to turn for help. I needed someone to talk with since Bev passed away, so I turned to the base chaplain and his wife. His wife and I had become friends through the base chapel. My family was over two thousand miles away, and I didn't want them to know what was happening in my life. I knew they would tell me to leave Phil, and I wasn't going to. So, I knocked on the chaplain's door of his house, crying for help. They had me come in, and we talked for some time. I left from there and went to my night class at the college feeling a little better about my marriage, but still very hurt and angry. God always puts people in the right place for me to talk to. During break I walked outside and Phil and the kids were there to see me. Phil felt guilty after drinking. He would act so pitiful that I would end up feeling sorry for him because he mistreated the kids and felt so sorry about hurting us. Phil had a way of always being the victim. I know this does not make sense in most people's worlds, but when you live in a crazy world, everything, yet nothing, makes any sense. I just got used to surviving this way.

Lueck started kindergarten and loved it. He was a very smart kid with a heart of gold. He did get in a few fights in school when other kids picked on a girl that had deformed fingers. Kids did not tease Lueck about his feet. We never made a big deal about them, and if anything was said, we tried to show the kids what a unique thing Lueck's feet were because he could turn them around backwards.

I was still in college and Kati was in preschool at the college. I stocked the commissary shelves at night to make a little extra spending money and to get out of the house. Between the GI Bill paying me to go to college, the commissary job, and Phil's income, we were doing okay for ourselves. We were not rich, but we were able to pay all our bills and still have a little fun. We had put an addition on to our house. People on the outside only saw the perfect family we pretended we were. Two kids, a nice house, smiles on our faces, friends to play cards with, and even a dog at times, made us look like the all-American family. My happy mask was beginning to stick so tight to my face that my skin was beginning to rot under the mask.

Near the middle of the year that Kati started kindergarten and Lueck first-grade, Phil came home with orders to Loring Air Force Base in northern Maine. He had requested a five-year tour because he, too, knew we had to move from California in order to save our marriage. We had to get away from family and the influence they had on us. They didn't run our daily lives, but they were a dysfunctional family that spilled over to ours.

We had to be at the base the beginning of May. I was so excited about moving. I felt like I was going home. I had missed the white Christmases I had grown up with in Minnesota. I got my ducks in a row and graduated after going to college for five years, with a two-year degree and a certificate in fashion merchandising.

Now we had to get ready for the move. We sold our house within one week of listing it with a realtor because Phil always had everything looking so neat. We traded in our pop-up camper for a motor home so the kids would be more comfortable driving cross country. We were off to a new place where were going to finally find contentment.

CHAPTER 7

MAINE

I could hardly get around because the muscles up in my back and neck were so tight from the stress of moving. I tried hard to have everything planned before we left, so the trip would go smoothly and Phil would not get angry at us. We pulled our Bronco behind the motor home and headed to Minnesota to see my relatives and take a break from the road for a few days. We pulled into Luann's driveway early in the morning. There was snow on the ground, and we slept in our motor home until daylight. We stayed at Luann's a couple of days, then headed to see Mom and Linda. Back on the road again, we stopped at the Canadian border, and Phil left his gun there, never to see it again. Why he had it with us when he knew he couldn't take it across the border was beyond me. I did not question too many things he did. It was his gun, and he could do what he wanted. At this point of the trip he didn't have many choices. We stayed a night in Canada and then headed south back into New York. On the last two hundred miles we saw at least three moose, and I knew I was going "home."

We arrived on Loring Air Force Base the first part of May and enrolled the kids in school for a month, which gave them a chance to meet some friends before summer started. Base housing was not going to be available for a few weeks, so we lived in billeting, which is like a base hotel. One of the first nights at Loring Air Force Base, Phil began crying as he lie on the bed. He felt scared and apologized for bringing us to this place at the end of the earth. I looked at him like he was crazy. I could tell I was going to love it there. The open air, fields, and moose were what I was looking forward to most. I knew for sure that Phil would quit drinking for good here. He had all kinds of animals to hunt. He had dreams of building a log home. We knew we were going to be in Maine for five years and did not have to worry about getting orders as soon as we got settled. How could he not be happy?

We got into base housing after only a couple of days of being in billeting. Our home was near the middle of a twelve-unit housing complex. It was a three-bedroom, one and a half-bath, and two stories. As we faced our housing unit from the front, our neighbors to the right had children close to our children's ages. The boy, Bryan, was the same age as Lueck and Shayna was two years younger than Kati. Ken and Deanne Koyles were our ages and welcomed us to the neighborhood. They had already been at the base for a couple of years, and Deanne hated it because of the long cold winters.

All the units in the row had the same inside layout except that every other unit was reversed. Our stairs joined the Koyles' and our bathroom medicine cabinets were also connected. I would shout at my children "go back to bed," because I could hear them coming down the stairs when it was really the Koyles kids using their stairs. We could talk to each other through the medicine chest, and I could smell what they were having for meals though the fan in the downstairs bathroom. There were not many secrets kept in base housing.

The Koyles' family and our family became good friends. On the Fourth of July, we all went to see the fireworks at the base softball field. Afterwards, while we were lighting candles out on the front steps of our home, Phil filled his belly button full of wax. He would do anything for attention. We all laughed about this for years. We were becoming a family again, laughing together as a family was supposed to do. Phil had not had a drink since we arrived, that I could tell.

The first year in base housing we entertained many guests. Linda and her family drove up from Minnesota. Brenda, a childhood friend, flew up to see Maine. My cousin drove up to see us while he was waiting for his semi to get fixed. But the best of all was when my sisters flew up to surprise me. They were going to come in February and then said they couldn't because something came up. But Phil and the kids knew they were coming anyway. Phil and the kids took off for an errand, and I stayed home to clean. I had been substitute teaching that week at the base elementary school. In Maine, I only needed a two-year degree in anything in order to substitute teach. I didn't know how to handle a room full of kids and just wanted some quiet time. I was hoping in the back of my mind that Phil was really going to get my sisters, but he promised me he would tell me if they were coming. This is one lie I was glad he told.

Phil and my sisters met the Koyles on base, and my sisters got in the Koyles' van so Phil and the kids could come home alone. When Phil and the kids walked in the house alone, with no sign of my sisters, I was a little disappointed. I then told Phil I was really hoping he had gone to pick up my sisters, and he reassured me again, that he would have told me if they were coming.

I was feeling pretty low. Loring Air Force Base, was in the middle of potato country in northern Maine where the winters were long and dark. I like winters for a month or two, but after awhile they were hard on me, since I needed a lot of sun. A few minutes later, both of my sisters walked in the front door. I stood there crying. They stood there crying. We were sisters to the very last teardrop.

The kids were in school and Phil at work, so my sisters and I headed to Canada to see what we could find. I got lost, which was nothing new, and we saw things we never expected, like moose along the road, and fun little stores that we stopped and shopped in. We did a little shopping and ate a little food and had a great time.

■   Some days I should not be writing, and today is one of those days. It has been almost sixteen months since Phil died and most days are pretty good. Today is pretty good, too, when it comes to the thinking part, but I still want to hide in the closet and forget the rest of the world. I don't want to think about the past, but I know I have to push myself to write this because otherwise I will never finish this, just like I never finish so many things.

Phil always wanted to live in a log home. That was his dad's dream also. I think Phil thought if we could build a log home and if his dad would come and see it and perhaps even live with us, his dad might finally be happy and really be proud of Phil. Phil was always trying to impress his parents. If he got any military award he would want to send the medal home to his dad. Phil played many sports in school, and by his words he was "damn good at them" too, but his parents never came and watched him do anything. He wanted his parents' approval even though he was thirty years old. He still needed that attention he did not get as a kid. Many times living with Phil was like living with a kid. If one of our children got something, he would say, "I didn't get one," and pout. He didn't pout nearly as often as he did when we were first married, since Kati did a much better job of pouting then Phil could.

We started getting ideas for a log home and looked at a few log home companies. We met a couple in Caribou, Maine, who sold log home kits, and they gave us a tour of their home. That was it; we fell in love with it. We got estimates from an excavator, a well digger, a furnace installer, and the people who would put in the foundation. I was the contractor for this job. It was up to me to line up the people we needed each day to get the job done. I loved doing this. We did most everything else ourselves and with the help of many friends. I found two acres of land for sale on the outskirts of Limestone, about one mile east of Canada and seven miles from the base. It was the perfect lot. It was walking distance to town, but far enough away that most of the kid's friends would call first before they came out.

We first got the driveway in and then on May 8, 1989, the excavating started. Things did not take long from there. We had the log kit delivered, and we had no way to unload the logs except by hand. We rented a forklift from the local hardware store, but it was not powerful enough to get the job done. Porky, the local city man, came and helped us unload with a forklift he had gotten somewhere. He did this without being asked, because that was what small town people do for each other. I knew for sure that I was home at last.

Once the logs were unloaded, the foundation set, and the well dug, we started with the work of putting our log home together. Our new neighbors stopped by, or at least drove by, to see how we were doing. Phil took vacation (leave) from the air force and worked many hours a day. Phil's co-workers wanted to learn how to build a log home, and they came out daily to help us, only expecting to be fed, and that was my main job. I was also the go-for for all needed material.

This was the best time of our marriage. We got along like married couples, like team players, like peanut butter and jelly, as we worked side by side building Phil's dream home. He was so easy going and would not get upset if someone did not follow the blueprint exactly. Tex and Rusty were two of the dependable guys that were out there every day, after working the day on the base, to help us build our home. Ken helped Phil do the electric work along with others from the base.

The plumber came to inspect the plumbing Phil did, and just shook his head saying, "That is not how I would have done it, but I guess it will work."

The hall was two different widths because the guys did not know how to read a blueprint. Some of the guys put the two-by-four on the inside of the chalk line, while someone else put it on the outside. It was supposed to go on the center. I am not sure what was inside all the walls because the guys liked to place different things, such as snuff and pop cans, in the walls as they were putting up sheet rock.

The men were working on a Saturday to put up the rafters. It took at least three guys and they had around five rafters in place when an immense wind blew them all down like dominoes falling after a small child teasingly hit the first one. They didn't bother measuring the center when they went to stand the rafter back up, so the center was now off-centered. After they nailed the plywood on the roof, this off-centered roof was quite obvious. The old timers from town would stop by and shake their heads, saying that we really needed to do something about the roof. What Phil finally ended up doing to fix the problem was put shims under the plywood ends to make the roof even. It was still off-centered, but the eaves looked better.

Phil's hands and arms were hurting each night after using a sledgehammer to nail the ten-inch nails into the logs, as well as working with his hands every day as a mechanic. He was losing strength in them and some days could barely hold a regular hammer or a cup of coffee. He was in a lot of pain. After several doctor visits he was diagnosed with carpal tunnel syndrome and was fitted with arm braces.

July 1, fewer than three months since the house was started, we moved in. The walls were not all up, but it was livable. We needed to get out of base housing so we could get basic allowance for quarters, BAQ, which is money the military pays for housing when military personal live off the base. We had a house payment to make, so we needed the BAQ. We lived down in the basement and placed the mattresses on the floor to sleep. I did dishes in the basement shower, and we had a great time. We awoke to birds hitting the windows upstairs. The birds got in through the eaves, because they weren't closed in yet, then they hit the windows trying to get out. When the birds knocked themselves out, we picked them up and put them outside. In a little while they came to and flew away.

I had gotten a job at the base dry cleaners doing alterations. I was working part-time in a temporary position. I liked my job, but my bosses were treating some of the other employees with disrespect and it deeply upset me. The way they treated other employees bothered me enough that I talked to both of my bosses about it. I could stand up for other people, but I could not stand up for myself. I worked with two gals in the alteration department who fought continually. It was a power struggle game they both loved to play. I did learn a lot of tricks about sewing while I worked there that helped me in the future of owning my own business.

It was starting to get cold again in northern Maine, and we did not have our ceiling up in the great room. One Saturday all the guys Phil worked with came out and put up our ceiling. We had so many people always willing to help. I don't know what we, or I should say, Phil, ever did that so many people were always there to help us. I guess it was Phil's charisma and people liked him. He was a good worker and a good supervisor. He was also a good storyteller.

■ My tears want to sneak out now, as I am writing this. Sometimes I feel like I have many people that care about me and I don't feel I deserve it, and still at other times I feel so lonely. I guess my lonely feeling is my own fault because I should be calling those friends that I know care.

Rick, Phil's oldest brother, called and said he was not working and would like to come and visit us to help with the house. The day Phil had to go and pick up Rick at the airport or bus depot, I don't remember which one, I was so nervous that I could not go far from the toilet. My stomach was tied up with memories from California with the radio and wine. Rick had to be one of the easiest going guys; none of his things meant anything to him and nothing of anyone else's meant anything to him either. He had been living on the streets and in his car surviving off of tomato soup he made out of ketchup packets.

He did show up at our house and helped us build the front porch and make curtain rod holders. After about two months of Rick living with us and me not getting much sleep because Rick was a loud night owl, Phil got him a job on the base working in the flight line café.

Rick was doing a good job and the pilots and other flight line workers loved him because he gave extra meat on the sandwiches. He found an apartment near the base and Phil lent his brother his bike, our TV, and other things he needed to live on his own. Rick worked his job a month or so when he got fired for taking old sandwiches home that were going to be thrown away. Again, it was not Rick's fault that he stole old sandwiches.

Neither Rick, nor we, could find Rick another job, so he decided to go back to Fresno. He was going to spend Thanksgiving with us and then head home the next day by bus. We went to the Koyles' house on base for dinner, and Phil picked up Rick and met us there. I don't remember this dinner at all. I can't figure out where I was. Phil was going to get our TV, his bike, and other stuff before dinner, but decided to get it after dinner instead. Rick told Phil his bike had been stolen and Phil could live with that; after all, it was his brother.

After dinner, when Phil went to drop Rick off and get all the stuff, there was no apartment there. A fire had consumed the whole place that afternoon. Rick had nothing left. He didn't have much to begin with, but now he had nothing. Not a thing except for clothes on his back, and we could not send him on the bus that way. The next day, Phil took Rick to the base thrift shop, and they donated enough clothes to Rick to get him home. They also gave him a suitcase and a few other things. We bought Rick the bus ticket and gave him money so he could eat on the long bus ride across the whole United States. Come to find out a couple of weeks later that Phil's bike was not stolen, but was sold for a few bucks to some GI on base.

Rick was afraid the fire was his fault in someway. He thought maybe he had left something on or a cigarette lit, but he had not. It was a young boy playing with matches under the stairs that started the fire. This time it really was not Rick's fault.

We made it though the first winter in the house. We had a wood stove in the basement so we got warm by carrying in the wood, splitting the wood, and burning the wood. Poor Phil, not ever seeing a real snowstorm, didn't think we would ever get out of our house again. He stood by the windows looking like someone was about to lock him up for life. He felt the snow would never stop and he would be in the house until spring, which might never come. Phil shoveled until his hands couldn't take anymore. Then he came in and stared outside. We all went out and shoveled, but we knew we could not keep up with millions of tiny flakes that were smothering the ground. I told him to relax and get a book, that someone would come and plow us out. I was not at all worried because I had lived though many snowstorms growing up in Minnesota. I loved a good snowstorm as long as everyone was home and safe. It must have snowed three or more feet that day and sure enough, when the snow stopped one of our new neighbors came by and made a single swoop through our driveway so we could get out. Later we hired someone to plow our driveway.

Our driveway had just enough of a hill to it that the neighbors were entertained watching us try to get into it. We learned that when it was really icy, if we took a good run for it and hit the first snow bank we would bounce off of it enough to get around the corner and hit the next snow bank to around the last corner into our garage.

That same winter Phil had surgery on his arm for carpal tunnel. He really should have had both arms done, but it is hard to go to the bathroom if they are both in cast. I sewed zippers in Phil's uniform pants and put Velcro on his pockets to replace the buttons, so it would make it easier to get dressed.

He had his surgery on the base in New Hampshire, and we ended up staying there an extra day because of a snowstorm. On the way home there was a semi that was stuck. Phil didn't think twice about helping the guy even though he had a cast on his arm. Phil got out the shovel and helped the guy dig under his tires. We did not make it home that night because of the snow and ended up spending the night in a hotel. At the hotel, one of the semi trucks hit our car with his tire as he was trying to turn, and put a dent in our door. Again, Phil was not upset and told the guy not to worry about it. We didn't even get the guy's insurance number because the man told us he would lose some award if he had any accidents, and Phil felt sorry for him. This is what made Phil so hard to live with, one minute he was the kindest guy I knew and the next he would be the meanest guy I knew. I felt Phil was really this nice guy deep down, but had been hurt so many times growing up that he didn't want anyone getting too close because they might hurt him too.

We did make it home the next day and someone had already been to our place and plowed out our driveway. We all went back to work or school and life went on at the Harris home.

Summer finally did arrive and we got busy getting to know the town. Phil took on the volunteer position of coaching the six-and seven-years-old soccer team, with our children being on this team. Phil was a good coach, and I was by his side being an assistant. I had never played soccer before and this was a good learning experience. He had a lot of patience with our children as well as the other inexperienced team players.

Also that summer I planned a grade school reunion in Lafayette, within the same week that my niece was getting married. The kids and I flew home after debating if we should drive. Phil was going to come with us, but something came up and he was not able to go. This worked out fine anyway, because I felt uncomfortable with him around my childhood friends. I felt he could not understand how I could have male friends without ever fooling around with them.

Two days after arriving in Minnesota, the town of New Ulm was having "Crazy Days," where businesses sell overstocked items on the street very cheap. Kati and Lueck spent the day with their cousin at her house while Mom, her husband, Harvey, and I went shopping for deals. We talked about lunch, but decided no one was really hungry, so Mom and Harvey decided to go home. Linda and Doug owned a store in New Ulm, and Mom and Harvey walked through the store to get to their truck, which was parked behind the building. After a couple of minutes, Mom came back into the store and said that Harvey was slumped over the wheel. I ran out the back door while Linda called 911. I started breathing in Harvey's mouth right away and the stiff body got a little softer. Doug came out right after me, and we pulled Harvey out of the truck and started performing CPR together. I believed I continued the breathing part while Doug did the compressions. The ambulance arrived, and Harvey was taken to the hospital where he never regained consciousness and died three days later.

I called back to Maine and told Phil what had happened. I am not sure if he was not listening to me, but he got the story all wrong when he went to tell his friends. He told people that Kati found Harvey, even though Kati was not anywhere around when Harvey became sick. I was learning not to tell Phil anything, because it seemed that he was in some other world when he went to repeat what he heard or saw.

When looking back at Harvey's death, I can see that if any death was meant to be, this was the one. Harvey was a wonderful man and had already had a couple bypasses and had a pacemaker installed. He was living on borrowed time. He had just put the key in the ignition when he slumped over. One more minute and Mom and Harvey would have been on the road with all the people shopping for "Crazy Days." My mom could have easily been hurt or killed in the accident. Harvey died the day before my niece's wedding, so Mom did not have to decide if she should stay by the side of her husband or attend the wedding. God had his hand on us.

I could not watch the show 911 for a long time after performing CPR on Harvey. I felt I did not do enough for him. I felt I let my mom down.

Phil wanted to know if he should fly down for the funeral, but I did not need him there. We did not have the extra money, and there was nothing he could have done to help. Lueck was one of the pallbearers for his grandpa. My mom knew she would be okay since she had done it before. I did not stay any extra days because my sisters were nearby and I needed to get back to work and to Phil and Maine.

When I got back up to Maine, things were not going well overseas. Things were not going well at my work. My bosses were treating people with little or no respect. The spring of 1990, I quit my job and opened my own business on Main street of Limestone, Maine. It was now called "C. Harris for Sewing," and I did alterations for people. The first day I opened the doors no one came. I cried wondering what I had done now. Then flowers arrived at my shop from my sisters wishing me good luck. I cried again. Phil was very supportive of me working for myself. I rented a small apartment that had a picture window that faced the main street of Limestone. This place worked perfectly for my shop. I liked being closer to the kids. They could come to the shop any time they wanted. I could again make sure everything was taken care of at home before Phil got off work. I could make sure the kids had not messed up the house too badly and there were not too many friends at the house. I tried to prevent problems before they occurred.

Sometime during the first year or two we were in Maine, Phil took the kids out target shooting. They would have been around six or seven. How the story is told to me years later by my daughter was that she walked in front of Lueck when he was shooting, and Lueck just missed her. Phil went off the deep end and beat and kicked Lueck. Lueck does not remember any of this to this day. I wonder how many other things Lueck does not remember and how many things I don't know about. Even though Phil was not drinking, he had not changed his attitude of life. I did not like getting calls from my kids while I was at work saying I needed to come home cause Dad was hurting one of them, mostly Lueck. I could not stand up to Phil, and this even hurt me more. These were my precious babies that he was hurting, and I was not strong enough to protect them. I wanted so badly to leave Phil, but I was hundreds of miles from home. Things would be going bad, but then Phil would have to leave for a short time because of military orders for somewhere. While Phil was gone I would always think he would realize how much he was hurting all of us and change his ways.

Desert Shield

Things were getting worse overseas with the fighting, and Desert Shield was becoming a household term. Phil was going to be shipped out. We filled out all the paperwork necessary for him to be gone for a long time and said our good-byes. He would be packed and ready to go, and then the plane would be cancelled. Phil would come back home, and then two days later the military would tell him he was going to leave again. We would say our good-byes again, and once again he would return home. The roller coaster of good-byes was harder than just saying good-bye once. Phil was finally leaving in August and again wouldn't be there for Kati's birthday. This time it was not Phil's fault he could not be there to watch his daughter turn nine, like so many previous birthdays where he chose to go hunting instead of spend time to celebrate Kati's birthdays.

I felt so many mixed emotions with Phil being gone. The tension was less in the house, yet I missed him. The children missed him, but they could feel the pressure was off of them too. I had no idea how long he was going to be gone. I was worried that heating oil prices were going to skyrocket, and we would have to live in the basement for the winter. I worried about having enough money to get by. The air force was going to pay Phil extra money each month while he was gone, but we also needed extra money because Phil needed more money where he was going. He could not tell me where he was or what he was doing. I sat by my kitchen table singing childhood church songs praying he would not start drinking again; praying he would be okay; praying that if he did start drinking again, he would not come home. Prices of heating oil did not go up, and I wasted my time worrying for nothing. I learned an important lesson.

I moved my business back home in the fall of that year. It was easier being home and working when Phil was not there. I also was hired to work part-time for a lady in Fort Fairfield, about twelve miles north of Limestone, doing embroidery. She was the greatest boss I could have ever had. Her husband was also an alcoholic, and we understood each other. She tried to talk me into going to Al-Anon, which is a support group for people that have alcoholics in their lives. She had a lot of patience in teaching me how to run the embroidery machine and often took me out to lunch. I wanted so much to be part of her family of thirteen children.

The neighbors and church friends were taking good care of me while Phil was gone. I wouldn't have been able to get through those times without the support of the people from church and from the town itself. One Sunday while I was sitting in church and was crying, a young lady came and sat next to me and put her arm around me. Jody became one of my best friends. She had daughters close to my children's ages and invited us to her home for dinner. One of the other church members checked my house every night, by looking out of their house window when they went to bed to make sure I did not have a chimney fire. Others brought us bags full of delicious Maine potatoes and invited the kids and me over for dinner. An officer from base, Major Knight, would call and ask if I needed anything. He mowed our two-acre yard with his riding lawn mower after the wheels kept falling off my push mower. He helped finish building shelves in Lueck's closet and did other odd jobs around the place. He enjoyed doing carpentry work and base housing didn't let anyone remodel it just because they liked doing projects.

Then it happened. I was at a city chamber meeting and the kids were home with Jessie, the kid sitter, when the news came that Desert Storm started. I called home quickly and asked Jessie to turn off the TV, but it was too late. The children now knew their dad was at war. The tears, the mixed feelings, the fears were all things that ran through me. By this time I knew where Phil was and what he was doing. Phil was not good at keeping secrets, plus it was pretty much general knowledge around the base that the troops were located on the island of Diego Garcia. Phil was in a pretty safe place where there was not any fighting, just B52s being fixed, ready for bombing.

The kids and I spent Christmas together. Phil spent Christmas with all the other military personnel on the island where he was stationed. He was able to call home at least twice a month. My mom wanted us to come home, but I needed to get things done. I decided to go to Minnesota in February and stay with my mom until Phil came home. I enrolled the kids in my old grade school in Lafayette, and asked Cyndi, a teacher and friend, to stay at our home while we gone. She gave up her apartment to move into our home with her two cats.

Two hours after we arrived at my mom's house in Lafayette, Phil called and said he was coming home. The war was over. I knew the war was over when I left for Minnesota, but I figured it would still be months before they sent the troops home. It took months for them to leave the states, and I thought they would have a lot to clean up before they came back. I was wrong. I didn't know what to do now. Cyndi was living in our house; the kids were enrolled in Lafayette School; we didn't have a lot of money to fly back home; and again, I could not just ask Cyndi to move back out when she had no place to go.

Phil had not met Cyndi, but was soon going to know her quite well. I decided not to fly home to meet Phil. His first sergeant told me they would send Phil to Minnesota as soon as he got home. Cyndi met Phil at the plane when all the other families were there to greet their loved one home. [This is something I regret to this day. Phil must have been so lonely getting off that plane after being gone seven months and not having any of his family there to greet him. Everyone else had family there, and we were not there for him. I am so sorry, Phil.] Phil spent the night fixing things in the log home, being unable to sleep. Cyndi spent the night there too, feeling awkward in the house with a stranger. Phil took the next plane out and arrived in Minnesota with most of my family at the airport to welcome him home.

My sisters rented a hotel home for Phil and me in New Ulm. Our children wanted to spend the night with us too, which was fine with me. Phil was really distant, and I felt very awkward. I think Phil was angry with me, but never said a word. I was always trying to figure out what he was thinking or feeling. I know I was scared. It had been so relaxing without someone mad at me all the time. I had seven months of thinking and feeling for myself. I wrote to Phil almost every day while he was gone. When he did call, many times he wanted me to have sex talk with him. I could not do that. It was not in me to say things I did not feel. I wanted us to be a family, but I still could not pull it together. Phil was home, and my life was hell once again.

We stayed in Minnesota a couple of weeks and then pulled the kids out of school and went back to Maine. Phil was getting back into life as a family and seemed to have changed some. He seemed to appreciate us as a family a little more. I was starting to love him again. He joined the Rotary Club and began getting involved in the community. I was so proud that I was not wishing him dead any longer, so I told him I used to feel that way but no longer wished him dead. I don't remember what his reaction was, but I should have known he would use this against me someday. At this time, I was glad he was my husband and the father of my children. Then one night it happened again.

It was February, near the anniversary of Jill's death when Phil left for a Rotary meeting. Phil was usually home around 8:00 p.m., and it was now 9:00 p.m., and he still wasn't home. I called Jody to see if she knew where Phil was because she was at the same Rotary meeting. She said Phil got called to work at the beginning of the Rotary meeting. It was below zero outside, and I knew Phil did not have much gas in his truck and there wouldn't be any stations opened when he returned. I don't remember if I called Phil at work or if he finally called me to let me know there were people problems at work and he would be home later.

I tried to sleep, but I heard him come home around one or two in the morning and he was puking in the shower down in the basement. I went down there and saw him sicker than a dog. I asked him if he had been drinking and, of course, he said no. He got very angry with me for even thinking he had been drinking. He said he had promised me he would not drink again. Never mind the smell of booze on him. Never mind the anger in his voice. Never mind the temper that was about to explode.

I went to bed and shared my tears with God. I was so scared. Phil slept down the basement on the cushions we had there. I figured God had something special in store for Phil since he did not die that night. He should have been completely out of gas and if he had to walk, he would have frozen. He was not dressed for the cold, and as drunk as he was, he should not have made it home. Who was I to second-guess God?

The next day, Phil was still sick. He was doing something in the basement when he threw up right where he was at. There was no warning, and he did not even try to make it to the bathroom. I started to clean it up for him, and he told me just to get away. I went back upstairs with fear in my body and tears escaping.

Phil told me he was disappointed in me for even thinking he would have a beer. His explanation for being sick was that the medicine he had just been given for his high cholesterol was making him sick. I knew better than that, but I did not question him to his face. I didn't talk to him. I wanted to leave, but where would I go? I went to work in Fort Fairfield with tears in my eyes. What was I going to do? I didn't want to live this way ever again. I didn't want my kids to live this way either. Where was I to go? What was I to do?

A few days later we still were not speaking to each other. It was late in the evening when Phil got called back to work for some reason. We were yelling at each other when he said, with so much hate in his voice it was like the devil himself talking and his eyes turning to glossy beads, "maybe you will get your wish and I will die tonight." He left the house rattling from the door being slammed. I was scared!

I didn't usually call my sisters and let them know what was really happening in my life with Phil, but that night I did. I was shaking. I had never seen that much hate coming from Phil. I hid all the guns in the house. I don't remember where I hid them. I was afraid Phil would shoot himself. I was afraid for the kids, and me, too. The kids were in bed when this all happened, and I don't know how much they heard.

Most things I didn't tell my sisters because I knew I was not going to do anything about my situation, so why complain. My philosophy was, if I was going to complain I better do something about it and not just bitch. They called the next day to see how I was doing, and Phil answered the phone. They asked to talk to me, but they knew I could not say much with Phil near by. They called again that night when Phil was at work, and I told them things were going okay. They knew better, but respected me enough to leave things alone. [I learned years later that my two brothers-in-laws wanted to come and take the kids and me back to Minnesota. I would have hated them for this. I thought I knew what I was doing and had to do it myself. That was why I would not usually tell them what was going on in my life.]

The next day I went to work in Fort Fairfield, and I told my boss about most of the stuff that had happened in the last couple of days. She was very understanding, being married to an alcoholic herself. I tried to work that day through tears. "Do I stay and put up with this abuse or do I try to make it on my own and take the kids and run?" was the battle racing through my head. I so badly wanted a normal happy family. I so badly wanted a friend, an equal partner as a husband, and, if I quit now, I would never get my dream. Battles raged in my head, battles raged in my home, and battles raged in my heart. When would there be peace?

That afternoon, while I was working, Phil arrived with flowers. He had talked to his first sergeant that morning and realized he didn't want to lose the kids or me. He knew I was about to leave him. I didn't want to make a scene at work, even though it was just my boss and me. I went out to the car with Phil, and we talked and decided we would talk more that night at our house.

I did not want to go home that night. I knew how Phil would act. I had seen the act many times before. He would be so sorry for everything. He would become the victim. He would be sick and throw up. He would cry and tell me he would change. I would feel sorry for him and try our marriage again because I could not stand to see him that way. Yep, that was just how it happened too. The kids were at a friend's house while Phil and I sorted out our life. I did not want to stay with him, but I felt I had no other choice. He made love to me that night on the living room floor. I cried. I did not feel the love, but felt manipulated by his sorry actions.

Not long after this, Phil had a doctor's appointment, and I went with him on base. I was holding his medical records and was afraid to look in them to see if he really had been to the doctor and was given new medicine for his cholesterol. In my heart I wanted it to be true. I wanted it to be the medicine that made him sick and not the booze. I wanted to be wrong. It was some years later that I had the strength to look in his records, remembering the date and finding nothing about him seeing the doctor and getting any new medication around that time. Another lie I was told.

Back to the honeymoon stage. Phil was loving and caring. But I was still scared every time Phil was late from work.

Phil's parents wanted to see their son after Desert Storm, and they were going to give Lueck Jim's El Camino. Jim was also dying and Phil wanted to see his dad for the last time. We all flew down to Fresno, California, from Maine and spent a week or so there. We drove the car back across country, taking our time and enjoying the road. The kids would take turns sitting in the back of the truck with me. We had bought a topper as well as cushions and seat belts for the back to make it fairly comfortable. Phil would stop when it got really hot and would look for a place for the children to go swimming to cool off. The only time on this trip that I felt really scared was when we got behind modular homes going slowly down the road and there was no time to pass with cars coming from the other direction. It was a busy highway, and Phil should have just pulled over and taken a break or relaxed and enjoyed the trip, but his temper took over his body, and we passed the trucks with cars coming towards us at great speeds that should only be used on race tracks. I forgot to breathe as I was saying my prayers in the back of the truck. I was ready to get out of the truck. I didn't say anything, because if I did I would just have heard "you think you can do better, you drive." [Thank you God, for taking good care of us.]

Since Phil had not celebrated Christmas with us because of being at Desert Storm we planned on stopping at Santa's Village, a small theme park in Vermont, to surprise him. It worked. We all had a great time on the rides and were becoming a family once again.

But just when I thought things were going smoothly, I got a blast of cruel life. One Saturday morning Phil was angry with the kids for something. I don't remember what, probably having messy room. He came down the hall yelling and ready for a fight. By this time I had pretty much detached myself from life and viewed things as if I was not there, but instead was looking at things from the other side of the one-way mirror. He was pounding his fist on the kitchen counter and throwing a fit. Looking at this grown man throw a fit instead of talking about a problem just hit my funny bone. If he could have watched himself make a fool out of himself, it would have stopped him from having tantrums. I stood there and laughed at him while he yelled and carried on. That was probably not the smartest thing I did on my part, but that was what I did. I laughed right at the fool throwing a fit. Talk about angry.

But Phil wasn't completely stupid, and he knew enough to get out of the house before he really hurt someone. I don't think he touched many of the steps as he flew down the basement to the garage to get into his truck and spin out of the driveway. When he left, the kids and I hurdled into a group hug of tears. Lueck asked me why I ever married him. What should I have said to an eleven-year-old child? I wanted the children to love their dad, but not act like him. I want them to know they couldn't get by in life by throwing fits to get what they wanted. I wanted them to know their dad was doing the best he could because of the life he grew up in and because he was an alcoholic. Why did I marry him? That was a very good question. But I did marry him and he was their dad and we were going to make the best of it we could.

He did come back home that day and, like the results of most of our fights, he did not talk to me for days. He did not talk to the kids either. The silent treatment worked. I felt I was worthless and invisible. Phil didn't talk to anyone, yet I always felt I was being watched out of the corner of his evil eye. He wouldn't say anything but just sit there and look at me like I was dumber than the muck between his toes.

Phil liked to be silent. He just stood around and watched us and not say anything. It wasn't a good observation, but more like we were being spied on. Lueck was in the shower when Phil walked in the bathroom, and without letting eleven-year-old Lueck know he was there, Phil watched him take a shower. Phil didn't keep this information to himself, but told our friends that he stood outside the shower and watched Lueck play with himself. There are two things wrong with this picture. What was Phil doing watching his eleven-year-old son take a shower and not letting him know he was in the bathroom, and why would he tell our good friends about this? Red flags waving all over the place, and I was trying to wash them enough times so they would fade and turn pink. Pink flags are not as bad as red flags. They are only little warnings.

The air force knew Phil did wonderful work, and they could always count on him to be there and give 100 percent of himself. He had tested for technical sergeant a few times and could not pass the test. The air force wanted to keep Phil, so they step-promoted him for all the work he did while in Desert Storm to E-6 as a surprise at a commander's call, a monthly meeting for personnel in a military squadron. His commander called me to see if I knew where Phil was to make sure he showed up for commander's call. I knew he was either out hunting or looking for donations for the Rotary auction that was coming up in a couple of weeks.

The children and I drove off in the El Camino to look for Phil at his favorite hunting spots. We did not find him, so we headed back home and I did some calling. I found him in Caribou, Maine, at a store and told him that he had to go to commander's call. I don't remember the reason I told him. The kids and I did not go, even though I wanted to be there, because then Phil would know for sure something was up. They wanted this to be a total surprise. It was. [Phil held this against me for years that I was not there. I really did want to be there to see him promoted.]

After his promotion I asked him what he had done in Desert Storm that no one else did to get him promoted. I am not sure how I meant this question, but Phil took it in a negative way and thought I doubted that he deserved it. Maybe I was? Maybe I wanted to really know what good things he had done. I just don't know. This is something else he threw back in my face for years. I just knew Phil had a way of making a small cut that needed a kiss and a band-aid into something that was life-threatening and needed stitches.

I found out from friends that were stationed with Phil during Desert Storm, Phil had been drinking while there. He stole, or borrowed, a military jeep and drove along the coast on Diego. Instead of getting into trouble for this, like most military personnel would, someone was just ordered to go and get Phil and let him sleep it off. He also broke a military personnel's finger when it was pointed in his face. Phil hated to have someone point a finger at him. Once again, Phil came out smelling like a rose. I don't know why charges weren't pressed against him. Probably because he was a good worker and whatever he did, he did it to the max. He was obsessive in most everything, work, play, anger, eating, not eating, lying, and drinking.

I felt something one day that I tried hard not to feel. I was collecting money for a fundraiser when I approached a husband and wife working on their lawn. The lady was sitting on top of the lawn tractor, and her husband asked her nicely to please not sit there because it was not good for the mower. My heart started to ache. Those were kind words that he spoke to her. He didn't say, "Get your fat ass off the mower. What's the matter with you?" He just asked her, as he would his best friend, with kind words, not to sit there anymore. I looked at my marriage and myself and realized that I did not look or really talk with other men because I would then see what I was missing. I didn't read romance novels or watch romantic movies because I would see what I was missing. If I didn't know something was out there, I couldn't miss it. I even played mind games with myself. I just wanted to survive.

The church we attended in Limestone had become our family. We both had become involved in the church, which we had never really done before. Phil was in the choir and the men's group and helped out where needed. The choir was teaching Phil to read music and how to sing. When the choir needed new robes, the members got together and did a lot of fundraising. Phil seemed to really belong and was enjoying church. The church family cared about Phil and about the rest of us too. They saw us as a good family. But, they did not know that when Phil went home after church and I was still there visiting with people, it was because Phil was angry at me or just did not want to take the time to wait for me as I visited with friends.

I was alone most of the week and church was my time to renew myself with friends. I acted like I wanted to walk home, which was really no big deal, but I did not have a choice in the matter. It was nearly a mile to our home from the church, and because Phil would leave without me, I walked the road several times. Sometimes our children stayed with me and walked home, and other times they took off with their dad.

A group of friends from the church decided to sell food for a fundraiser at the Fourth of July picnic. Phil and I were involved, as well as our children. We set up our tent at the festival for a place to cool down or get out of the rain, whichever happened to be in God's plan for the day. It was the last night of the festival and the fireworks began. We stayed by the booth to keep in eye on things and when I happened to look around for Phil, I couldn't find him. I went and checked in the tent and there he was, all curled up in the fetal position in the corner of the dark tent. He was scared. I tried to talk to him, but didn't get very far.

I don't think I tried too long because I never knew with Phil what was really true and was only true in his mind. Later I found out that the fireworks reminded him of Desert Storm, which didn't make sense because where he was stationed he shouldn't have seen any fighting. [I wish the air force could shed some light on this for me.] The next Fourth of July when we were at the same picnic again, Phil started to act strange by getting very quiet and staring off into space when the fireworks started. I asked him again about this behavior, and he said he didn't realize he was acting strange and never did it again in the following years.

I needed to talk to someone, so I talked to the pastor of the church about my marriage, and she understood how I was feeling. I am not sure why we didn't go to counseling there. I don't think Phil realized how depressed I was in the marriage. I knew we had talked about counseling at one time or other, and Phil said he would never go. He would state that he did not have any problems and, if I wanted to go by myself, I should go. I wanted out of the marriage, but it was not the right time.

I can't remember why I flew to Minnesota alone. I usually didn't leave the kids with Phil unless I had to, but I don't remember them coming with me to Minnesota on this particular trip. I felt this was going to be the last time I was going to see my sisters and mom. I just knew that I was going to die. Maybe it was because I wanted to die so badly. I wanted out of this hell of a marriage, but knew it was wrong to divorce Phil. I was just so worn out from living scared and being mentally abused that I wanted to die. Maybe the children were with me, but I know Phil was not there on this trip.

Coming back from Minnesota I sat in an airport on the East Coast, not wanting to go back to Maine. I closed my eyes and prayed and when I opened my eyes, there was a man sitting next to me that looked like my dad. I knew it was my dad. I looked at him and closed my eyes again. I felt like I was in a dream. I only had them closed a few seconds and when I opened them again he was gone. I could not see him anywhere. I knew he had been there. I knew that whatever would happen to me, I was going to be okay. If the plane crashed on the way home, as I was hoping it would, my dad would be there to take care of me. If I made it back to Maine to live in a large wood box, my dad would be at my side telling me I was a beautiful person and I could get through it. God was listening to me, but had given me my own brain to use on deciding what to do with my life. It was my choice to stayed married or leave Phil.

BACK IN MAINE AGAIN

The rumor was that Loring Air Force Base was going to close. We didn't believe it would. We decided we were going to retire in Maine. We loved our log home. We loved the people there. We had many friends, and the church was our family. We both belonged to the community. I was on the budget committee for the school as well as a chamber member, and Phil belonged to Rotary and we were both involved in the church. The kids were involved in school and sports and had made many good friends.

It was voted on and Loring Air Force Base was closing. We had to sell our home and move once again. We had a couple of choices of where we could move to from here. We chose to move to Whiteman Air Force Base near Knob Noster, Missouri, along with our friends, the Koyles.

There was no market for housing with everyone having to move and no job market to bring new buyers to the area. We basically gave our house away and the government made up some of the difference. We moved back into base housing for ninety days. Bob and Dot Phair, our elderly friends, helped us move from our home in Limestone back to Loring Air Force Base. Phil and Bob carried in the heavy objects like our couch and chairs, beds and mattresses, and washer and dryer. Phil was pushing to get all this done at a very fast pace. Bob was not looking good. It was hot out and Bob was in his seventies and had health problems. Still, Phil would not slow down and give Bob a break. Bob finally had to stop anyway because he was sweating and not feeling very well. Phil was not thinking about anyone else. He just wanted to get the job done and the truck returned. The rental was good until the next day, but Phil wanted it returned by noon. There really wasn't a rush to get the furniture moved into our house in such a short time. I felt so bad for Bob and Dot, but I did not want to say much because I knew it would only cause a scene.

I continued working in Fort Fairfield for Mary, driving the twenty miles each way, while we lived in base housing. The kids spent most of their last summer days with their friends in Limestone. One day as I was working, Kati called and said that Dad was hurting Lueck. Phil had pulled Lueck's ear and yanked him into the truck for some reason I don't remember. When I got home that afternoon, Phil was at work. Lueck was upset, but never complained about his dad hurting him. I asked the kids if I should leave him and they both said no. I realize now, that I put the weight on their shoulders if I should stay or go. I wanted to leave Phil so badly, but did not want to take the kids' father away from them. The next day, I went to the library and got a book on how to raise kids. I needed answers on what to do, but the answers were not in the books, but in my heart. I did not listen to my heart, or did I?

Phil was working the night shift again and tried to make all the kids' events in school. He was lacking sleep and when Phil was overtired he walked and talked in his sleep. I was upstairs in the shower when I heard a crash. The kids came running up the stairs and shouted that their dad had fallen. I grabbed a towel and wrapped it around me and ran down the steps to see what was going on. I found Phil at the bottom of the steps and as I stood over him, dripping water on his face from my wet body, he came to enough to tell me that he was okay. He had just gotten up too fast and was overtired and passed out. I went back up and finished my shower. After the shower I called the base hospital to see if there was anything I should do for Phil. They said to just keep an eye on him and, if any other problems occur, I should bring him in. He was fine. He got some sleep and was at work the next night.

When military members live in base housing, the members have to have it cleaned to certain standards before they can move out. When the final inspection came for us to move out, the inspector found a *Penthouse* magazine on the top shelf of our bedroom closet. Phil denied it was his. I didn't believe him, but I wasn't going to challenge him. I just pretended I was dumb and let him think that once again I believed his lies. Whatever?

For the move to Missouri, we both drove a vehicle. We had the Bronco and Lueck's El Camino that were both full of our stuff. Yellow Trucking Company took the rest of our things to Missouri. The Koyles left a couple of weeks before us and were moved into their house near the base.

Okay, now things were going to be okay. Phil would be happy now. It was me that was upset about moving. I did not want to leave Maine, and I moved to Missouri with a chip on my shoulder. I was not going to like it there. Maine was supposed to be my home.

I drove the El Camino and followed Phil because Phil had a small trailer he pulled behind the Bronco. Halfway to Missouri, Phil decided we needed new tires for the trailer. He installed them himself after buying them at some tire place. As I was following him that day I thought they looked like they were wobbling. I told Phil about the tires, so that night in Ohio Phil tightened the tires to make sure they wouldn't fall off. As I followed Phil up the on ramp the next morning, the tires froze up and flipped the trailer. Our guardian angels were with us that day. We were lucky it did not flip the whole Bronco. I drove around the city and found someone that would come and help us get the trailer off the side of the road. We rented a U-haul trailer and had to move our things from the trailer to the U-haul. Phil thought he needed to keep the new tires off the trailer cause we were just going to leave the old trailer at the U-haul place.

As Phil was loosening a tire, the lug wrench slipped and Phil fell over a five-foot wall into the bushes. The kids and I looked at each other and didn't know what to do. We didn't know if he was hurt or if he was going to be mad at us for something we did or didn't do. We did not expect the reaction we got. Phil came up out of the bushes laughing. He was really laughing at his own fall. We all laughed, and I felt that once again we had a chance of being a real family. I wanted us to be the caring family I grew up in, where mistakes were laughed at and love was given even when I messed up. I didn't want us to be the scared family we were. I wanted hope. Now I knew things were going to be different. They had to be different. Phil had to see how much we loved him and we just wanted his love in return. We didn't want to live scared anymore. He didn't have to be perfect for us to love him, and we didn't want to be perfect for him to love us. I knew things were going to be okay now because we had laughed together over a mishap when Phil fell over the wall. I grasped at anything that gave me even a smidgen of hope.

One tiny tree does not make a forest. One tiny laugh does not make a family.

CHAPTER 8

WARRENSBURG, MO

Before we left Maine the air force authorized Phil a one-week special leave to look for a house in Missouri. Phil found a new sub-division that was building houses and picked out a floor plan. We would get to choose the floor coverings and paints. The house should have been almost done by the time we arrived in Missouri, but there was miscommunication with the contractor and the bank, and it had not even been started.

Our ol' friends, the Koyles, said we could stay at their house in Knob Noster, about twelve miles from Warrensburg, Missouri, which is located forty-five minutes east of Kansas City. After we talked to the bank and got things going with the house, we took off for a week to see my family in Minnesota. When we returned to Missouri, our basement had been dug. It felt great to have that started. We asked the Koyles if we could stay with them for a month until they got our house finished. They were great friends and gave Phil and I their daughter's room. The girls slept on the living room floor on cushions, while Bryan shared his room with Lueck. Our kids started school in Warrensburg and the Koyles went to school in Knob Noster. After one month, our house was not nearly completed, and it was the end of October. I checked on the house every day when I brought the kids to school. Deanne was not working at the time, so we had many good talks. We worked well together, taking turns cooking, shopping, and cleaning the house. The Koyles were an easygoing family, and I always felt welcomed there. I had a great time at their house, playing many games of cards. Phil and Deanne flirted with each other, and this was a great moral booster for him. Ken didn't mind, and I didn't mind at all either. Deanne was my best friend, and I knew she would never do anything to hurt me. Phil, on the other hand, would get very upset if I flirted, even the tiniest bit, with anyone. I felt I could not talk to anyone of the opposite sex for even a few seconds without Phil giving me "the look." This might have been my imagination, but to me it was real.

Another month passed and our house was getting closer to being done, but was still not ready for us to move. It was the first of December when we finally moved in, three months after we asked if we could stay with the Koyles. We learned a lot about each other. I learned the Koyles were very easy people to live with, and I could depend on them for anything. I am not sure what they learned about us.

One evening when we adults were sitting around their living room talking, I was telling Phil that I thought I would go back to college and get my teaching degree. I had a couple thousand dollars my mom held for me after my dad died, and I felt my education would be a good thing to invest in. I still remember how I felt slapped in the face, punched down to nothing, when Phil discouraged me from going back to school, by saying, "Why should you go back to school when you never used your first degree?" To most people this is probably no big deal, but to me it was a statement that said I was worthless. I had used my first degree, which was an AA in general education. I also had a certificate in fashion merchandising, which I used to have enough self-esteem to start my own sewing business in Maine. My AA was what allowed me to substitute teach in Maine. I wanted to be encouraged to go back to school. My self-esteem was low to begin with when it came to going to college. That is why I had not gone to college right out of high school, even though my whole college would have been paid for though Social Security and veteran's benefits. I listened to Phil and did not go.

The tension between Phil and me had not changed. I did not want to be in a room with him any more than I had to. I hated having to watch everything I did and said. Phil's evil eyes burned a hole right through my heart. His head, shaking of disapproval, was taking its toll on my self-esteem. The silent treatments that would last for days were getting harder to ignore. I would, at times, carry on a two-way conversation with Phil, answering for him, just so I could pretend I was living a normal life. Ken, Phil, and I sat up many nights watching TV. Deanne went to bed to watch something else or be on the computer in their bedroom. When Ken went to bed, I headed to the other computer room and played games. Phil was very jealous that I left the room when Ken left and confronted me on this before he chose the silent treatment for my punishment.

Phil was correct when he thought I didn't want to be alone in the same room as him, but it was not because I liked Ken, it was that I didn't like being with Phil. We could not talk, we could not flirt, we could not argue, we just could not communicate. If I ever flirted with Phil, he thought he had to jump my bones right away. That is not what I wanted, but could never get him to understand that.

When we moved out of the Koyles' house, Phil was not speaking to me except when there were people around us. I found Phil the prefect card about how much I loved him and wrote on it that the only person I loved was him, and he did not need to be so jealous. It was true. I didn't love any other guy, and I wanted to love Phil and did the best I could, but it was never enough. I did not give him the card, but placed it in the glove compartment in his truck instead. I am not sure if he ever read it and, after a couple of months, I threw it away. I was not sure what his response would be if I gave it to him. I did not know if he would be kind to me and thank me, or just call me a liar.

■ I have not written anything for over three months. I just want the rest of this to be someone else's life. I do not want to admit that the things that follow happened to my family. I wanted the family other people thought we were, but they saw only our masks.

Lueck and Kati were getting involved in school. They were both in band and on the park and recreational soccer team. I had gotten a job with a family-owned business doing embroidery, and Phil was flourishing at his job in the military. We met our neighbors and started to belong to a neighborhood. The children had friends in the area, and the school was only a mile or so away. We had been in our house a few months when it was Lueck's birthday. Lueck invited about twelve friends from school for an evening party. Phil knew the teenagers would drive him crazy, so Kati and he went to the Koyles' for the evening while I chaperoned the party.

The teenagers just kept coming. There were nearly twenty kids in our basement. I ordered a super extra large pizza that barely fit on a card table. I made brownies and drinks for everyone. I was down in the basement the entire time with the kids except to answer the door and get more food. The kids were great—no trouble for having twenty kids in the house and not knowing any of them.

After they all left, Lueck and I were cleaning up the basement when we found a sports bottle that had had beer in it. I was upset, not with Lueck, but with me for missing it and with the kid who brought it in. I was worried what parents were going to think of us and what Phil would say to Lueck and/or me. We were new to town and if the kids go home and tell their parents that Lueck had beer at his thirteenth birthday party, the parents might think we approved of this.

The next day I made phone calls to a few parents of the kids that were at the party and explained what happened. No one seemed too upset, and one parent thought it was no big deal at all. I figured this was the parent of the kid who brought the beer. I finally told Phil about this, but I don't remember any reaction from it. There were many things I did not tell Phil because I didn't know how he would react. Again, it was February, and this was Phil's time of the year to explode.

My job as an embroidery machine operator was about to take a turn. I was to work only in the back of the store doing embroidery. I did not get to talk to the customers, which I found very difficult when it came to understanding what needed to be done. I wanted my own business, and still had the money my mom had put aside for me when Dad died. I tried to talk to Phil about me starting my own business and purchasing a $12,000 machine and equipment. He was not for this. I needed collateral; I did not have it. Phil would not let me use his stocks for collateral, but I later found out it wasn't allowed anyway. I think he thought I couldn't do this, or maybe if I had my own business and succeeded, I wouldn't need him. He did not like me working, yet he liked the money coming in. I finally asked to him to look at people on the street and notice everyone's clothing, as they all had something on that was either embroidered or screen-printed. I convinced him I could do this and make it work.

I took out a loan, but had to have Phil co-sign, and we used our two vehicles for collateral. My next step was to find a machine, and after some searching, I found a nearly new one in the Kansas City area. Lueck and I drove to look at it and talked to the owners. They had planned on working with the machine on weekends, and the day they bought the machine they found out they were going to have a baby. The baby won out over the machine for their time. I called the manufacturing rep, and he picked up the machine for me and hauled it forty-five minutes to my home. The rep took the time to show me how to use certain things on it and got it set up for embroidery. I was off and running.

The basement of the house was perfect for the business of C. Harris for Embroidery. The front door led right to the basement door and the basement was a walkout, which made it easy to get the machine in and out. The first week in business I set up in the base exchange where people could see my machine, and I got them hooked. I was never without customers, and I was never late on a payment.

My first large embroidery order was caps for an air show coming to the base. I was still learning and had a few problems with the tension of the machine. I asked Phil to help me color in some of the bobbin threads that showed on the top with a permanent magic marker. I noticed one of the caps he was working on he had gotten a pen mark on the front of the cap and just asked him that if he notices if he makes a mistake to put the cap aside. He would not admit that he had made a mistake. Phil did not make mistakes. Everyone else could mess up in life, but Phil was not allowed to. He never allowed himself to mess up. I couldn't imagine living with that kind of pressure on myself. I could never assure him enough that it was okay to mess up as long as he admitted it. I gave up and learned not to point out things he did wrong. Somehow or other it would always end up being my fault anyway. I would be the one that was wrong, even if he hurt me.

Being home and running a business was great. I could be home when the children got home from school to hear about their day. I would be home when Phil got home from work to defuse any situation that might occur between him and Lueck. Kati was Phil's favorite, and she could hardly do any wrong in his eyes. The neighbors across the street had a four-year-old boy that Kati baby-sat, and when she couldn't baby-sit, I would. Another good part of being home and working was getting to watch small children once in awhile. Phil seemed to like the kids too, and the kids liked him. He played with them and took time to talk to them when he was out working in the yard. Phil liked to do yard work and took pride in our new yard. He was also good at doing carpentry work and finished off the basement for my business and built Lueck a bedroom in the back basement.

Talking to the neighbor across the street, I found out they played the "Harris Family" with their four-year-old son, Billy. Billy thought we were the best. He loved Phil's Bronco and how Phil talked to him and told him what he was doing as he fixed the truck. This was really scary that a little kid was looking at us as the perfect family. He had not a clue what was going on inside the house behind the wooden two-by-fours that could hide voices and tears and feelings of a dysfunctional family.

Kati and Lueck wanted another dog. I did not want a dog, period. I thought we argued enough and did not need anything else to get angry about. We were not home enough for a dog, and I could not have dog hair on any of the clothes I was embroidering. Phil and I talked about this, and he agreed with me that we were not home enough for a dog and it would be just another expense.

Phil really did want a dog because he grew up with a dog, but he still agreed with me that this was not the time or place. It felt good that we had discussed this like real parents and supported each other, or I should say he supported my feelings about a dog. Wrong! While I was out, Phil took the kids to the pound to "just look" at the dogs. Right! Just look, my butt. You can't go to a pound and see all the animals that need homes and will be put to sleep if one is not found and not be thinking about taking one home.

Phil knew what he was doing when he brought the kids there. He would be the wonderful dad that got the kids a dog, and I would be the hateful mom that said no. They dragged me out to the pound to see the puppy that would stay small. I can't remember if I finally said yes, but I knew I lost the battle anyway. They returned to the pound to get the dog and then purchase over $100.00 worth of dog stuff. This made me angry because there were many things I felt I went without so Phil and the kids could have things they wanted. Now a dog was getting more money spent on it than I was getting spent on me.

Guess what, this was not a small dog. This was no surprise to me. It was not a huge dog either, but a pointer of some sort. It was now Christmas time, and we were going to go to Minnesota for Christmas.

We paid to have Phil's mom fly in from California to spend Christmas with us. Phil's dad did not want to fly and was not feeling well. I had to put the dog in a kennel for the four days we were gone. More money spent on the dog. I had to get the dog fixed and the shots up to date. We agreed the dog was not to be on the couch, but when I was away Phil and the kids let the dog on the couch. When the dog did not do something Phil wanted it to do, he hit the dog with a rolled up newspaper or something else. It made me cringe when he did this. This was another reason I did not want the dog.

Lueck and Kati enjoyed having friends stay overnight, and I usually loved having their friends over at the house, too, because that way I knew what they were doing and where they were. Both children had friends over one night. Lueck had a neighbor boy from down the street that was maybe one or two years older than him. Kati had a neighbor girl stay over from a couple blocks away. Phil, the kids and their friends, and I all watched a movie down in our basement and ate popcorn.

The boys were a little too anxious to get to bed, and Phil caught this. We all were getting ready for bed, with the girls upstairs in Kati's room and the boys downstairs in Lueck's room. I had gone to bed thinking Phil was following me there. As I was lying in bed waiting for Phil, I heard screaming and yelling. I didn't have a clue what was going on. I went downstairs and saw Phil yelling at the boys, grabbing Lueck and going all crazy because the neighbor boy had brought a *Penthouse* magazine over for the teenagers to check out.

I am not sure how long Phil yelled at the boys, but he told me to get back upstairs. The girls were awake and wondering what was going on. They were scared too. I tried to protect Phil and explain to them that he was just protecting them as females because the boys had a dirty magazine in their room and those magazines only made women look like sex toys and not real people with real feelings.

Phil sent the boy home at that time and told him not to return. I can't remember if Phil walked him home and woke his parents or if Phil sent him by himself. I did not get much sleep that night, and Lueck had to face his friend the next day in the neighborhood. To me this was an overreaction to what teenage boys do—explore what women are about. I did not like them having the magazine, but to yell and carry on and hurt someone because they had normal desires to look at women was a little excessive. Phil could have just taken the magazine away and checked to make sure they did have any more while talking to them and explaining why this was wrong.

Things like this made it so hard to live with Phil. I never knew how he was going to react to a situation. I tried to never have situations where I had to find out. I tried to keep peace at all times among everyone, and I was getting tired of being a peacekeeper. I wanted a husband, a friend, where we could trust one another and work out problems together. I had to hide most problems from Phil. I wanted a real family more than anything in the world. I wanted a husband where we could disagree and still talk to each other, where we would sit down with the children and include them in conversations that made them think for themselves. I wanted a husband where we would always back each other and support each other's dreams. I wanted a husband I could depend on to make loving decisions when it came to disciplining our children. I wanted someone to laugh with, to cry with, to share secrets with, and know my feelings and thoughts would be safe.

Many times I grounded the children and didn't tell Phil about it. It took a lot of work to ground the kids and then not let Phil know why I didn't want the kids to go out with their friends. The kids knew their dad didn't know and usually followed my rules. They did not have to worry about being grounded long because I would forget I grounded them and let them do things anyway. I know this did not help the kids, but I was not one that stayed mad long, and I had a lot of other things to think about.

Not knowing how Phil would react to situations not only affected us, but other people also. The town recreation program needed soccer coaches, and Phil took on the job. The kids loved him as a coach because he would get in the practice and play with them. He knew the game well. As a coach he protected his team. There was a coach from another team that was very negative towards Phil's team. During one of the games the two coaches got face to face in an argument, and I thought for sure Phil was going to hit the guy. I was sitting on the bench behind Phil and shouting at him in my mom voice to "stop it now!" I think Phil called the game quits, and he took his team home.

About this time Phil started drinking again. He was coming home with all kinds of weird stories, and I have no idea how many were true. He was telling me he was working for the military OSI (undercover police) and was doing uncover work and had to meet some of the people in a bar in Warrensburg. I asked him about his booze breath when he came home, but, of course, he always denied drinking and turned it around to make me feel like I was crazy to even think he was drinking again. Sometimes he admitted he had an O'Douls or some other non-alcoholic beer. I could tell right away when he had been drinking, not only by his breath, but his actions and his personality would change from being a halfway nice guy to someone who thought he was funny but was just plain mean.

I was not the only one who saw Phil was acting strange. Phil stopped at the Koyles, and Deanne was home alone. He told Deanne he had just returned from St. Louis and was driving over one hundred miles an hour, but it was okay because the police had called ahead to let the state patrols know he was coming. He was on some OSI mission. When Deanne told Ken about this, Ken became concerned and talked to the OSI agents on base. They said as long as Phil was not hurting anyone, there was nothing they could, or should, do. Phil was just getting stranger by the year.

It was February again, and we had lived in the house a little over a year. It was time for Phil to blow again. Besides being February, Phil was going to be leaving for Saudi in three weeks and would be gone for three months. He hated traveling and would usually get mean and hateful before he left on any TDY. By the time he left, I was usually glad he was gone. This was becoming a real pattern, and after twenty years of marriage, I could see it coming again, but I never dreamed it could have been this bad. I had gone grocery shopping on the base and ran into Phil in the parking lot at the commissary. The kids had come home from school before I left the house. They had received their report cards that day. I was not pleased with their grades, and I knew Phil wouldn't be either. I thought that if I told him about their grades, he would have time to cool down before he got home. He did not seem very upset about the results of their grades, and I went on with my business of grocery shopping.

Screams and crying and sobbing is what I heard as I entered my home. My home had become a hell. What was happening? I walked into Kati's room with a panic inside of me so tight I could hardly breathe. I found her wailing and crying uncontrollably. I tried to find out what had happened. I got Kati calmed down enough to find out that Phil had beaten her. She showed me the bruises on her lower back. It was not a spanking, but a beating. I had never heard Kati cry like this before. Someone she loved and trusted really hurt her. She told me that Lueck was hurt.

I headed for the basement, not wanting to know what I was going to find. The first thing I saw was Lueck's bedroom door and it had a hole in it. If his door had a hole in it, what was I going to find when I saw Lueck? Lueck was in his bedroom with anger written across his face and pain showing on his shaking body. Lueck would not show me what Phil did to him. He would not talk to me and tell me what had happened. Lueck will still not talk about this to this day. Lueck doesn't remember if the hole in the door came from his head or Phil's fist.

I still don't remember where Phil was when I came home. I can't remember if he was in the house or if he was out. He was not my concern at that time. There was no medical attention needed and the children were getting calmed down. I needed to talk to someone. I was shaking and crying and didn't know what to do. I called the local pastor and he was not at the church, but I was told where I could find him. I found him at a local nursing home, and we talked. He asked if we needed a safe place for the night. I told him we did not because it was the district-wide church lock-in that night at the local university, and I was going to be a chaperon and my children were going to be there too.

I had to get back home. I didn't know what was going on there. Was Phil going to hurt them again because they told me what he had done? Lueck was getting more angry by the minute. He was not only angry at his dad, but at himself for not protecting his sister. I was angry with both Phil and myself. I was angry with me for not being there for my children and stopping this crazy man from hurting our children.

At some point I finally talked to Phil, and he said Lueck had smarted off to him about school, and he just blew up and hit Lueck. Then he felt he had to be fair to the kids, so he hit Kati too. Wasn't that nice? He wanted to treat the kids fairly so he made sure he beat them both equally. Hell, we should have beaten him. I heard a different story from Kati—that Phil hit her first, then hit Lueck. I don't know if they were both in their own bedrooms when this happened or if they went there afterwards. No one talked about it much. We were all scared. I felt lost in life. We were surviving, but no one was living.

You know what the kids and I did that night? Yep, we put on our happy mask and went to the lock-in. Kati was so sore and hurt anytime anyone touched her. Lueck would not complain about anything, but he was hurting. At the lock-in, I hurt on the inside so bad I should have been bleeding on the outside. The father of my children hurt them. How could I ever trust him again?

Where was I to go? How was I going to support the children if I left him? How would Phil survive if I took the kids away from him? How were the kids going to have all the things Phil bought for them? The kids would become a statistic, a broken home family. The elephant is dancing around the living room, smashing all the furniture, and I am sitting in the corner with my head between my hands, trying to figure out how to hide it so no one sees it, or the damage it has done, as they enter the room. If I leave the elephant and take the kids, the elephant will not disappear but only reappear with more anger and destroy more things and more people. I put on my smile and talked to the people at the lock-in, but I was not listening to anyone. I had to do something, but what?

The lock-in was over, and we had to head back to the walls that kept our secret hidden. We slept most of that day. When we came home I saw Phil sitting in a dazed stupor, and he looked terrible. I could tell he had been up all night and had either been drinking or crying or both. He was a mess. He was feeling sorry for what he had done. After we all had some sleep, all four of us tried to talk. I think it was Phil who did most of the talking. He was trying to get our pity because he felt so bad for what he had done. It was Saturday night and we were all trying to get some sleep because we were all mentally drained and still physically lacking sleep. I don't remember where I was sleeping when I heard the awful noise of someone falling down the basement steps. I ran to the stairs and there was Phil lying at the bottom on the cement floor. He had scared the dog, and she crapped on the floor as he landed at her feet. Kati got up from her bed, and we both tried to find out if Phil was hurt and what had happened. He seemed to be okay, but really out of it. I went into Lueck's room and told him his dad had fallen down the steps. He could have cared less and would not get up and help Kati and me get Phil back upstairs.

Phil was talking a little, and Kati and I got him back to bed. The next morning when I went into the bedroom, Phil was bruised on his face and other parts of his body. Kati and I were standing near him and asking him if he remembered anything about last night. He did not remember anything. When he woke up that morning and realized how sore his body was, he thought I had beaten him. He felt he deserved whatever he got.

While he was out of the house I took pictures of Kati's back and butt in case I had to go to court in a divorce hearing. My kids wanted me to leave him, especially Kati. I was scared to leave him for many reasons. I could not give the kids all the things they were accustomed to getting and doing. I could not be the soccer coach their dad was or go to all of their events if I had to get a job outside of the house. I knew Phil would not, or could not, survive without us. I knew that was one of the reasons he was trying so hard to control me and discourage me from going to school. I felt he was afraid that if I were able to take care of the kids and myself that I would leave him. He had to make me feel like I was worthless and dumb. He would only allow me to get a job outside of the home if I could still take care of everything in the house, and I would have to be the one to take off if the kids were sick or needed something. My job would never be as important as his was. My mental health would never be as significant as his was. I always had life easy by Phil's eyes. I had no reason to complain about anything.

I still didn't know where to go and what to do. I didn't have the energy to flee. I didn't have the energy to fight. I only had enough energy to survive. I only had enough energy to put my arms around my children to try to protect them. I only had enough energy to put my hands to my face to protect myself from the blow of words. My mind wasn't allowing me to think beyond surviving. The only thing I could think of was to go to church that morning and pray. It was Sunday and I went to the second service and sat in the second to back row. I cried through that whole church service. Tears did not stop once. I had learned many years ago how to cry without making a noise, and that day my tears hurried down my face screaming for someone to help me, but were not heard by anyone. The people around me might have seen the steady flow of water leaking from my face and ask me after the service if I was going to be okay, but no one had any knowledge of what was causing the mess. People wanted to help clean up the water damage, but not find out what caused it. I did not want to share anything with anyone, and no one wanted to really know anyway.

The silence of the walls that screamed with pain were more than I could fix. The silence was so loud. I needed to hear words of kindness bouncing from walls around me. I was living in a box where silence was thought of as a solution to problems. I talked to the pastor again. I told him that Phil really came from a messed up family and this was the only way he knew how to act. Phil thought he was doing well as a parent because he was not beating his children as often his dad beat him. I was never beaten, and I didn't understand this kind of action. I told the pastor that Phil was always trying to please his parents and make them proud. Phil knew he had a drinking problem but since his dad had quit on his own he thought he could quit by himself too. The pastor suggested I go and see a family counselor. So I did.

█ This part alone makes me what to scream. I want to scream so I can hear there is life within me. I want to tell the world I am alive and have feelings. It has now been another month since I have written anything in this book. I have tried so hard to forget everything from my past and get on with life. When I go back and feel those feelings of being afraid again, my chest tightens up and I want to sit and cry. I am still so scared that I will have someone angry with me for thinking my own thoughts, or feeling my own feelings. I am still afraid of the evil looks and eyes of hatred. I am afraid of disapproving words that have been bedded in my heart and echo "you did it to me." Maybe I did do this to Phil. Being told what a rotten wife I was maybe holds some truth. Maybe if Phil had a better wife he would be alive and happy today. I try hard to smash the self-doubts before they consume my mind, but once in awhile those thoughts sneak in. This morning I was going to wake early and write, and so I had dreams again last night and I stayed in bed two hours after my alarm went off hoping the day would go away. It did not, and here I sit, making myself remember things I worked so hard to ignore.

I went to the crisis counselor in the city and told him my story. I got the feeling he thought I was blowing this all out of proportion, and I was the one that needed the help. I went home and talked to Phil. He knew I had seen the pastor. He had gone on his own to see him too. I told Phil about the counselor, and he was willing to go and talk to him with me. Phil knew what he did was wrong, and I think he really wanted help this time. We could not go to the air force mental health clinic because that could jeopardize Phil's career, and his career meant a lot to him, and to us as a family. After we talked to the counselor together, he sent us to the neighboring town to talk to a paid professional family counselor.

We were called into her small square office where the walls were closing in and told her about Phil losing his temper and beating our children. After everything was said and done, her comments were that Phil and I came from two extremely different families and neither one of ours was the norm or healthy. I came from the family where there was no fighting, and not much physical love either, and Phil came from a family where there was fighting all the time. Phil had often said his dad beat him if he needed it or not because his dad thought he must have done something wrong. She also concluded Phil was under a lot of stress with work and the TDY to the desert that was coming up, so she slapped his hand and told us to go home and not come back. She told Phil he needed some sleep and that was about it.

There! All of our problems were now solved. I felt she was telling me we could go home and have a happy life. I felt like once again it was me expecting more from Phil than what was the norm. I was wondering if it was only me that could see the harm Phil was causing my family. Poor Phil was just overworked and that made it okay for him to beat the kids. I should have known. The counselor made me feel like I should have more understanding of what Phil was going though. I should allow him to put us down because he was tired and overworked. Phil had this way about him where he always came up on the positive no matter how much trouble he should have been in. He had charisma and had the art of manipulation down to a science. He could charm anyone into believing he was really sorry for what he had done and he would never do it again. If Phil couldn't make someone understand he was sorry, then he could make them feel it was their fault that Phil did whatever he did that was wrong. So, we went home and we didn't talk about the bruises he left on our children after that day. Poor Phil didn't mean to hurt us or did he? Maybe it was my fault or was it?

I did come up with a plan and talked about it with Phil, and he seemed to give it some thought in his pitiful way. The idea was that the kids and I move into an apartment and Phil could live next door in his own apartment. That way we would not drive him to his anger with our needs, and he could get the rest he needed. Phil did promise to start going to AA as soon as he got back from the desert.

The kids were not as quick to forgive and forget this time. He had done some serious damage. I thought that while Phil was back on the desert for his three-month TDY, some of the children's wounds would be healed, but I don't think three months was enough time to heal wounds that went so deep. Time only hid the wounds below layers of skin, deep within the soul, hiding where no one could pull them out and make them look at them ever again.

Phil left for the desert and the kids and I got on with life. I worked my embroidery machine in the basement of our home, and the kids had a life of friends and school. Phil and I wrote back and forth to each other, but we never talked about what we were going to do when he got home. I knew, and he knew, that I would be a good wife and would be there for him when he returned. He wrote and told me he was reading books about anger management and was going to church, but never mentioned AA.

I did have enough of the dog that I ended up taking care of, so I found a new owner for the dog and gave her away while Phil was gone. I didn't want the dog in the first place, and if Phil thought I was going to do everything for him, he was wrong. Some things I felt strongly about and having a dog to be concerned about was something I could live without. Good-bye dog. Maybe Phil will go find a new home too.

I don't remember the day Phil came home from this TDY, but the elephant in the living room was growing so large that I had a hard time hiding it when people came over. If anyone saw the elephant, they were polite enough not to mention it to me. Maybe if we traveled somewhere, the old beast would get lonely and go away on its own.

We took a family vacation that summer and flew to California to see Phil's folks. Phil's dad, Jim, was still dying, and Phil was sure this was the last time he would see him. Jim was sick in many ways. The whole family had of way of making little sores into life threatening events. Jim did have bronchitis and other lung problems, as well as needing a lot of attention. We knew before we left for California that we would have to have plenty of money with us because his parents did not have any extra money. Phil's mom was getting a good retirement check and his dad was collecting a disability check, but that money had a way of finding little holes to fall in and disappear when a handle was pulled on the slot machine. There were times when they would call and say they had little or no food in the house and still had another two weeks before they would get a check. We then had to wire them money. I didn't mind so much that we had to give them money, but the idea that they always seemed to wait until the last minute to ask meant we had to pay the wire fee besides giving them money.

Home again and the summer was over. The kids were getting ready for school, sports, and band. They were really getting into school and meeting a lot of good friends. We thought Whiteman Air Force Base was our last base and Phil would retire here, so we got involved in life again. Both children were in marching band and played high school soccer. Kati played on the junior varsity boys' soccer team along with one other girl. She ran cross-country from 6:00 a.m. to 6:45 a.m. and then would head to the school by 7:00 a.m. for marching band where she performed with the flags and then after school played soccer. Kati was about to crash. She was always tired, and we could have told her she had too much on her plate, but she was trying to please her dad and be the jock her dad seemed to want her to be. She was daddy's little girl and was trying so hard to make him happy. Or, maybe she was running from her home life and this way she didn't have to be in the house with her parents. I took her to the doctor and, with a lot of common sense, the doctor told her she was putting too much stress on her body and needed to give up one of the sports. She gave up the cross-country.

While she was running cross-country, we tried to get to all of her meets. Phil always cheered her on and only encouraged her, never saying negative comments. At one of the meets Phil was not able to attend, I went alone to cheer her on. I could never figure out why people would run the never-ending distance that they did. They would run, puke, and get up and run some more just to cross a little line near the same place they started.

I watched Kati run at one of her meets and she was exhausted and was trying so hard to finish the race. Even though she was exhausted and did not give up, I could see the pain in her face. I wanted to yell at her to "Just stop it. You don't have to do this." When she crossed the finish line she had just enough strength left to let the tears flow from her eyes. We held each other in hugs, and we both let our tears relieve the tension we felt. I cried for her, for the desire she felt to finish the race even though she ended a few feet from where she started.

Things were not all cheery at the Harris home even though I had a good business, the kids were involved in school, and Phil could retire in a few months. Phil came home from work all upset because he felt he could be kicked out of the air force for lying on his enlistment papers. I never did understand everything he was telling me, but the best I could tell was there was another person on the base that had the same name as Phil and close to the same numerals in their social security numbers. The hospital was getting their medical records confused and this other Phil was doing drugs and they put it in my Phil's records. The air force did some investigation and found out Phil had tried to comment suicide before he came into the air force and lied about it. Phil's family doctor lied for him, too, when he signed the papers.

Phil came home from work sobbing and, at first, was not going to tell me anything except that he might not have a job. He would not tell me why or what was going on. I stayed calm and told him things would work out. He would just get stranger in his actions, and it was like living with a totally different person. At the end of this strange episode, the air force told Phil that because he had been in the ranks for nearly twenty years they would not [or maybe could not] press charges against him for lying on his enlistment papers. They seemed to do more investigation on the other Phil Harris, and I don't know what happened to him. It was so ironic that there were supposed to be two Philip Harrises with social security numbers with the same last four numbers, and living with my Philip was like living with two completely different people.

Another one of our fights that became a routine was that Phil would accuse me of trying to change him. That part was true, but I only tried to get Phil to look at things in a different way. He usually seemed so sad or mad, and I thought it was my job to make him happy. I knew I could not change him. He had to change himself, but maybe I could get him to see that things were not as awful as he thought they were.

The other fights were usually after he had been drinking. I knew he was still drinking, but now I was told he was only drinking "near beer." If he was only drinking near beer, it still had enough alcohol to change his personality. He thought he was funny with his cutting comments to the kids or me, but they were hurtful. Phil told me I did not have a sense of humor and I was the one that needed help.

I knew I could not handle Phil's drinking by myself any longer. I knew about Al-Anon, but I also knew that if I went to a meeting, I would then be admitting I had an elephant dancing in the living room. I would then have to clean up the mess this huge mammoth of gray wrinkles left as evidence while living in my home. I went to Al-Anon to learn I was not alone in wishing my husband would die so I did not have to live this way anymore.

I did not really want Phil to die, but it was more just wanting the pain to stop and the mind games to go away. I knew I could not leave him because he would not survive without the kids or me. I learned I was helpless in doing anything for Phil and the only person I was responsible for was me.

My children started going to Teen Al-Anon where they learned they were not the fault of their dad's drinking either.

What was wrong with this picture was that the children and I were going for help because of Phil, but Phil would not go for help. He had conveniently forgotten about his promise to attend AA, and I was not going to remind him because he had to want to go on his own in order to make AA work. I also didn't want to hear another lie from Phil. I didn't want to be even more disappointed if Phil told me he would go and then didn't go to AA. We all seemed to have the problem except for Phil. I met some wonderful friends that helped me detach myself from Phil's actions. I knew, and Al-Anon confirmed, that Phil had to make the decision to attend.

Detaching me from Phil was not always easy. There was a knock on the door and the UPS guy was at my door again. To most people this would not be a problem, but Phil was so insecure, he accused me of having an affair with the guy. I received packages on a regular basis because of the embroidery business and got to know the driver on a first name basis. While Phil was on another TDY, he had a dream about the UPS guy and me where I was peeing on this guy's face and other strange things. Phil wrote to me about this dream in detail and was quite upset. He was still upset with me when he came home from his trip. After that letter I felt very uncomfortable even saying hello to the man when he delivered packages while Phil was home. If I saw the UPS truck while riding in the car with Phil, I pretended I did not see it and looked the other way.

Phil was not only jealous of me but of our friends, the Koyles. In the service it was not allowed for officers and enlisted to be friends. You can go to parties together, be on sports teams together, but not be friends where you go to dinner together as a couple. The Koyles had a friend that was an officer. They opened up their house to him and his wife, just as they did for us when we moved to Missouri. This upset Phil enough that he turned the Koyles in to a first sergeant on base. I am not sure what happened to the Koyles and their officer friend, but if something did, it was because of Phil.

If I was going to survive another four years of marriage I had to learn some tricks. It would be four more years until Kati graduated. One of those tricks was to ignore most of my feelings, to ignore the red flags that were planted all around. Another trick I learned in surviving was that if I liked what I was doing and seemed happy, that only made Phil treat me worse, so I could not be happy around Phil. He would become jealous that I could find happiness in what I was doing, while he hardly ever seemed happy. He blamed the kids or me for most of his problems in life. I had also learned to detach my body from the rest of me. My body was only something that held my thoughts, provided me a way to get around, and a hole for Phil to have sex. The real me was not a part of this body. The body could be abused because I was not in there. I was standing on the side watching the whole thing.

Phil once again showed me his kind caring side. If he had always been hateful to live with, it would have been easy to leave. This is called crazy making and it was working to drive me crazy. He could be the best father and husband at times. I just never knew what he was going to be like from minute to minute. And if he did do something nice, I was always afraid he would use that against me for not appreciating him at all times. One of the very special things he did was encourage me to go skydiving. Ken Koyles had also wanted to jump, so our two families arrived together at the small airport to watch Ken and I leap from the plane. First Ken and I had to go to several hours of classes and then pass a test while Deanne and Phil entertained the kids. Phil and Deanne's joke was they were going to sit on the ground with our life insurance in their hands so they would be ready to cash them in case we did not land safely. Skydiving was one of my greatest moments.

I loved floating in the sky. The part I hated was getting out of the plane. In order to get out of the plane I had to walk on a small strut and then hang onto a bar until the jumpmaster told me to let go. The wind was supposed to hold me up while I was hanging on the bar, but my butt must have been made out of lead because I was not being held up. My hands were slipping off the bar and the jumpmaster just kept shaking his head telling me it was not okay to let go. Oh well, what was he going to do? My hands just kept slipping, and then I was on my own, floating towards the ground. The chute opened safely when it hit the end of the line that was hooked to the inside of the plane. I was wearing a headset so the ground crew could talk to me and tell me how to hit my target in landing. I had so much fun that I did it again a few weeks later. I wish someone would tell me how to hit the target with life.

Phil liked things neat and clean. I tried to keep things that way for him so he could be happy. It seemed the only way I was capable of keeping things really neat was not to do anything all day. If I worked on projects, like sewing, I would let everything else in the house go for the day and leave the project right where I left off when I quit working on it. This would drive Phil nuts, and he would complain. This made me feel the things I liked to work on were not important and he just as soon not see me or hear me. If I left my shirt on his side of the bed or our dresser he would always move it to my side. His side was always neat. Many times he made his side of the bed and left my side unmade. In the mornings when I made the bed I would make both sides of the bed. I tried to tell myself he was just trying to help me by making his side only and not saying that I was worthless because he could not do something for me.

Sometimes the house would not be thoroughly cleaned for a couple of weeks, but it seemed as soon as I took time to really clean it, Phil would clean right after me. I felt I could not do a good enough job for him. What was so funny about this whole situation was that when customers came over, they remarked how organized I was, but Phil could not see this. One of the things Phil did learn when we saw the family counselor was to pick his battles with the kids, and if they wanted to live in a messy room, just close the door. This worked out fairly well and until their rooms got so bad Phil and/or I could not stand it anymore and one of us would have to say something to them.

Phil was the thrower and I was the keeper. I started out in our marriage keeping many things that meant something to me. I kept the first flower he gave to me and cards he sent to me. But as the marriage went along and these tokens reminded me how I was being controlled and forced to live in a situation that was unhealthy, the sentimental part of me disappeared. I no longer wanted to keep things to remind me of the past. I wasn't quite the thrower Phil would have liked me to be, but I did not keep a lot of new items to remind me of special events in my life either.

Phil had not had any major fits in some months. Often he did not speak for days, and I usually had no idea why he was mad at me. I learned to ignore his silence and put on my "I don't care" mask, but deep down it really hurt.

Phil was going on twenty years in the military and thinking about retiring. Maybe retirement was just the thing Phil needed to be happy. Maybe the military was too much stress for Phil. So after two years of living in our house, the four of us drove to northern Minnesota to check out towns we might want to move to in the near future. We looked at buying resorts, checked out schools, and scoped the housing market near Walker, Minnesota. There was a screen-printing business for sale that Phil thought was a good idea to buy. The schools were not what I wanted for the children and the houses were very expensive. We talked about this on our way home and again after we arrived home.

Phil was ready to move. He told our friends and me that he had read everything there was to read about screen printing and wanted to buy this business with me doing the embroidery. I never saw Phil with a book about screen printing this whole time. The thought of Phil and me working together really scared me because I knew we had two different ways of treating customers, and they would not jive. I also knew Phil had a way of taking over whatever I did, and I would not let him near my business now, much less work side-by-side everyday in a business. We did not see life the same way, and I was afraid he would ruin everything I worked so hard to achieve in my embroidery business. I could not tell this directly to Phil so I discouraged him from moving there by telling him I did not like the schools and was not ready to move to Minnesota. He was not happy about this, but seemed he could live with it. I didn't really care if he retired and got a job in the area. I just did not want to move and give up my business and have the kids change schools again.

Once again, Phil had to leave for a TDY, and the kids and I could relax for awhile. I don't remember where he went or how long he was gone this time, but it was long enough that I bid on an order for sixteen thousand name tags for the air force and got the bid. By the time he returned I had gotten a loan on my own and purchased a three-head embroidery machine. I hired a woman to work with me a few hours a week, and my little business was really booming. About six months after I bought this machine Phil came work from home and told us he would like to take us all out to eat, including Lueck's girlfriend. This was not like Phil, and I knew something was up.

Sitting in the restaurant with all of us around the table, Phil spoke up like he memorized a script and said, "If you wonder why I have called of you all here tonight, it is because I have orders to Alaska." Right there in the public's eye we had to keep on our smiling faces and act like this was good thing. Phil did give us a choice. He could either retire or we could move. At least he did not make us decide right there on the spot.

I felt this was not a decision for me to make. I knew, even though Phil would change his story depending on who he was talking to at the time, that he had changed his military dream sheet so he would get orders to Alaska because I did not want to move to Minnesota. A military dream sheet is where military members tell the people in charge of orders where they would like to live. If the military can use your career in that location, there is a good change you can do an assignment there. My business was going great and the kids were adjusting to a place they thought they would be calling home until they graduated.

Lueck was upset about the move. He only had two years left of high school. He had made many friends. He had bought the little orange VW of his dreams, after I had talked him into selling the El Camino a year or so before he turned sixteen. I couldn't see paying insurance on something that wasn't being used. Lueck was working on fixing his 1964 bug. None of this mattered to Phil.

In order to convince Kati to move to Alaska, Phil sat down and told her there were horses on the base, and it was going to be great. Kati was not excited about moving, but would do so because she knew it was what her dad wanted.

And me, well, I knew Phil had always wanted to live Alaska and there was no way I could live with him forever if I asked him to turn down the orders and stay in Missouri. In less than five months we would once again be on the road to a new home.

I had to sell my business because I could not move my three-head machine. It was too big, too costly, and the air force would not pay to have it moved. I sold the business within a couple of months to another military family, and I kept my single-head as a hobby machine. My customers knew I had a good thing going with my business, and I had no trouble selling it.

I felt Phil really did not want me to succeed in anything I did. He wanted to control me. He knew if I could support myself, I would not need him. One of our fights was over this. That day I was at the bottom of our basement steps when Phil started telling me what my thoughts were and what I was feeling. I told him I had made this business succeed on my own, and he was instantly angry and told me I could not have succeeded in the business without him. I tried to explain what I meant was that I had not taken any of his money to pay for the machines or bills that had been accrued by my business. I did acknowledge I could not have supported the family on my income, and I appreciated that he allowed me to keep the money I earned to pay the business bills. The money that came from the business was our fun money. This is what we spent for vacations, fixing broken vehicles, the kids' soccer fees, and musical instruments for school band.

Phil could not, or would not, hear what I was saying. All he could hear was "I did this without his help." This conversation somehow got turned around to his parents, and he proceeded to tell me I did not like his parents or family and never did. I once again tried to explain to him that I did like them. They were good to me, and I had nothing against them except they could not manage money. I always thought of them as my parents also. But Phil was trying to tell me how I felt about his parents instead of listening to me on how I felt. His true feeling always had a way of becoming someone else's thoughts.

Phil should have been truly happy now we were moving to Alaska and I no longer had a way of supporting the kids and myself since I sold my prospering business. In only two months we would be leaving for Alaska, so we bought a new "whoopdee van" as the kids called it. It was a conversion van with everything a teen-ager could want as a dating vehicle. It had cool lights that dimmed. It had a bed in the back, and we bought a small TV to have in it. It had four captain chairs.

Before we left for Alaska we needed to make a few trips to say good-bye to friends and family. Two days before school was out for the summer, the four of us drove to northern Maine to see our old friends for a few days.

After arriving back home from our trip to Maine, Lueck had one more soccer game to play in Columbia, Missouri, before we took off to our new home in Alaska. We picked up some of the team's members in our new van and headed to the games. While watching Lueck mess up on a kick, Phil walked away from the sideline and stated to me in his angry voice "that is not my son." The disappointment in Phil's voice was so chilling it made me want to cry. I was thinking that this was only a game, and I did not understand how he could not be proud of his son for playing. I don't know how many other people heard what Phil said or saw him walk away with anger in his steps. It put a damper on my spirits, and I wanted to put a huge shield in front of Lueck so he could not be hurt by his dad's hateful words. [Lueck, I am sorry if you read this. I tried to protect you for so many years. You will have to decide now how this is going to affect you. It is your choice.]

After the game we took the guys and headed home. Phil did not say anything to Lueck directly about his playing. As most times, I was the only one that heard Phil's comments.

Another trip I had to make before we moved to Alaska was to Minnesota to see my family. Phil stayed home that weekend and had a yard sale. I knew that was going to be a mistake to let Phil sell our things, but I did not have much choice in the matter. We needed to get rid of things before the packers came in a couple of days, and I needed to see my family before we took off. My things had no value to Phil, and if he didn't like something he would almost give it away. But, if Phil liked something, he would pay anything for it, even if it was worth nothing.

My fears were correct. He sold our bedroom dresser, most of his wood working tools, and other things we still needed. We talked about selling our dresser, but had not settled on if we should or not. The part that bothered me most about selling the dresser was that Phil had to clean out my drawers, and I knew he had looked at everything in them. I felt I had nothing private in the house.

I came home to a cold Phil. Another silent treatment was in store for me. I had an idea what was wrong this time, but was afraid to ask. I had pictures of Kati's bruised back hidden under a cover of a shoebox in my drawer of the dresser he sold. I had the pictures in case I ever got the courage to leave Phil and needed to fight for my children. Phil did not say anything about the pictures, but they were moved so I was pretty sure he saw them. Phil did not find Lueck's shirt I had stuck in a sewing box that he had ripped when he grabbed Lueck while living in Maine.

The tension in the home was pretty high. Lueck did not want to leave, and Kati was standing by her dad and was excited about the trip. The children were hoping I would throw a party for them before we left, but I did not have the time to plan one while trying to find buyers for our house. [Lueck and Kati, I am so sorry about this.]

The packers came and put all of our stuff in boxes and the boxes in crates. What were they going to do with the elephant in the living room? How many pounds did that thing weigh? Guess what was found under our dresser in our bedroom? Yes, you have it right. There lay a copy of a *Penthouse* magazine. How ironic? How do you suppose that got there? Phil couldn't have done that, not since he made such a big deal about Lueck and his friend having one. I knew better to say anything about it. I just made sure Phil knew that I saw it. I was not as dumb as Phil thought I was. I did know what was going on. I just chose not to say anything. I knew that whatever I said would come back in my face someday—somehow.

We sold Phil's Bronco that he had for ten years. Sold Lueck's cool VW bug that he and his dad had worked on it together, as father and son should. Said good-bye to all of our friends and took off on a trip of a lifetime. We headed south to Oklahoma and then west to California to see some military friends we met in Maine. They now lived in southern California, and we spent a night or two with them. Phil was anxious to see his folks, so we needed to get on the road again. We planned on spending a week or so with his parents, but after a few days of both parents smoking and the California heat, we were all ready to take off again. We then headed north to Oregon to see Phil's Uncle Norman and family, and Phil's brother Rick. We stopped in Oregon, but did not spend the night at his uncle's house because they did not have room for us.

As we traveled, like always, I was the one in charge of the map and directions to where we were going. I had gotten fairly good at this and always tried to have things go smoothly so Phil would be happy. He hated being lost. I didn't mind being lost as long as we did not have a time schedule and we had plenty of gas. It was during times I was lost that I found the most exciting things to see. Phil liked to know where we were going, when we were going to be there, and what we were going to see along the way. The joke was that he wanted me to know what I was going to order in a restaurant before we even entered. I was a "fly by the seat of your pants" kind of person. I liked adventure [that was safe], while Phil liked things planned to the tee. This made for tense situations when I messed up and could not always figure out where we were by the map.

Phil's uncle and aunt went with us to Seattle for a day of adventure. Just driving there was adventure enough for me. We followed Uncle Norm and family on the freeway. Trying to stay behind another car on a busy interstate was not always safe. Phil managed to drive crazy, like the rest of the people on the interstate, and we spent the day on the wharf. I loved Seattle and the commotion as long as I wasn't the one doing the driving.

One more day and we would be on the ferry on the trip of Phil's dream. This assignment should finally make Phil happy. If this does not work, nothing will, I thought.

CHAPTER 9

ALASKA

—■—

■ I don't want to go here.

On the ferry we had a small cabin with four bunk beds, a compact shower and toilet, and a window to see the sea. We were on the ferry for three nights and four days. Lueck was Lueck and decided to make the best of this trip by sleeping on the deck with a sleeping bag we had bought for this trip. On the deck people put up tents and taped them to the floor with duct tape. Other people slept on the deck chairs under the stars or under the roof that extended out over the deck. There were huge heater ducts that blew warm air from under the roof. Inside the ferry there were reclining chairs for people who did not have cabins. Towels could be rented if you needed a shower and did not have a room. The cafeteria was very expensive. We planned ahead and brought a couple of ice chests full of drinks and snacks.

Things were not all wonderful in the Harris cabin. Phil was not speaking to me. I was really confused by this because up to now we had a fairly decent trip. Everyone was getting along, and we were on a new journey in life. Phil's dream of living in Alaska was coming true. He should have been on the top of the world. It must have been something I said, but what? Maybe it was because he felt guilty we are moving again? No, I really doubted that, but just maybe?

I slept a lot on the ferry. I loved the peacefulness, and the rock of the waves put me right to sleep. Phil and our children spent most of the time on the deck looking for whales and other sea creatures. Phil enjoyed video taping the trip so he could send a copy to his parents and make his dad happy.

The small ports we stopped at all had short tours we could pay for to see the surrounding area. They had these planned so we would not miss the ferry, even if we only had a little more than an hour stopover. Lueck was the first to take a trip. Phil was upset because he was worried Lueck would miss the ferry. I received the evil eye, the "I wish you would die" eye, because I allowed Lueck to go on the tour in the middle of the night. My self-esteem was getting smaller and smaller. "Why was he always mad at me? Why couldn't Phil have a little adventure with us? Why did I always feel I had to be perfect? Why did I move with him?" were all thoughts that raced around and around in my head. No wonder I was tired and wanted to sleep all the time. Sleep was my escape from life. Maybe I would wake up and my nightmare would be over, but it never seemed to end.

When the ferry stopped at Juneau, I went on the tour with the kids while Phil stayed on the ferry to make sure he did not miss the boat. The tour was another quick trip to see the glaciers and the capital city of Alaska. This would have been a beautiful place to live if you liked the rain. When we arrived at our port, Phil drove our van off the ferry, and we started on our two-day trip to Eielson Air Force Base near Fairbanks.

I don't remember much about the trip except for a lot of trees and seeing a bear or moose now and then. I don't remember where we stayed or where we stopped along the way except for one small café that looked more like someone's house and kitchen then it did a café. I am not sure if I am just blocking things out or if I slept the whole time as an escape to the remarks and looks I so often received.

Driving up to the south side of the base on one of the few highways Alaska has, we saw vast flat land with planes dotting the concrete base aircraft runway. It was midsummer, and the sun knew in a few months it would be damn cold and dark, so it stayed shining all day and night to help prepare us for winter. The military base did not have housing for us, so we were assigned billeting. We could live there three months at the most, and then had to find place to rent until a house on base would be available. The billeting was old base housing and came completely furnished. There were two bedrooms upstairs. One room was small with two single beds and the other room larger with a queen size bed.

Lueck took one of the single beds and moved it down to the basement to make his own room. He was one not to complain, but after sixteen years, learned to blend into the room at home so he would not be noticed and be smashed down by his dad's words. With the money Lueck had for selling his car in Missouri, he bought a used little red car. Now he had a car he didn't sit around wasting time, but went and looked for a job. It was soon fair time in Fairbanks, and Lueck got himself a job running a gaming booth. He had to take a drug test to get the job, but they should have been taking drug tests during the fair instead. While working at the fair, Lueck started smoking pot. I don't believe this was his first time.

With the money Phil received for selling his Bronco, he bought an old green gas guzzling four-wheel-drive truck. The vehicles he bought usually caused problems between us, and this one was no different. I learned over the years to just keep my mouth shut because I would just get that look or be told he makes the money and he can spend it how he likes. If I got angry, he told me I had no reason to be mad. He never thought I should have a reason to be mad at him. My thoughts and feelings were not important.

While living in billeting we met our neighbors. Most of them were just arriving on base as we were. We were starting to get into a routine.

The kids were meeting new friends, and our temporary home was becoming the gathering place. I bought a new computer with the money we received for moving. Before we left Missouri I bought new software for digitizing embroidery designs with the money I made on selling the business. I spent my free time learning this program.

It was now August and the soccer program for the high school was about to start. Both kids tried out for the team and made good impressions on the coaches. Kati especially did because she had become aggressive after playing on the high school boys' junior varsity team in Warrensburg. Our three months in billeting was almost up and there still was not a base house available for us. I was looking for a landlord that would rent to us for just a short time and found one about four miles from the base.

It was starting to get dark at night after being light twenty-four hours a day. The darkness was growing fast. All of our stuff was still in storage. We were able to keep it there and still get a few things we needed. We rented a dungeon from a wicked witch that constantly bitched at her husband. Her drunken husband survived life by working in his garage, tinkering with stuff. It was a split-level house, and they had the top floor. The basement of this house came completely furnished with sheets, towels, and all cooking utensils. It had three bedrooms and an open dining room, living room, and kitchen. The washer and dryer were in the garage, and we were allowed to use them on certain days when the witch was not using them.

The kids were in school, and Phil had become comfortable with work. And me, the tears were coming more and more every day. I was home alone, in a dungeon of a strange place, many miles from friends and family. I did not have a job. I was not looking for a job either. My plans were to start my embroidery business as soon as we got into base housing. I liked to be able to go to all the kids' games and would not be able to do that if I worked for someone else. I still wanted to be home so I could defuse any situation that might arise.

The days were getting colder and shorter. The walls were getting closer and darker. I tried to keep busy by sewing a teddy bear by hand, working on the computer, and getting out whenever I could. The witch and her mate were going to go to the states for a week or so to gamble and needed someone to take care of their two old dogs. I said I would do this for them because none of their friends would. Come to find out their friends knew the witch better than I did, and they knew that if that old dog died while they were away, the witch would blame them and put a curse on them. Well, maybe she would not really put a curse on them, but she would definitely curse them. I could hear her yelling at her husband all hours of the day. He spent hours in the garage drinking and smoking and talking to his friends that would stop by to visit. The dogs didn't die, and I cleaned up a lot of pee from the little mutt that had a temperament of its owner.

After living in the basement for a few weeks, we were offered a house on base, but turned it down because the garage and the house were too small. Another week or so passed and we were offered another house across the street and down four houses from the first house we looked at. If we did not accept this house our name would go on the bottom of the list for housing and it could be a year before we got another house. We took this one and movers delivered our stuff that we had not used in five months. It was funny how little I really needed in life to survive and how much stuff accumulates that just takes up space.

I stopped at the witch's house to get our deposit back, and she gave me only part of it back because she found bread crumbs on the counter and I didn't move and vacuum under the couch when we moved out. Oh yes, and there were little blue spots all over the shower. That was because I had used blue cleanser and left it on too long. The water in Alaska was full of sulfur and iron and left ugly stains all over the tub. I had to scrub to get the rust off the shower wall and I let the cleanser sit on the shower walls and tub too long.

We moved into base housing just before the snow came and before Halloween. I met our new neighbors and I unpacked boxes, made curtains, unpacked more boxes, wiped up puddles of my tears, and unpacked more boxes.

We might have moved thousands of miles from our last home and we might have had a weight limit and we might not have had our stuff for five months, but that damn huge gray wrinkly pest of a beast followed us. It didn't come out and dance in the middle of the living room, but instead the sneaky thing hid around the corner and when no one was looking would throw its trunk out and trip me.

While paying bills I noticed an odd charge on the master card bill. It had been recurring monthly since we left Missouri. Since we had so many different charges on the bill from the move, I didn't give it much thought before. I called the company to see what this charge was from and found it was from an Internet site in California that offered teenage porn. Someone in my family had used my credit card to join this site and was paying $29.95 a month. The code name that was used was "yohar." I got the company to drop most of the charges since we did not even have Internet access for the last four months. I was shaking inside to think that someone would use my card and sign up for this site. I knew that neither Lueck nor Phil would admit to this, and I was sure it was not my fifteen-year-old daughter that signed up for this site. I had to confront both male figures and get to the bottom of this. Phil denied signing up for this site, but did not seem too upset about it. He was angrier with me for thinking he would even do something like this, but did not seem to want to find out who really did it.

I knew my place and did not question Phil too hard about the subject. I didn't want him to blame or hurt Lueck for something he did. Lueck also denied it. I explained to Lueck he had nothing to lose by admitting he had signed up the site. I could not ground Lueck, and I definitely was not going to hurt him or tell his dad. Lueck still denied it. I figured if Lueck was going to look at a porn site, it would not be a teenage site, and I really didn't think he would use my credit card. I wanted it to be Lueck, instead of my husband who was the father of my children, a Sunday school teacher, a coach, and a respected military member, but in my heart I thought I knew who had signed up for the teen porn site.

■   Again, I don't want to write anymore. My chest is fighting with my stomach for attention. I am not sure who is going to win. I want a hug. I want to know I am going to be okay. As I sit here and type, I keep stopping and placing both hands over my face to make my thoughts go away. I tell myself I have to keep typing to make this real. I ignored my feelings for so many years that for the first time I am allowing myself to feel scared. I should be angry, but I am more frightened than anything.

Base housing was beautiful. We were in the middle of a triplex with a double heated garage, three bedrooms, two and a half bathrooms, full basement, and carpet throughout the house. I set up my embroidery machine in the basement and started sewing on uniforms as a business. Phil's boss's wife also sewed on uniforms, so I agreed not to compete with her and did not advertise that I did sewing and alterations. I got involved in the children's school and the booster club.

We flew back to Minnesota for Christmas. We landed at the Kansas City airport, rented a car, and visited our friends, the Koyles. After a couple of days, we drove back to the airport in Kansas City to return our rented car. Linda and Doug drove eight hours down to meet us at the airport and then drove the four of us to Minnesota to celebrate Christmas with my family. We celebrated Christmas at Shetek Bible Camp, near Slayton, Minnesota, in the southwest corner of the state. Each family had their own bedroom. Phil was Santa, as in years past, and, as always, did a good job. And also, as always, Phil would not be the one to initiate conversation with my family. He sat in the corner and waited for everyone to come to him. He had Kati by his side and pointed out to her how no one liked them. If someone talked to him, he told them some tall tale, a lie, a story that was meant to impress them on what a wonderful guy he was. He convinced Kati no one in my family liked her either. None of this was true. My family liked Phil and they loved Kati. But, they could see what Phil was doing to me after twenty-one years of marriage and did not like it. They did not say anything to Phil or me because they loved me enough to support me.

The first winter in Alaska went by fairly quickly. Lueck and Kati joined an indoor soccer team in Fairbanks. The days were now getting longer. I made it through the first winter.

We had been in Alaska for a year and Phil could get his resident hunting tags for the fall. This also caused a problem between us. I didn't mind that he would go hunting, I just could not see spending all the money to look good or having four or more different guns while they all did the same thing. I hated having dead animals hanging on any walls of my house. I hated seeing Phil spend so much time reading hunting magazines and learning how wild game think and act, but never touching a book to see how wives or children think. I told him that at times, but, of course, I was just looked at like I was crazy. I hated hearing the hunting stories that I knew were not true. But I did like the game meat.

I went shopping with a friend from base and, after we left the base, she could not remember if she had closed her garage door or not. She called her husband at work and asked him to go home and check the door. I was amazed by this request of hers. She was not afraid he would tell her to do it herself or make her feel stupid that she had forgotten to do something. He did not try to make her feel guilty by saying his time was more important than her time. He did not say, "What is the matter with you? Can't you do anything right?" I looked at my friend and was wondering what I was doing wrong in my marriage. What had I said or done to make Phil so angry with me all the time?

Lueck got a job that summer working for Pizza Hut in North Pole, Alaska, about twelve miles south of Fairbanks, delivering pizza. He traded his cute little red car for a piece of metal, called a Scout, that was old and needed repair. Lueck also tried out, on his own, for the Fairbanks Junior Symphony Orchestra and was accepted. He would do anything so he did not have to be at home. While playing his French horn in the orchestra he met a young lady, Kyle, who played the violin. These two individuals were very much alike and became good friends. I never knew what color hair either one of them had from day to day. They both dyed their hair odd colors, including bright pink, orange, or green. Lueck drove to Fairbanks in his Scout with the top off, rain or shine, to take her out. When he arrived at her place, after driving in the rain, he looked like a drowned kid with no sense, and her mom would not let her get in his truck. Smart mom.

Kati tried out for a traveling soccer team in Fairbanks, and made the team. The team had games in Anchorage and in Fairbanks. One of the best times I had with Kati was when she had a game in Anchorage, and the two of us tented in order to save some money. Kati and I were on equal basis when it came to doing something, so we did not tell each other what to do, but worked together instead. We put up our tent and tried to figure out a way to put a tarp over the whole thing because of the rain. The first morning we woke up, our sleeping bags were soaked from the rain. That morning while driving to soccer games, I put the bags in the back of our van with the heater on and dried them. We also bought camping cots for the next night. It felt good to be friends with my daughter.

I was realizing how peaceful the weekend was without having to worry that I was going to get the silent treatment or "wish you were dead" eyes or other comments that made me feel worthless. I didn't have to make love and act like I was enjoying it. I didn't have to worry about Phil getting out of bed and sleeping on the coach because I said no to having his body thrust upon me. I didn't have to worry about waking in the middle of the night to have fingers fondling my body or a hard muscle stuck between my legs. The more places I could go by myself, the more relaxed I became. The only thing I had to worry about was that Lueck was home alone with Phil, and I never knew when Phil would lash out at him. Lueck had a car and could leave whenever he needed, which helped me not worry quite so much.

Then he came again. That sneaky elephant was playing mind games with me. He left a beer bottle behind the couch while I was away. I didn't know what to do with the bottle. If I had confronted Phil with it, I was sure he would blame Lueck for it, and I had no idea what would happen from there. I knew Phil would not admit it was his, so it was no use asking him. I wanted Phil to know I found it and I knew what was going on, so I put it in the trash where he would see it. I figured if it wasn't his, he would ask where I found it or if I had been drinking. There were no comments about the bottle. I knew in my heart where it really came from. The red flags were waving. The elephants were marching. The parade had never stopped. The poop was piling deep. The world was about to end. I hid in the dungeon. The kids hid in school.

I wanted to run away. Linda and Doug were in Papua, New Guinea, and I seriously thought about flying there to see them. I had applied for my passport and was looking into the shots I needed when Kati approached me and asked me not to go because she did not want to be alone with her dad. I knew I could not live with myself if anything happened to her while I was gone, so I cancelled my trip. No one knew why I cancelled my trip except for Kati and me.

I knew then that I needed to make plans on supporting myself when the time was right to leave Phil. I decided to go back to college and get my bachelor's degree. After I completed a couple of classes, Phil also decided to get his degree before he retired from the air force. When I sat down to do homework, Phil continued to interrupt my studies. I felt he was trying very hard to prevent me from graduating. I was more determined than ever to graduate. I knew I could do it. I could not live scared any longer. I was starting to get seriously depressed, and I knew I had to do something about it because no one else would. I was in charge of me, and I was going to make it. I had made it this far and Kati would be graduating in two years; I was going to be ready to leave Phil if he did not change.

The darkness of Alaska and the darkness of Phil's words were strangling me. The classes were not enough. The words Phil threw at me were killing me like spears being thrown at an animal being hunted. The looks of disgust that Phil controlled me with were like receiving hate mail from my best friend. The head shaking of disapproval when I said or did something Phil did not like was like getting on stage in front of my own family and having them boo me right off the stage. I was hurting. I knew where all the cliffs were around Fairbanks, and I knew that if I drove the car off a cliff no one would find me for quite some time and it would look like an accident too. My children would not know any difference if I killed myself or if it was an accident. Oh, my children! I could not leave my children. Who would take care of them? I had tried to protect them for so many years, and I could not leave them now. But, I also could not live the way I was much longer.

Phil and Lueck both bought hunting licenses, and with a group of men, headed up north to hunt caribou. They each killed a caribou, and Phil went behind my back to get his caribou's head mounted. Lueck paid to get his own caribou rack mounted. I did not mind so much Phil was going to get it mounted, but I just wanted him to wait until we got back into the states to see where we were going to live. I thought he could get the hide tanned then, so it would be ready when we got back. It is hard to put a four-foot head of a dead animal in a closet when it becomes an eyesore or when there are no walls tall enough to display it on. Once again Phil lied to me when we had previously agreed we would not buy anything while we were in Alaska, but would instead use that money to travel together and see the sights while we were there. His dead trophy was more important to him than I was. Once again, Phil got what he wanted without much thought to anyone else. Maybe what upset me wasn't so much that he got what he wanted, but I didn't get what I wanted, a husband that was a friend.

Christmas was just around the corner, and it would be lonely with just the four of us. I made plans for us to drive to Alyeska Ski Resort, nearly two hours southeast of Anchorage, for snow boarding and cross-country skiing. The high school soccer coach, Scott, had parents that lived one hour north of Anchorage, and he invited us to stay a night at his parents' house. This was a good stopping place for us. Lueck and Kati spent the night in the soccer coach's room while Phil and I slept in his parents' bed. This was a mistake, but I did not find this out until a few years later. That night while Phil and I slept, the military man and trusted soccer coach, who was twenty-six, pulled my sixteen-year-old daughter off of the floor and on top of him while Lueck slept on the floor. I don't believe the bastard touched her in other ways, but this alone was like being raped when she trusted a coach and a friend to care about her. I did not know that Scott did this to Kati until four years later, and after Phil's death, when Kati told me about it and showed me the love letters Scott had written to her. Scott told Kati not to tell anyone about his feelings towards her. I don't think Phil ever knew about this, or he would have killed Scott, if not, at least filed charges against him. [Kati, I am so sorry about this.]

Scott and a friend of his came to the hotel to snowboard with the kids. They spent the day with us, and they drove the four hours back to his parents' home that night. I felt uncomfortable with the two guys there. I never knew if they would say something to me that would make Phil think I liked them. I never knew when someone would see we were not the happy family we pretended we were. Christmas day arrived and we opened presents in our room and went to a Christmas pageant at the hotel. As a family we were doing well, until Phil and I went cross-country skiing together. As I am writing this I don't remember what happened to have Phil angry with me again, but my chest is tight and I know things were not right. I can see us skiing at night under the lights, but I can't think of what happened to me to receive the silent treatment again. I felt so lonely. The next day we packed up and prepared for the ten-hour drive home. We stopped at Scott's parents' house again and thanked them for the presents they gave us. I don't think we spent the night, but I don't remember for sure.

Life still went on in the Harris home. I worked in the basement on my embroidery. We had two phone lines into our house, one for the basement only, which was my work line, and one for the family. If I needed to make any personal calls when Phil was at home, I would use the basement phone. Many times I felt he was listening on the phone. If I was in the basement talking, I felt he was sitting on the steps at the top of the stairs listening. These were more red flags I was trying ignore.

If Phil was home alone, he would not answer the phone, and if we were home, he would be the first one to answer. The only reason I figured out that he did this was to see who was calling and for whom. He was getting stranger and stranger every day.

One day while working in the dungeon, I realized Kati would be graduating in only eighteen months, and then I would be able to escape the hell hole I had decorated with colored fabric in order to camouflage red flags. I climbed the stairs of the dungeon with a smile on my face, realizing I would soon be free. Phil noticed my smile and commented on how nice it was to see me happy for a change. Little did he know I was happy because I would soon be free.

I gave a lot of thought about if I really wanted to leave Phil or not. I still wanted to love him and be the happy family I always dreamed of. I decided that six months before we left Alaska I would give my whole self to Phil. I would woo him with everything I had. I would try every way I knew how to make him feel secure in my love so that in return he would love and trust me. I had to wait because if I gave all I had at that time during our assignment in Alaska, I would have no place to go if he did not respond how I had hoped. I could not pull Lueck and Kati out of school and move again. I had to graduate from college myself. I had to prepare for the worst and the best.

I could not take Phil's actions any longer. I was majoring in human services and was learning what I already knew I knew, but tried to ignore, about unhealthy relations. I confronted Phil about my feelings of being afraid of him and feeling that he didn't care about me. I told him how his lies were upsetting me, how I felt controlled, and how scared I was to talk to him. I really poured my heart out. I tried telling him how I was really feeling. This took a lot of courage for me because I never knew how he was going to react. What I wanted was for Phil to say he was truly sorry and he did not know he was making me feel that way and he would try not to do those things anymore. That was not the reaction I got. His words that he smashed in my face were, "Oh well," as he turned walked away from me. I felt my concerns, my feelings, and me, meant nothing to him. I then knew I would not be able to woo him like I had thought of trying. I just gave up. I was nobody. I was an object Phil used to show to his friends, someone to take care of his kids, something to stick his cock in when the desire hit him. I was nothing. If it wasn't for my childhood and the foundation my parents gave me, I would have ended my will to fight for me right then.

By this time, I had even more detached myself from life. I was only a shell with no feelings. I was not there. I still put on a smile when I was out in public. I didn't want anyone to know what I was really thinking. Between the cold and darkness of Alaska and the coldness I felt in my heart, I was getting more and more depressed. I was scared because my goal of staying married until Kati graduated was getting near, and I didn't know if I was going to stay alive, or married that long. I tried to keep busy with my work and by getting involved in the school. I volunteered to work with the scholarship program in the high school. I joined the booster club and worked at the games. I continued taking classes. I was going to survive for another eighteen months. Lueck was going to be graduating in a few months, and I had to be there. I was going to be there no matter what.

What was really scaring me was that I might actually go through with one of my plans to kill myself. As I sat in the bathtub trying to hide from Phil, I thought of all the pills in the medicine cabinet. Again, the thoughts of my children saved me. But, that was that day. What about tomorrow when those death thoughts return? I was not sure if I would be able to fight them off the next time. I needed God's help. I prayed. I cried. I prayed. I cried. Life went on.

I wrote in my journal once in awhile. I usually hid the papers in strange places, like the pocket of a dress or the inside of a shoe. I also wrote in a notebook and then placed it someplace I hoped Phil would not look.

Jan. 24, 1999
More tears. I don't like who I have become. There are no laughs on the inside, only a lot of tears. I asked God to take me home tonight, and I told him if he isn't coming for me, I'm coming on my own. I then pictured Dad, Harris [my childhood neighbor], and Grandpa holding me down here on earth and hearing them tell me God has plans for me yet, just hang on. I don't deserve their love. I wish these tears would just stop. I think I'll read now and then try to sleep. I only took one Tylenol PM. See ya in the a.m.

Feb. 5, 1999
This last week as been much better. There haven't been as many tears. Very few for a fact. It's been super cold here, negative forty to negative fifty degrees Fahrenheit for the last week. I'm no longer panicking about the cold. The days are getting longer. I still have no feelings. I don't want to get in much detail because if anyone ever reads this, I want them to still remain my thoughts only. I have many things going on in my head that I would really like to share with someone, but there is no one around here that would

understand. I just want a friend I can depend on to listen to every one of my thoughts and take the time to explain themselves without saying, "What did I just say?"

We attended the base chapel where Phil became a Sunday school teacher and a youth group leader. The chapel offered a couple's study course, and Phil and I joined that also. I had hoped Phil and I could maybe, just maybe, make things work. I had hoped we could both learn something about a healthy relationship. The chaplain in charge of the class was a male pig and used his family to get what he wanted. In one of our classes he told us the only reason a wife was ever allowed to leave her husband was if he committed adultery. I asked him about being abused by a spouse, and he stated that was no reason to leave a marriage. I asked him if he would feel the same way if his own daughter was being abused, and he replied that he would. He believed men should be the head of household and control everything and everyone. Lueck lost all respect for this man when he gave his sermons at church about judging people that were different. I lost all respect for this man when he told me it was okay for men to abuse their wives. I did continue to go to the group classes. I figured it could not hurt and maybe we would learn something that would save our marriage.

One thing that was talked about in the group was listening to what the other person was really saying, then paraphrasing back to them what was heard. A card was given to the couples on how to disagree with respect and how to take turns listening. I thought this card was a great tool and just maybe Phil would start listening to what I had to say. Just maybe he would? And just maybe I would understand what he was saying. Just maybe I would? A little hope was better than no hope.

I knew my children were also struggling along with Phil and me. I was talking to Lueck and I don't remember what he said to make me think he had, or was, smoking pot. While Lueck was in school and Phil was at work I went into Lueck's room and the first place I looked, which was in an old pair of his shoes, I found a bag of weed. It was old and stuck together, but it was in my hand on federal property in base housing. I was beyond scared. My stomach turned in knots. I didn't know what to do. I could not tell Phil because I did not know what he would do to Lueck. I didn't know if he would sit down and talk to him, turn him in to the security, or beat the crap out of him. I had to talk to Lueck, but what was I going to say? I prayed. I cried. I prayed.

I talked to Lueck and was informed that this was old stuff from when he worked at the fair as a "carny rat." It didn't help me feel much better. It was old. I could tell that from the bag, but now what do I do with it? If the military finds out Lueck has drugs in our house, we could all get kicked off base, and Phil could lose his rank. Really, Phil would not lose his rank for this small offense, but I knew Phil would make a huge deal out of it and blame Lueck if he was not promoted next time he tested. I had to handle this situation myself. I wanted a partner who I could talk this over with and we could come to a sensible solution, but that was not happening in our family.

I thought of many different ways to get rid of the weed. It could not just be thrown it in the trash because if it was found in our trash bag with our names on any items, the military would know where it came from. What I ended up doing was having Lueck hide it in the middle of some used cat litter when he threw it out. It was gone, but was the problem of Lueck using drugs?

I couldn't trust Phil not only with how he would treat Lueck, but how he would treat me. Both kids were in band and there was a competition a few hours away that they were attending. Phil and I made hotel reservations and went to see them. I had been on an antibiotic for something for about a week, and I noticed my body was not feeling well that night. I tried to explain this to Phil when he wanted to make love but he thought this was just another excuse. We went though with the act of having sex, and all the while I was trying to decide what my body was telling me. It was like all my nerve ends were on the outside of my body. It was easier to have sex with Phil than it was to live with the anger or the silent treatment, even though I wasn't feeling well. I didn't ache, but my skin was very sensitive to touch.

We went home the next day and the following morning when I got up and looked in the mirror I found the problem. I saw this red-faced blotchy person looking at me in the mirror. I was red hot, and I had broken out in hives. I broke down in tears. I felt I was burning. Phil was already at work, and the kids were getting ready for school. I made a doctor appointment and headed for the clinic. When they brought me in the office I once again broke down and cried. I was exhausted from the heat. I was immediately seen by the doctor who gave me a shot in the rump, and was told I should not be alone in case my windpipe swelled up. I was not allowed to drive home either.

I called the school to see if they would let Lueck out to come and get me and then stay home with me the rest of the day. When I got home I called Phil to let him know what was going on. I didn't ask him to come home because I did not want to bother him. I did not want to be a burden to him in any way.

When Phil came home that evening I was in bed sleeping and the first thing he did was not to come up and see how I was doing, but he started the vacuum cleaner to clean the living room instead. Besides being upset that Phil didn't care how I was feeling, I was hurt that he accused me of not letting people sleep when it was really him that couldn't stand to see me sleep. I was still having the blame put on me for things he did. This was getting really old.

The porno stuff still hadn't gone away. One evening, while saying goodnight to Lueck, I noticed Lueck quickly hid something as I walked into the room. I asked him what it was, and he would not give me an answer I could believe. I hated lies more than anything. I could not make a scene, for again, I did not know what Phil would do. While Lueck was in school I found a couple porno of magazines in his room, under his bed in a suitcase. I threw them away, and Lueck could not say anything to me because then he would have to admit he had them. This made me doubt who really signed up on the web site with the teenagers. Once again I confronted Lueck to have him tell me if it was him. I wanted it to be Lueck. I wanted to believe my husband was not a pervert. Again, Lueck assured me he did not sign up for the teenage porn site. I felt I knew in my heart that Lueck was telling me the truth. What had he to lose if he told me the truth? He would be moving out in a couple of months anyway. I could not ground him, and he knew I would not tell Phil. It gave me a horrible feeling to think Phil would do this. He was now teaching Sunday school and working with the youth group. There was nothing I could say to anyone. This was just another secret that would rip my insides to pieces.

People on the outside looking in would not have any idea how unhappy I was. My happy mask was painted on tight. I thought if I pretended I was happy, maybe I would really be happy. My tears knew the truth—my silent tears that dampened my pillow at night after Phil had sex with my body. He was good at sex, but that did not mean I wanted it whenever he did. I felt I did not have a choice and that made it feel like rape. I was just a sex object. It seemed the only time Phil was nice to me was when he wanted sex. I was becoming colder towards him, and his words were becoming more controlling. This was not a good combination. I tried to stay up later than Phil to make sure he was asleep when I came to bed. I tried to get up before Phil so he would not use me for his sex hole first thing in the morning. I slept to the edge of my side of the bed. I slept as far away from Phil as I could. I wanted to die. My kids needed me. I could not die yet.

My kids and their friend Jenny were supposed to be home from snowboarding on the army base. My phone rang and Jenny said Kati was in the hospital. They had just brought her there by ambulance. I said, "Yeah, right? You guys better be on your way home!"

They were not on their way home. Phil and I were on our way to the army hospital twenty-five miles away.

Kati lie in the emergency room with this blank stare on her face. Her brother and Jenny were outside in the waiting room. She had fallen off a twenty-five-foot cliff. They had been in an area that was off limits for snowboarding and while Kati sat at the edge of the cliff with her snowboard at hand, she fell forward off the cliff. To this day Kati doesn't remember if she tried to slid down the cliff, or if she walked off the cliff, or what she really did to get herself in that situation. Lueck and Jenny ran around and down the cliff to get to her, and she was not moving. Lueck ran the half-mile back to the ski lodge and told them what happened. They sent the snowmobile medics to her right away and from there to the ambulance.

When Phil and I walked into the room, Kati was lying in bed and quietly complaining about her elbow hurting. She looked at us as if she had no idea who we were. Her subdued complaining was not like Kati. She liked attention and normally cried when she was in this much pain. The doctor talked to us to let us know she had hit her head and had a concussion, hurt her knee as well as her elbow. It was the concussion that had us most concerned. The hospital ordered a CAT scan for her and started an IV in her arm. This IV was enough to bring out the Kati I knew. As Kati and I sat in the CAT scan room, the liquid from the IV hit her and she had to go pee. She was not going to pee in a bedpan, and she let everyone know that. She felt it was her body, and they better let her up and use the bathroom. She was feisty and back to being the Kati I knew. She recovered from all of this after weeks with crutches and taking it easy.

The long dark, really dark, cold, really cold, winter was almost over and we were getting ready for Lueck's graduation. Negative sixty was cold whether the wind was blowing or not. Luann and Bruce were going to fly up to see Lueck graduate, but had to come a few weeks early instead. I was always nervous when family was staying with us. Phil could be the nicest guy and everything could go smoothly, or he could be a jerk and let people know just what he was thinking and it wasn't always pleasant. Phil took time off of work, and we took Luann and Bruce up to Chena Hot Springs for the day, a two-hour drive northeast of Fairbanks. I had a great time with my sister and brother-in-law and all went well.

Lueck could not wait any longer to live on his own. One week before graduation Lueck moved out of the house and into an apartment with Kyle. He had been working full time all during his senior year for Pizza Hut and continued to do so while going to college in Fairbanks in the fall. Lueck had wanted to live on his own for a long time. When he was only fifteen years old and we were living in Warrensburg, he had planned on moving out and living with a few friends. At that time, Phil was very hurt by Lueck wanting to live on his own and took this personally. Maybe it was personal.

I didn't like being with Phil, and I see now that I used Kati to entertain her dad so I didn't have to feel guilty about not wanting to be with Phil. It was our last summer in Alaska, and the two of them would do some fishing while I made every excuse I could think of not to go and spend time with Phil. I didn't like being in the car with Phil any longer than I had to. His negative comments about other people and about our kids could suck all the positive thoughts out of me in just minutes. Being afraid to voice my opinion and the silent treatments made trips very long, even if it was just around the block. Being told how dumb I was or being asked "what is the matter with you" was taking its toll on me. Having something break because it was old and then being beaten with the questions, "Why did you break it? Things don't just break on their own. You must have done something to break it." These questions made me afraid to touch anything that was not mine. I did not want to drive Phil's truck, or use anything of his.

I did get to see some of Alaska, but not nearly what I wanted to see. Kati was still on the traveling soccer team, and I made a few trips that last summer to Anchorage for games. Most of the time Phil had to work, so I made these peaceful trips with Kati. I became friends with the mother of one of Kati's teammates. I could confide in her how I was feeling about my marriage. I wonder whom Phil could confide in. I felt for him. I don't think he had any good friends in Alaska, or anywhere else, for that matter.

This was the last year Phil could go hunting. Lueck and his dad made plans to go up north again for a caribou hunt. Phil's back was in bad shape, and he knew he would be having surgery in a few months, but they went anyway. The idea was to tie a rope around their waists and have the other end or the rope tied to the canoe. They then pulled the canoe upstream to their campsite. This would have been a good idea if the river was straight. They walked many extra miles winding around each curve in the river. They were both exhausted by the time they reached camp. Lueck was sick and throwing up and Phil was in extreme pain, so the next morning they decided to come back home instead of hunting. They took their time and stopped to fish along the way and got to know each other. Phil came back with many stories of their trip, but never told them when Lueck was around. Lueck knew the truth of the trip, and Phil knew the lies. I can't remember the stories because I learned to ignore Phil's stories. When he started telling one, my ears tuned them out. If I was to question anything he said, his words of "woman, you got your mouth open again" would put me back in my place. It was best not to listen and not to comment about anything Phil said.

One more year and we would be leaving Alaska. One more year and I would make my goal of surviving until Kati graduated. I could do it. It would be nearly one of the worst years of my life. I didn't have much more to give. I had given all of myself to Phil and my kids and there were only little pieces of me left.

CHAPTER 10

THE LAST YEAR IN ALASKA

■ I am not a bad person. I was told I was bad many times by Phil. Maybe I am. Maybe I was. Just maybe it was me that caused all of the problems in Phil. Just maybe? These thoughts still have a way of sneaking into my head. I need a hug. I need a tissue. I am so sorry.

There wasn't a girl's high school soccer team for the second year, so Kati once again played on the boy's soccer team. Kati was voted the captain of the team. She wanted her dad to coach, but I don't think I had encouraged it. I was always afraid of what he would do. The district coaches also voted her to the All Conference Boys' Team. Her dad was very proud of her. She was fulfilling his dream of playing soccer. During her last soccer game, Kati started to feel sick and could not catch her breath. I believe this was the result of tension in her life. She wanted to be popular. She wanted people to like her. She had to be a great soccer player so her dad would love her.

One of Kati's goals in life was to become homecoming queen. She was voted one of the candidates. The night of homecoming Kati was still sick and had a hard time breathing. She had gone to the emergency room only the week before when she started coughing and hyperventilating. While in the emergency room they gave her a shot of Valium to get her breathing under control. This time it did not work, but caused Kati to quit breathing altogether. The doctors now had a real emergency on their hands and tubes were being prepared to enter Kati's throat when Phil commanded her in a loud voice to "breathe!" It worked, and Kati came around. After a couple of hours we all went home exhausted.

Kati and her younger date, Chris, headed for the homecoming dance. Phil and I were going to be chaperones at the dance. When the queen of the ball was announced and it was not Kati, she started to pass out. She had held up just long enough to find out who the queen was and that was all the energy she had left. Phil saw her going down and picked her up, hoisting her over his shoulder like a sack of potatoes, and carried her outside. She had worn a very short slinky black dress that night and it lacked fabric when it came to covering her butt as she rode on her dad's shoulder. Once outside, Phil got her calmed down enough to get her home. We put her in Phil's truck, and we drove the mile home.

When we got Kati to the house I called the army hospital and asked them what we should do. They said to bring her in. Phil went into the garage to start his truck so we could once again rush Kati to the hospital, but it did not start. Chris and his friend followed us home, so Kati and I got into the vehicle with the guys while Phil worked on his truck. On the twenty-five-mile trip, Kati stopped breathing, and I had to get her calmed down and get her breathing back under control. Phil arrived shortly after we did. The two guys had carried Kati into the hospital, The boys stayed until they knew Kati was going to be okay, then left for home. [Thank you guys.]

Kati not only fought for her health, but Kati and I were fighting more and more too. She hated me and told me so in no uncertain terms. Phil never seemed to stand up for me and tell our daughter to knock it off, but got upset with both of us instead. I felt Phil really enjoyed Kati telling me she hated me because many times he egged her on by telling her I would do something for Lueck and not for her. If I let Lueck do something when he was a certain age, but I did not let Kati do it because I learned it was not a good thing, Phil told Kati, "Well, your mom let Lueck do it." He liked it when we fought because then he would be the good dad. Phil did whatever Kati wanted him to do. If Kati called at midnight when Phil was sleeping and asked him to pick her and her friends up and take them someplace, he did it without any questions. This action of Phil's also raised red flags, and I was wondered what kind of hold Kati had on her dad that he would do anything she asked, even if it was not the best for her.

If Kati brought home Ds on her report card after she was failing the class at midterm, Phil praised her and told her what a good job she had done. I didn't agree with this at all because I knew she could do better than Ds. She was a smart person but was not doing her homework because she didn't like the teachers. Phil made excuses for her instead of encouraging her to use her talents. I tried to explain to Kati she was not hurting the teachers by not trying in class, but only hurting herself.

I saw and knew things were not healthy in our home. I should have taken Kati and Lueck and run. I still knew Phil could not, or would not, live without us. Besides leaving their dad, our kids would also have had a funeral to go to. We only had to make it a few more months, and we would all be on our own. I would deal with my children's emotions afterwards. If they were on their own when I left Phil, then it would only be me that would have to deal with the guilt of leaving him. Children are supposed to grow up and leave their parents. Wives aren't supposed to grow up and leave their husbands.

I knew the real reason Kati hated me was because I had not protected her when her dad beat her when we lived in Missouri. I tried to let her words bounce off me and give her hugs to show her I understood. There were times when her words hurt more than I could handle and tears of exhaustion drowned my heart. I knew deep down that she loved me, but she had learned words of hate from listening to her dad talk to me. Kati probably felt if it was okay for her dad to talk that way to me, it must be okay for her.

Kati wanted a car. Phil and I talked this over like normal parents and agreed she would not get one until she had a B average. That is the condition we made with Lueck, and it helped keep his grades up. Auto insurance was less expensive if young drivers earned good grades and insurance for teenagers was costly enough. I knew Kati could get good grades if she really wanted them, but Phil once again went behind my back.

Phil and Kati had been talking about cars and one day Phil came home and told me he found a car for Kati and was buying it for her. He was using some money he had put aside, giving the seller his pistol, and Kati was paying the remainder with her saving bonds that were supposed to be for her college. He drove me to the lemon lot where the car sat and told me all about the car. He told me how he had test driven it yesterday and how well it ran. I looked at the snow around the car and could see there were not any tire tracks leading in or out of this parking space, and it had not snowed in a few days. Either Phil was really strong and lifted that car in and out of its parking spot or he was lying to me. I asked him again, just to make sure I heard him right, and he said he had driven the car the day before and it was running fine. I knew better than to argue with him because he would make me feel dumb for questioning him. He would just come up with another lie. I could not take any more lies, so Kati now had a car of her own.

I hated being lied to! I hated feeling like a fool. I wondered if other people thought I actually believed what Phil was telling me. I wondered if Phil would go to work and tell all his co-workers how dumb his wife was for believing him. I wondered if Phil believed his own lies. I wanted to be equal in our relationship. I wanted to trust the partner I lived with. I didn't want to be better than anyone else, and I didn't want anyone else being better than me. By Phil lying to me, I felt he thought he was smarter and better than me. I felt he thought I didn't matter and I was just someone that got in his way. The car did work fine, but that was not the point.

Phil was getting lazier and lazier, and he was one that had to keep busy in order to be halfway happy. The more I did for him, the more he expected and the lazier he got. This is called "care taking," and I was very good at it. After being yelled at for not having his uniform ironed on a Monday morning after he sat around all weekend and did nothing, I put my foot down and told him I quit. He tried all of his techniques to get me to feel guilty, but this time I did not back down. He tried a few weeks later to make me feel guilty after he had forgotten to iron his uniform, but once again I did not back down. I did not say anything to him when he gave "the look," but I didn't go and iron his uniform either. Saying something to him would only give him the excuse to say something hurtful back to me.

I once again stuck my neck out and questioned Phil. I should have known better. One month before we were supposed to go to Fresno to see Phil's family for Christmas, and eight months before we were to leave Alaska, Phil decided he wanted to buy a heavy air compressor. It was Sunday morning and Phil was looking at the Sunday paper when he saw the compressor he wanted. I questioned him about why he wanted a compressor now, when he knew we were close to being overweight on our move back to Minnesota. He became instantly angry with me, threw some quick words at me, then applied the silent treatment. I could feel myself shrinking lower and lower. Being the family of disguises, we put on our happy masks and went to church.

After church we went to the base chow hall for a cheap meal and chatted with other members of the church like we were a normal family. Arriving back at our house I knew I had to get away for awhile and get myself back together. I felt hurt and angry too. I knew all I had done was ask Phil why he needed an air compressor now, and all I wanted was an answer I could understand. I needed to get away for awhile so I could get a better perspective of the situation.

Kati was life guarding at the base pool. I thought it would be a good idea if I worked out some of my frustration by swimming laps. The water felt good, and it was nice having some quiet time without being ignored. I was refreshed after the swim and ready to deal with Phil again. I was in a good mood when I got back home, but that didn't last long. Phil had brewed the whole time I was gone and was ready to explode. I got it all. For three hours he yelled at me, told me what a worthless person I was, told me everything I had ever done wrong in the twenty-two years we were married. [I didn't think that was so bad. It only took three hours to list all my faults in life.] We were in the living room when he started shouting at me. I asked him to stop shouting and informed him I was not deaf. I told him yelling only made him loud, not right. In a calm voice I asked him again not to shout at me. He continued to yell. I was surprised the neighbors didn't call the police since the walls in base housing are fairly thin.

Kati came home from work and heard the angry words being launched at me. I tried to ignore Phil and keep busy working. I knew to stay calm because if I got mad it would only be used against me. I knew if I got nasty too, it still would not stop his words that were trying to deflate my spirit; it would only put me at his level and I refused to go there. I put up my shield, my plastic bubble, and my huge brick wall, and let the words bounce off of me. Phil started reminding me what a terrible person I was in bed. He was talking about our sex life in front of Kati! I could not understand how he could do this to me or to her. Kati couldn't handle any more and left for a friend's house.

I walked into the kitchen after an hour or so of being insulted in the living room. I had to get homework done, and Phil's mouth followed me into there too. I finally convinced him I was not deaf, and he could insult me in a normal tone of voice with as much hatred trailing from his words as if he was shouting. I tried using the arguing card we received in the couples group. I tried to rephrase back to him what he said, but the executing words that he finally did kill the conversation with were, "What did I just say?" This meant I had better listen the first time he told me something because he was not going to repeat it. It was another way of calling me stupid. His words were telling me I was not smart enough to understand what he said.

I had had enough, and my shield was getting blasted full of holes. I can't remember what the exact words were, but I finally said something about his past to him. I think I said something about Jill. He took those words I said and threw them right back at me, telling me I should have known better then saying things like that to him. Since I had taken psychology, I should know how much damage this could cause him. Never mind the things he said to me.

Kati returned home to us still fighting and hid in her bedroom. I start talking about Phil's drinking. He told me he had been going to AA for ten years. I looked at him with disbelief, but didn't dare say anything. I knew he had never seriously gone to an AA meeting. If he had, I would have seen an AA book or heard an apology. I had been going to Al-Anon and knew the twelve steps to the program. I had not seen Phil take any of those steps. I told him I knew he lied about test driving Kati's car. He still continued to lie to me and told me he did test drive the car before he bought it. I informed Phil I had talked to the previous owner who told me that Phil did not drive the car before his purchase. That put a stop to that part of the argument, but Phil found other things to remind me about what a rotten wife I was.

After about three hours of Phil trying to break me down, he finally succeeded. I started bawling with sobs that took my breath away. I told him I planned on leaving him. He asked how long I had been planning this, and I replied with an answer of a very long time. I then proceeded to choke out the words that I had also wanted to kill myself. Out of this whole three hours of trying to knock me down to nothing, the only thing he got out of that whole conversation was that I wanted to kill myself. He didn't hear anything else I tried to tell him about our marriage. He didn't hear that I had planned on leaving him. He didn't hear how unhappy I was. He didn't hear the sadness in my voice. Phil only heard what he wanted to hear. Phil was the only victim in his mind. Phil ended the conversation with low growling words of hate that stuck in my ears, "Don't you ever question me again. If I want to buy something I don't need your damn permission. It's my money."

I pulled myself together and headed for the dungeon to work. I needed some space. I needed to dry up the lonely and confused tears that were lost on my face. I needed to figure out what I was going to do with my life. I didn't know if Phil was going to tell me to get out of the house now or what he was going to do. I just knew I was not going to question him about anything ever again. I would become that wall that I worked so hard to build a wall without feelings. Walls could survive, while my feelings couldn't. I was not going to ever be hurt like this again.

While I was down in the basement Phil had gone upstairs and talked to Kati. He told her I wanted to kill myself. This was more manipulation on Phil's part. He looked like the caring husband by telling Kati I was unhappy. She came down crying. I reassured her I was not going to kill myself because she and Lueck were too important to me. We hugged each other with the strength it takes to tell someone they are going to be okay.

The next morning Phil went to work, and I went to my temporary part-time job working with a school photographer. Another lady from the base and I worked, and often rode, together. She had become a good friend, and I could confide in her. Her husband worked with Phil and out-ranked him, but I knew she would not say anything to him. It was good having a friend. I worked that day as if nothing had happened at home. Little did my boss know that my marriage of twenty-two years was maybe coming to an end. My smiling mask was glued on tight.

In two weeks I was leaving for Minnesota for my cousin's wedding and to check out Southwest State University for Kati. Kati wanted to play soccer there, and we had sent the coach a tape of Kati playing soccer in Alaska. I would be leaving Kati alone with her dad. She had a car so she could leave and go to her brother's if she needed to. She had money in the bank and could take care of herself.

Kati slipped a note into my luggage as I was leaving. This was something we started many years ago. When someone went on a trip or if Phil had to go TDY, we hid notes in their suitcases to show them we missed them. This note Kati sent stated she was going to be okay while I was gone, but if anything happened between her and her dad, she could always go to her friend's house. She was scared about being alone with her dad. There was no note from Phil this time.

While in Minnesota I contacted the soccer coach at SSU and talked about the video of Kati playing soccer I mailed to her earlier that month. She seemed very interested and wanted to meet Kati in person to see how she would get along with the team. Kati would have to meet the team in the next couple of months.

I also attended my cousin's wedding while in Minnesota. By now I was comfortable doing things by myself. Matter of fact, I preferred doing things by myself instead of with Phil at my side bursting my positive thoughts. I could be myself and not have to worry about entertaining him all the time. Phil was usually not able to attend things with me because of his job, and I liked it that way.

At the wedding reception most of my cousins I had not seen in many years were there. One cousin I used to be very close to was also in a very unhealthy marriage. She married a Baptist minister who said men are to be the head of the household and wives should be their slaves because that is what it says in the Bible. He picked out all of her clothes, cut her hair, and when they traveled as a family, he and their son flew first-class, while their daughters and she flew coach. She seemed happy enough to everyone else, but as she was walking towards me, our eyes met and I swear she had the same pleading signs in her eyes I felt in mine. My smile was painted on my face, but I wanted someone to read the message that my eyes were trying to illuminate, the message that read "Help me! I'm hurting." No one could see the message, or if they did, they chose to ignore it. I knew I had to save myself because in my heart I knew no one could do it for me.

One more stop while in Minnesota. I went to visit Luann and Bruce and brought some of my diary writings to put away in a safe place. I was afraid Phil would read them, then use them against me. I also had Luann keep some of my money for me. I confided in her that I had planned on leaving Phil in the summer if things did not change between us. One night while visiting with Luann after Bruce had gone to bed, she asked me if I was concerned about leaving Kati alone with Phil. I told her yes and was going to leave it at that, but something inside of me told me to find out her why she asked.

Luann continued to tell me about the time we were at their old house and her daughter Cammie was about thirteen when Phil sat on her and rubbed his hand over her chest. She didn't know if it was an accident, as he was reaching for her hands, or if he had done it on purpose. It had really upset Cammie at the time, and she had finally confined in her mom. I remembered that day. I knew something had happened that day because I remembered her running into the bathroom, crying, after Phil sat on her in the middle of the kitchen floor. Phil had been drinking, and he always thought his niece was cute. They would horseplay and pick on each other, but Phil never realized his strength until someone got hurt or mad. This time he went way too far. [Sorry, Cammie,]

I don't remember how I got back to the airport, but I do remember the flight home to Alaska and how I cried sitting in the seat of the uncaring airplane. Tears of panic rushed over my face. I didn't want to go back to Phil, but had to because my children were there. Kati was going to graduate in six months from high school, and I was going to graduate from college. I had to finish what I started so I could get a new life. Lueck was also in college, and I didn't want to leave him there by himself at this time. He would have been left to deal with his dad and that would not have been fair to him. I was the one that had chosen Phil as their father, and it was up to me to make this as pain-free for the children as I could. But, I did not want to go back to being abused. I did not want to go back to being ignored. I did not want to go back to the dark cold winter. I did not want to back! I had to go back. I was going back. i was back. [I use the small "I" on purpose to show how I felt.]

In just a few weeks we planned to leave for California to see Phil's family for Christmas. Phil came home from work and told me we were going to have a family of three come and live with us until the home they were having built was finished. He did not talk this over with me first, just informed me. I guess he knew I would not buck at the idea.

They stayed in Kati's old room since she had moved into Lueck's room after he moved out. They stayed with us for about three months, did not even write us a thank you note when they moved out, but made sure they didn't leave a morsel of the food they bought behind in our house. They had a little girl who was about one year old.

Both Phil and I found we were leaving our own home because they had a way of taking over the living room and the TV. Instead of confronting them, we both became silent complainers and let them have our home. I am not sure what that says for both of us, but I don't think it was healthy on either of our parts. Phil was her supervisor at work. I don't know why he asked them to stay with us. I think he felt sorry for them because they didn't have a place to live. They were getting a housing allowance and, by living with us for nothing, they saved that money and put it towards their new home. We could not charge them rent because we lived in base housing, and we would have gotten in lots of trouble if we rented out something the military was paying for. We did not actually pay rent, nor electricity, nor water. Base housing was part of Phil's benefits.

In the meantime, I made Christmas presents for the family and attended all the sports events at the school. I worked in the concession stand whenever Kati was not playing basketball. All four teams, varsity boys and girls and junior varsity boys and girls, played on the same day. There were few schools in Alaska and the teams from what schools there were had to normally travel a long distance to another school, so all teams rode or flew together to play at another school. Many times the teams stayed overnight at the school and the booster clubs fed them.

I hated sitting by Phil at the games. He sucked all the enjoyment out of me by his negative comments. He usually said them quietly so I would be the only one to hear them. Sometimes he would be obnoxious and yell at the ref, but mostly he was just complaining quietly about how the players were playing. I had to work so hard on being happy, just a few minutes with him made it almost impossible to feel good.

Afterwards Phil got upset with me for not talking to him. He accused me of talking to everyone but him. It was true. I didn't like talking to him. I didn't like being near him. We looked at things two totally different ways, and they were not meshing. I felt bad for the kids when they messed up. I knew what it felt like to be in front of people and do something stupid and then have someone like Phil judge me. I knew I was doing the best I could at that time, and I figured other people were doing the same. I also thought that about Phil. I thought Phil was doing the best he could, but his best was hurting me. The young players did not need to be reminded of how bad they did, but they needed to be encouraged to get out there and try again. He never said anything negative to the players in person; most of the negative comments he made were directed my way.

Lueck did not go with us to California for Christmas, but instead joined some friends in Germany to go snowboarding. Before we arrived in California, I figured we would have to buy some, if not most, of the food while we stayed at Phil's parents' house. I didn't think we would have to buy it all. It wasn't that it broke us. I just didn't understand that when they knew their kids were coming home, whom they had not seen in two years, why they had not planned ahead and had some food in the house. They did give us each $100.00 for Christmas that year, which didn't make any sense to me.

Almost immediately, Phil spent his money on himself buying new fishing things. I spent some of mine buying food. This did not make me a better person or Phil a bad person. It just shows once again how different we were. I did not need anything. I had learned years ago that things did not make me happy. I would not wake every morning happy because I had bought a new something. Afterwards that something would become a burden and just be something that needed fixing or dusting. All I wanted was my freedom to be me and money was not going to buy that. Also, I was hungry, and I was a caretaker. I felt I had to take care of everyone but myself. I knew I would be okay, but I wasn't sure if everyone else would be okay without my help.

While talking with his brothers, Phil told them what he did at work in the air force and how many people he had working for him. Phil then proceeded to brag he was good at manipulating people to get them to do things for him. That was one statement he made that was not a lie. Phil was the best at manipulating people. He could make anyone feel they were the ones who had done something wrong, even if it was totally Phil's fault. He was good with words. He would take the blame for nothing.

I usually complained about Phil to his mom, but this year I did not say much about Phil at all. I had become completely numb to thoughts and feelings. I was hoping she could see how sad I was, but she had her own problems to deal with.

We made it though the 2000 New Year's Eve without any lights going out and without all the computers crashing. Kati went to bed before midnight, and we weren't far behind. A few days later we flew back to Alaska to finish the last months of our three-year tour. Kati could get back to school and see her friends and play basketball.

Chris, Kati's boyfriend from homecoming, and Kati were getting rather serious with each other. He had given her a pre-engagement ring, and they had planned on living together happily ever after, even though he was three years behind her in school. He was not much younger than she, but had failed a few classes and was held back a year in school. He was not a dumb kid, but came from a dysfunctional family.

Kati and Chris were getting too serious, and their relationship was leading into things that only married or older couples should have been experiencing. Kati approached me about birth control pills. I told her I could not do that for her because I didn't think they should be having sex. I explained to her I felt it would be the same as if she wanted to rob a bank. If I stood outside of the door of the bank as a lookout person while she robbed the bank, then I would be telling her it is okay to steal. I couldn't stand outside the door and watch her make a mistake that might affect her for life. I wouldn't go to the clinic and get her pills. If she chose to do that on her own, then it would be her decision and she knew how I felt about it.

In a few short months Phil would be retiring from the air force, and he needed to get any medical problems completed while he was still on active duty. Phil was still having a lot of pain in his back. This pain started while we were at Whiteman Air Force Base and Phil was catching for a squadron softball game. He was plowed over when a player was running for home plate. His pain got worse each year and many times he could barely stand. The doctors told Phil he needed surgery on his back for ruptured disks. This surgery had to take place at the base hospital in the state of Washington. I had to make a difficult decision. I didn't feel I should leave Kati because I didn't trust her and Chris alone together, but I should also be by Phil's side when he had major surgery. Phil had been so nasty lately, and I didn't really want to be with him. I put some of the blame for his disposition on the pain he was experiencing. I just couldn't understand why anyone would be so hateful otherwise.

A friend of ours, who had this same surgery a few months before, was going to Washington the same time Phil was going. Because someone would be there for Phil, I chose to stay in Alaska. I called Macky, Phil's old roommate from Iceland who lived near the base in Washington, and asked him to check on Phil too. He said he would love to see Phil again and agreed to check on him.

I knew my choice to stay with Kati really upset Phil, and I didn't blame him. I would have been upset too, but I had become empty walking flesh and would do almost anything to save the little bit of self-esteem I had left, even if that meant not being at my husband's side.

Phil survived the surgery, and I could tell he was bitter at me for not being there. He healed fast, but not fast enough for him. He hated being down.

It was Valentine's Day and the base chaplain that headed up the couples group was planning a special dinner at the army base ski lodge for anyone who wanted to go. He didn't tell us what to expect during the dinner so Phil signed us, as well as Kati and her boyfriend, Chris, up to go. When we arrived at the lodge everyone was dressed in evening wear except us. We wore nice pants, but nothing fancy. After the dinner the chaplain surprised me with the announcement that all married couple were going to renew their wedding vows. I panicked. I wanted to run. I wanted out of there. This was not being fair. I did not want to do this. I did not love Phil. I did not want to be married to this man anymore, and now I was expected to swear in front of everyone, and God too, that I loved this man. I only wanted out of the marriage. I wanted to dash out of the door, into the freezing cold and run until I collapsed.

I didn't run or scream or even leave. I was a good wife who didn't cause a scene. While saying the vows I looked at all the room instead of at Phil. He took my head into his hands and forced me to look at him and told me with a cold voice filled with hatred and hurt that I could at least look interested. I wanted to puke. My body was stiff and the panic grew like a weed given fertilizer. "Noooooooooooooo," I wanted to shout. "No, I will not marry you. No, you have hurt me too many times. No, I didn't want to marry you in the first place, and I don't want to do it again," my head was thinking, but my trained mouth kept still. On the twenty-five-mile drive back to our house the tears in the dark escaped down my face in silence. I was relieved the whole night was over.

At the end of February, Kati and I made the trip to Minnesota so the soccer coach at the university could see Kati's skills for herself. While staying at my mom's house, we went and played bingo in the town hall for such wonderful prizes as a roll of paper towels or a bag of pretzels. If we were really lucky, we won as much as five dollars. On long winter nights people in Minnesota would do just about anything to get out and meet with friends. One of my old boyfriends was working at bingo that night, and I introduced Kati to him after the games. I knew he had left his wife. He was very handsome. He was close to six-feet eight-inches tall. He had a body of a well-fit carpenter with a full dark brown beard to cover his forty-year-old face. I told Kati about his old name of "Hot Lips" and how he had gotten it when he was eating pizza I spiked with hot sauce. He turned a little red and mumbled something back. When Kati and I got into the car to drive the three blocks back to my mom's house, she turned to me and said, "Mom, you should go out with him." I looked at her and replied with surprise in my voice that I was married.

I didn't know where she got the idea I should go out with someone other than her dad. I never told her, with words, that I was planning on leaving Phil or I how unhappy I was. She was seeing more than I gave her credit for. My happy mask that I wore around the kids must have had rips in it.

I called and talked to Phil and let him know how things were going with Kati and college and, while on the phone, he told me he had sold all of our vehicles and his canoe. He would not tell me how much he received for the stuff. I told him I needed to go visit with my mom and her husband, Armin, because Kati and I were leaving in a couple of days. He hung up without saying good-bye. His anger was so strong that even thousands of miles away it could still grip my chest and squeeze it until it made my eyes leak.

We flew back to Alaska for the remaining three months of the tour. Kati and I got ready for graduation, Kati from high school and me with a BA in human service.

We arrived home to a Phil that was getting stranger. We had only been gone a few days, and I noticed Phil had washed the bedspread and put a different one on the bed. I don't know for sure, but I believed he got drunk while we were gone and puked the good ol' flu in the bottle routine all over the bed. It just wasn't like Phil to change the bedspread for no reason. He was not into decorating the bedroom. He might move the furniture around in the living room, but not the bedroom. Phil didn't have anything sold, as he said, except for his canoe. More lies in the home sweet home.

When Phil was at work he bragged about me to the guys he worked with. Once he even came home from work and told me the guys told him they couldn't figure out why I stayed with him. Phil admitted he was a jerk and lied. It was as if he admitted it, then it made it all okay because he knew the facts. It was like being an alcoholic, admitting you're an alcoholic, and then going to the bars to drink because being an alcoholic gave you the excuse you needed in order to drink.

Phil was also using the Internet in strange ways. After Kati and I went to bed, or while we were out of the room, he turned the screen so only he could see it. No one else could view it unless we walked in directly behind him. If we entered the room he quickly closed whatever he was working on. Most times he just shrunk to the bottom of the screen, but sometimes I was faster than him and I could see what he was doing. It was enough to make my stomach panic inside. I could see the site he was on was a sex chat line for teens. When I asked him if he was chatting on there and how it worked, because I had never been on a chat site before, he replied he was just looking and not chatting himself. Never mind that his initials were on the side of the list of people chatting or, at other times, used his call name of "Lonewolf." I knew better than to question him. He would just come up with more lies, and I knew I didn't want to hear the truth. I wanted to believe my husband wasn't a pervert.

Other times when I came home from school at night and Kati had been at work, Phil sat at the computer. Once again he had it turned away from the door, in case someone entered the house they could not see what he was looking at. Phil also closed the blinds behind him so the neighbors could not see in at what he was doing. Sometimes I found a rag, either in the living room or on the steps to the basement, where we many times threw out dirty clothes, stuck together as if someone wiped a body part off that had mild glue on it. I knew what he was doing. I knew the sites he was on.

I confronted him on this and asked him outright if he was on porno sites when we were gone and then jacking off. He didn't deny this, but stated in an angry voice he could not believe I thought he would do that. What I heard him say was that he did it, but that he could not believe that I knew what he was doing. I did not find sticky rags after that. I don't know if he stopped or if he just got better at hiding them. [To give Phil the benefit of the doubt, because I don't want to think of my husband as getting turned on by teenage girls, and I don't want to accept the fact that I had married a pervert, I will tell you what he wrote in his journal while he was getting counseling after I left him. He said that what he was really doing on those sites was telling the teenagers about Jesus and that they should not be on those sites. He also stated he did not tell me what he was doing because I had told him in the past that a good deed was not really a good deed if someone bragged about it. You decide, because I want to believe one thing, but my heart tells me something else.]

Life was not passing for me fast enough, while for others it was passing too fast. Because of volunteering in the school, I came to know most of the students. It was getting close to spring when two teenage sisters were in a car accident. One was driving and the younger sister was the passenger when they pulled out in front of another car. The younger sister died, and I went to the funeral by myself. I knew this would be a tough funeral, so I brought along plenty of tissue. I was crying before the funeral even started. On the short drive back to the house I fought with myself about going back at all or just staying in the van and driving forever. I did not want to go back to a lonely house. I wanted to go somewhere I could share my feelings and not be afraid of the cutting remarks they would bring. I wanted to go somewhere I could be held and feel safe. I wanted to go somewhere a warm caring smile could heat up the whole house. I did not want to go back to our house. But I had to go back. The tears that blurred my vision were not only for the young teenager that died and wanted to live, but also for me because I wanted to die, but had to go on living.

■ I had nightmares again last night. They were so real that I could not go back to sleep. I can't remember what I was dreaming, only that fear returned to my body. My feet rubbed together as if they are running a race for my life, and my body began to itch from the bottom of my frightened feet to the top of my malfunctioning head. I wanted someone to hold me and reassure me it was all over. I sang Sunday school songs to myself hoping that would relax me and put me back to sleep, but my singing was so bad I couldn't even stand it. I finally got up and watched old black and white game shows and fell asleep on the couch early this morning. When will the nightmares stop? Am I really crazy like Phil said I was? Was I really seeing things that were not there? Was I the one with the problems? Will anyone ever want me as that special person in their life, or am I too damaged? Will I always be alone? I know I am a good person, or, anyway, I try. I believe Phil tried to be a good person too, but he didn't know what good was. I try to tell myself I will be okay again, but then the question creeps in asking if I was ever okay. Someone please hold me! Am I making too big of deal of what happened to me? Does everyone go through this, and I just can't handle it like everyone else? I am tired today, and I have so much work to get done. I will try not to think. God help me! When I am awake I think too much and when I try to sleep, the nightmares hurt. I tried to stay up late and get up early, but that is not working either. I don't want to be strong today, but I will do it for one more day.

We are getting ready for the move back to the lower forty-eight, Kati's graduation, my graduation, and Phil's retirement. Kati wanted someone to come and see her graduate so badly that I came up with a plan to go to the Fairbanks airport and have Lueck pretend he was getting off the plane just so Kati could say someone flew up to see her. I told Kati and Phil about my plan, but the real plan was I was paying for Phil's mom to fly up so she would be there for Phil's retirement and Kati's graduation. It worked. They were totally surprised when we went to the airport to pick up the guest and it was Donna.

I had a good time with Donna there. It was the first time she had come to anything of her son's. Jim did not come because he was dying. Jim had been sick for fifteen years or more and would probably outlive most of us. It was good for Donna to get away from taking care of her husband. We showed Donna around the area, and Kati had her grandma watching her graduate.

Phil had a small retirement ceremony. His mom, Lueck, Kati, and I were the only family at the party. Phil talked about us, and how he could not have made it through the last twenty-four years of the military without our help. He told how proud he was of Lueck for being able to be himself, brightly colored hair and all. He told Kati he loved all the spirit she had and the talents she had as an athlete. He had a really nice speech written up and did a great job a sharing it. I think Phil wanted to believe what he said in his speech, but his actions at home didn't back up his thoughts.

Phil seemed to be getting more depressed. I think he was having a hard time thinking of retirement. I think he was excited about it and still scared. The air force was all he had known for twenty-four years of his forty-two years of life. Phil didn't like the unknown; he liked things black and white. He liked things all planned out and knowing what was going to happen once he arrived at his planned destination. Phil did not know what kind of job he wanted or where he was going to get a job. I tried to find out where he really wanted to live if I was not in the picture, but he would not say. He just told me it was now my turn to choose where to live, and he was going to follow me because I had followed him for all those years. I felt he knew in his heart that I was going to leave him, but did not want to admit it. I told him during our fight in November that I planned on leaving him, and he blocked it out. I don't think he really believed I would leave him. He did not think I would do a lot of things I did, like start my own business and make a go of it and then complete my four-year degree. I was a stubborn person, too, and when I set a goal for myself, I tried my hardest to meet it.

Phil was becoming stranger and stranger. More lies and more stories didn't make any sense. Phil came home from work one day and told me about the people that lived behind us in base housing. This guy had a Chow dog, and Phil proceeded to tell me how this guy told him it was such a friendly dog. Many times I had seen the dog tied in the front of house lying on the driveway letting the sun warm him. While walking one evening I saw the dog lying on the driveway, and I began thinking about what Phil said about the dog. I walked up to the dog to pet it, which is so unlike me because I didn't even like dogs. When the Chow got to the end of the chain, just within my reach to pet him he launched at me and bit my knee. He bit a hole in my pants and drew blood. I was so embarrassed I had let this happen that I looked around to make sure no one noticed, then headed for home to see what damage was done. I was shaking when I entered the house. I went to the bathroom to look at my wound and to clean it. The dog bite wasn't very deep and did not need stitches, but my self-esteem needed medical attention. I couldn't believe I allowed Phil to do it to me again. I should have known better than to believe anything Phil told me.

I thought about what had just happened and decided I should talk to the owner of the dog in case he didn't know his dog bites, especially since he told Phil the dog was friendly. I walked back over to the guy's house and told him about his dog. I knew it was my fault because I should not have gone up to a strange dog or walked on the man's driveway. The owner of the dog told me the dog had bitten people before, and he was not surprised. His story was not making sense. Phil had just told me he had talked to him and it was a friendly dog. Who was lying? Why would this guy tell Phil the dog was friendly when it was not, and would Phil make up a story to tell me the dog was friendly when it was not? Why would Phil make up most of the stories he did? I couldn't believe that once again I listened to Phil and believed what he said. I had to go to the base clinic to have my knee looked at, then a police report had to be made. I was told this dog had bitten children before and, if the dog bit one more person, they would either have to get rid of the dog or move off base. The owner of the dog had orders to another military base and was moving in a week or so anyway, so nothing was done about the dog.

Phil's anger towards me never seemed to stop. Phil sold his truck a month or so after Kati and I got back from Minnesota, so we were down to one vehicle. I needed the car one day, so I drove Phil to work. As I pulled around in front of the Phil's work, he realized he had forgotten his hat at home. We had to turn around and go back to the house to get his hat. Remember, this was the military and one could not go outside without the uniform hat on. Phil criticized my driving the one and a half miles back home, and then back to his work, he told me again that I was stupid and I should not be going this route. He said he could not believe I was not smart enough to go a certain way.

After I dropped Phil off and went back home to regroup for the day I traveled every route in my head that I could have taken to make the short trip to Phil's work even shorter. I was always thinking about ways to get somewhere so he would not be angry with me for going the wrong way. I was always thinking about how I was going to word something, everything I was going to say to him, so he could not turn it around and use it against me. I felt I had to be perfect, and I was not. Almost everything I said to Phil I thought about how it would sound to him and how he could turn it around and degrade me with my own words. Even if it was a positive statement, it could come back to haunt me. Not knowing how he was going to react to anything was like living with a bomb and knowing it could go off with a tap of a button. Phil's favorite words to stop me from telling him something he was doing or saying was bothering me were, "Well, you do it."

We constantly hurt each other. I know I didn't set out to hurt him on purpose, even though he said I did. I had come to a point in my life that my shield was the only thing protecting me. I felt I did not have a weapon, but only a shield. I felt I could not fight back, but only put more bricks in my wall to protect me. I felt so alone behind my wall. I would peek out of the cracks and watch other people have lives. I wanted a life without a wall too, but it was too dangerous with all the acid words hurled at me. I needed protection to survive.

Phil complained I didn't flirt with him, and I really didn't very often. If I did flirt with him, he always was ready to hop into bed, and I wasn't. I found it more fun just to flirt and leave it at that and then flirt some more and then see where things would lead. Sometimes when I flirted with him, he got nasty towards me, then not speak to me afterwards. We were in the kitchen and, with a gleam of mischief in my eyes, I licked my finger to smooth down his eyebrow. Anger, pure anger, is what I saw when I went to touch his eyebrow, followed with another bout of silence. I was afraid to flirt. I was afraid to live.

I was fighting with myself and then with God and then with myself almost everyday. The battles were so draining. I tried to reason with God about leaving Phil. I tried to reason with myself about leaving Phil. I did not try to reason with Phil, because there wasn't any communication with him. I told God I would stay if Phil quit drinking, but that was not working either. Phil might have quit drinking for awhile, but he was still a dry drunk, and I never knew when he would start again.

I knew marriage was supposed to be forever, in sickness and in health, and Phil was definitely sick. His sickness was killing me. I was losing me. I no longer loved him, and I hated myself for this. I wanted to love Phil. I wanted the marriage to work. I wanted us to be a family. I didn't want to leave. This was the hardest decision I ever had to make. I pleaded with God to change things. I knew I could not change Phil. The only person I could change was me. I didn't know how to change me. I knew I was normally a nice person, but I could not give any more to Phil. I had nothing left to give. He had already told me I was not to question anything he says or does.

He was trying to make me a yes wife. I was not a yes woman on the inside. I had my own feelings. If I thought he did something and I asked him if he did, he got angry with me for accusing him of doing something that was no big deal, then leered at me until I apologized. He barked at me, "Tell me you're sorry!" This could be something as small as asking him if he just farted, after smelling a foul smell. I felt angry after his words were thrown at me. All he had to say was he didn't do it. He wanted me to apologize to him just for asking him if he farted. Sometimes I answered back that I was sorry or, other times, I could be a jerk too and reply back, "I am sorry you're a jerk." This didn't help the situation any, but it felt good.

If I had done something I was really sorry about, I told Phil, "I am really sorry," and I meant it. He then gave me his evil "I wish you were dead" eyes and with death-wishing words, say, "No, you're not." I could not win. He told me when I was sorry and when I was not sorry. I didn't have to think or feel anymore because he was telling me how I should feel and think. I was really losing me. I had to make a decision if and when I was going to leave. I really didn't want to leave Phil. What I still wanted more than anything was for us to be a healthy family, but I didn't see it happening.

God and I kept going around and around on me ending my marriage. I knew what I was supposed to do, but in the same breath, I figured God gave me a brain, just as well as he gave Phil a brain. If God did not want me to use my brain to feel and think, he should not have given me one. God put common sense in me also. I knew if I told my story out loud to someone, I would hear the words and know how sick I was for staying. I did not want life to be this hard. I wanted to read a book and know exactly what to do. The marriage vows say to love your spouse in sickness and in health, but I did not love my spouse. Hell, I didn't even love me. I knew what Phil was doing to me and the kids was wrong. But what was even more wrong, was me staying and letting this crap happen again and again. I could not find the switch that turned on the love. It was broken the first month I met Phil. Of course, there were times in the marriage that I truly loved Phil, but it seemed he didn't want to be loved. So many times Phil sabotaged any love for I had him. After twenty-some years of being abused, the love switch was ripped from the wall. I didn't know if God would still love me if I left Phil. I did not know if I could ever love myself again if I left Phil. I did not have much self left to love. Just maybe things would change by the time we moved to Minnesota. Maybe something in my heart would see things differently.

I hardly ever got sick, but on Mother's Day in 2000, I was feeling pretty lousy, and I thank God for that. I was dizzy and nauseous and planning on staying in bed all day when Phil and Kati came upstairs to my bedside. I knew he was up to something. Phil, with Kati at his side for more manipulation, gave me a huge gaudy diamond and told me he loved me. I wanted to throw up. I had not been able to tell Phil I loved him for some time. I couldn't say those three little words without meaning them. He was trying hard to get me to say something I did not feel or mean. I didn't like the ring, and I didn't like our marriage. The ring was not going to buy my happiness. Most wives would have loved a big diamond, but I did not like to show off anything about me. I wanted to hide in a closet so no one would notice me. The last thing I wanted on my finger was this huge diamond so Phil could say what a wonderful husband he was. He knew I did not like big diamonds. He knew I was a not a person to show off what we had.

I didn't have to be nice to him that day with hugs and kisses and, "oh, thank you," because I was sick. I was sick in more ways then one. I felt Phil had Kati by his side so if I acted like a real jerk and gave him the ring back, he and Kati could hug each other and talk about what an awful person I was. He knew I would not do that with her at his side. I couldn't do that even if she wasn't at his side. I might have wanted to give the ring back, but I could not do it and still live with myself or with Phil. I had a plan, and if Phil told me to leave right then, I would have had no place to go for three weeks. I only had to survive three more lousy weeks in Alaska and then we would be on the road, to a new life, in a new state.

Phil had saved his money from different things he sold to buy this ring. This was the first time he had ever saved money to buy me something, but it was too late. It was not the ring I wanted. It was a friend and husband that I wanted. He said I could return the ring for something else so we went to Sears where he purchased the ring, and I found a much smaller one that I loved. But it still was not the wedding ring I wanted. I wanted a magic ring that put real love into our marriage. I would have been happy with a plastic ring from a gumball machine if it would have changed the way I felt about Phil, our marriage, and me. I felt guilty taking the ring. But just maybe the marriage would work out. Maybe once Phil got out of the military I would see a change in him. Maybe he would finally be happy.

Phil liked to play mind games with me. He liked to see if I would admit I was wrong about something, even if I wasn't, just because he thought he had the power to do so. Phil was usually bad with directions, and I had to be halfway good at them so I could tell him how to get somewhere without getting us lost, or Phil would lose his temper. We were talking about the fire station on the base and where it was located in reference to our house. I stated it was behind our house, and Phil said it was in front of our house. There were only houses in front of our house so, to prove my point, I suggested we go for a walk to the fire station. We left out of the front door, turned right on our sidewalk, walked about three blocks, swung right again, and walked another three blocks, which put as at the fire station. I tried to explain to Phil that if we moved all the houses and the trees that were in between the fire station and our house, we would see the backside of our house and not the front. This was just a fun disagreement, but Phil was going to win this no matter what it took. He told me he didn't think I could be that dumb. He was not sticking to the point, but trying to make me see it his way by making me feel inadequate about myself.

When we got home from the walk, his words were trying to sneak in the cracks of my self-worth and tear me apart. I was fighting with myself and telling myself I was not dumb. I told Phil he was lucky I had enough self-esteem left that I could take his words. It was a strange look he gave me, a look kind-of-like, "I can't believe you are still feeling good about yourself after all those negative things I said about you."

Since my plans were to leave Phil, I tried to get my personal belongings I had in the basement in a group. There were not many things I wanted if we separated. I only wanted my freedom to be me and not lived scared anymore. Things I knew I could not replace and meant a lot to me I mailed to my sister's house for safekeeping. In one of the boxes, along with my dad's WWII army coat, my great aunt's confirmation dress, and some letters, I placed a letter I wrote to my whole family in case Phil killed me when he found out I was leaving him. I was very calm the day I wrote the letter. I knew Phil had done his best and I had done my best, but I could not live with him any longer. Our children would be safe and on their own, when I would tell Phil that I was leaving him. I addressed the letter to me and hid it in the coat. I figured if I died, my sister would look through the box of things and find the letter. I did not want her to open it unless I was dead, so I put my name on it instead of hers.

April 10, 2000

Dear Mom, Armin, Luann, and Linda,

If you read this letter, then you know I am dead. Yes, dead, like a doornail. Please don't be sad. I might not be with you physically, but I am here spiritually. Believe me, I will see what is happening. There are three very important points I want to leave with you.

1. Please forgive Phil. He is just sick, and I had a feeling it was going to come down to this and I did nothing about it, so that makes me just as sick. Please make sure my kids forgive him. You know, we are here on earth to learn, and I learned a lot. All we can do is our best, and sometimes that just is not good enough.

2. Like I told Lueck (please remind him) that when you smell brownies baking or fresh bread and you don't see any around, that is me telling you I am okay and there is a God that loves you very much. Please tell Juston.

3. I want you all to know I love you very much. I could not have asked for a better family. You are all special in your own way. Step back and see how you are making a difference in someone else's life. Be happy with yourself. You are the only person in the whole world you have to live with. Make sure you are a good roommate.

(I am not even crying writing this. I am looking forward to seeing all my friends that always made me feel special. I get to see Dad and my little girl I never got to know. God still loves me and thinks I am ready to go home now. Please have a party for me where everyone comes dressed in something they always wanted to wear but were afraid to. Sing "Jesus Loves Me" and the "Hymn of Promise." Drink wine and tell a lot of good stories. Laughter heals the soul. I love you.)

The movers came and packed all of our things for the last time. Kati was to stay in Alaska a few more days after Phil, Lueck, his girlfriend, Kyle, and I left for the lower forty-eight. Kati stayed with her traveling soccer team, and they were going to fly to northern California for soccer tournaments. We drove our motor home to a port in Alaska and took the ferry to Bellingham, Washington. Lueck and Kyle planned to stay with Phil's Uncle Norm and his wife while they found a job and a place of their own to live. We planned on meeting up with Kati in California and watch her soccer games. But, I always had more than one plan in mind in case I had to make a quick exit from life with Phil.

CHAPTER 11

WHAT I THOUGHT WAS THE LAST AND FINAL CHAPTER

As much as I didn't want to relive the Alaska chapter, this next and last chapter are going to be pure hell. I am scared to write and to relive it. Maybe I can just stop now?

After Phil, Lueck, Kyle, and I got off the ferry in Bellingham, Washington, I made a few phone calls to friends who lived in the area. I called Phil's old roommate from Iceland, Macky, and thought we could stop and see him and his wife. They had other plans they could not change, so we continued on our way to see Phil's brother Rick. Rick met us at his work and treated us to a wonderful dinner at the county club where he cooked. From there we followed Rick to his home where he gave Lueck a car that needed repair. Rick had always been good to Lueck. When Lueck was just a tot and Rick didn't have much money, he still saved all of his silver dollar tips he received bartending in a casino, and gave them to Lueck. We left the car with Rick for now, planning on Lueck and his great-uncle Norman to drive up to Washington state and get the car at a later date.

The four of us drove a little farther that night and stayed at a campground. We got up early and headed for Oregon where Lueck and Kyle would live with Uncle Norman and his wife. It made leaving them there a lot easier for me knowing they had someone to help them get started in their new lives. Lueck wanted Kyle and him to sleep in a tent until they found jobs. I would not have been able to leave them there, alone, without income, without a way of getting a hold of them, without worrying myself sick. I was so thankful to Phil's uncle and aunt for opening their home to my kids.

Phil and I hit the road again, leaving Lueck and Kyle at Norm's, to meet Kati in Sacramento, California, to watch her regional soccer games and pick her up for the rest of our journey. Kati had flown with her Alaskan traveling soccer team to California about the same time Phil, Lueck, Kyle, and I left Alaska. The team had to get used to the hot weather before the games.

I was already missing Lueck. It was so hard to leave a child behind, but I understood why he did not want to go with us. He liked Oregon because of the mountains, the artistic people, and the liberal marijuana laws, and it was far away from his dysfunctional family.

This trip with Phil was no different from any other in that I carried hidden cash with me because I never knew when I might decide to leave or have an emergency. Now that Phil and I were alone, who knew what would happen? As we pulled up to the pump for gas, Phil told me to get out and get what I wanted in the store. I didn't understand him. I didn't know if he wanted me to get out right then, or if he was going fill the tank first, park the motor home, and then want me to get out. I asked him if he wanted me to get out right then to make sure I followed his directions correctly. Most normal people wouldn't haven't even given this a thought, but I was always trying to make sure I did things the way Phil wanted me to. He gave me the "I can't believe you are so damn dumb" look and, with a low growl, spit out, "What did I just say?" I wanted to run.

I had money with me, and I could just take a bus to some place, any place. I did not go. We had to meet with Kati the next day and what would she have said if I was not there for her? What would Phil have told her? I felt he would lie and tell her what a rotten person I was and that I did not care about her or the family. Or worse yet, I thought, maybe Phil would not show up for her at all. I had to be strong. I could not think about myself yet. That time would come. I wiped the tears from my eyes and slept so I would not have to think or feel.

When I awoke, I didn't know what mood Phil would be in. I didn't know if I should act as if nothing had happened, as I usually did, or if I should show Phil how I felt and just stay mad. I knew staying mad wouldn't help my cause. If I stayed mad, it would only make Phil mad, and then we would be chasing our tails. I chose to act as if nothing happened. I chose to act like I was not mad or was not hurt. I put the smile on my face, talked a bit, and then slept some more. We decided to spend the night in a motel instead of the motor home. The next day we got up early and headed for the soccer tournaments.

We arrived in Sacramento and found the hotel, without getting too lost, where the team was staying. The hotel was full and there were not any extra rooms in the city because of the regional soccer tournament. The hotel manager was kind enough to let us plug our motor home into Kati's room that she shared with three other girls. Phil and I used the shower in their room after the girls left for practice. It worked out quite nicely.

Phil and I still didn't talk much about anything, which was nothing new. I knew the chaperones that were with the girls, so I spent as much time as I could with them, without upsetting Phil.

After the girls lost their games, the team decided to go to Santa Cruz, a couple hours southwest of Sacramento, to the beach boardwalk for the day. Phil stayed behind since it was just females going on this road trip. It was a very relaxing day, except I worried about what Phil was doing. I worried he might be drinking, or just sitting around getting depressed because he was alone. The girls' soccer coach was at the hotel, but I didn't think Phil would be assertive enough to ask to hang around with the coach for the day. Phil was quiet when we returned, but seemed okay. He had spent the day walking around the area looking at stores and sitting in the motor home reading and watching TV.

The next day we packed up the motor home and, with Kati now traveling with us, we took off for Phil's parent's house in Fresno. Kati said good-bye to her Alaska teammates knowing she would probably never see most of them again. It was a hard time for her.

Kati and I slept most of the day as Phil drove the motor home. I did not drive very much when Phil was with me. I made him very nervous, and he made me very nervous, which, in turn, caused me to make more mistakes. We made it to his parents' that evening and stayed a few nights with them. We were very anxious to get back on the road, to find a home, jobs, and get settled in life, one way or another.

First we planned to stop in Knob Knoster, Missouri, to see our friends, the Koyles. I wanted to confine in Deanne about my plans to leave Phil. I wanted someone to tell me to stay or to go. I still had a very small hint of hope that Phil would change in the next few hundred miles, and we could communicate as a healthy married couple. Besides, staying at Phil's parents' house was making me uptight. There wasn't anything to do there, it was hot, and I didn't have anything to say to anyone.

We decided to take the back highways to Minnesota which would make it more relaxing, at least until we hit Kansas. While Kati and I were escaping life in the motor home by sleeping, Phil took a wrong turn, or missed a turn, and when I woke up I asked him where we were located. He did not realize he had taken a wrong turn and driven at least one hundred miles out of the way until I figured out on the map where we were.

When Phil stopped for gas, Kati and I got out to use the bathroom and get some snacks. While we were in the bathroom Kati asked me why I didn't say something to Phil about driving hours headed the wrong way. She told me he would have said something to me. I told her he would just turn whatever I said around and he would figure out a way to blame me for it, so it was best if I didn't say anything. Getting back into the motor home Kati gave her dad a hard time about taking the wrong road, and sure enough, he blamed me for it. He said I should not have been sleeping, but watching the map instead. I said out loud to Kati that I had told her he would find a way to blame me for his mistake. It was not the smartest comment I ever made, but it was the truth. A few miles down the road, after Phil cooled off, he tried to make a joke out of the whole thing and said it was okay he took this road because it was more scenic. I know we stayed at least one night in a motel before we arrived at our friends, the Koyles.

Our plans were to stay just a couple of days at their house and then head up to Minnesota. We gave the Koyles a hard time and told them just one more day and we would be on our way. Six years before we had told them "just one more day" and it turned out we lived with them for three months. The four of us played cards and joked with each other just like we used to. It felt good to have friends. They knew both Phil and I as well as anyone did. I knew I could confide in Deanne about my plans of leaving Phil. I also knew I had to set a date to leave Phil or days and then weeks and then years would slip by and I would still be in the same place.

I came up with a date of November 1, 2000. I thought four months would give Phil enough time to make some friends who could give him support after I left. I didn't want to leave him right before Christmas or our anniversary, December 10, because that would be way too hard on him. I wanted Phil to be okay when I left him. I wanted to make things as easy as possible for him. When I told Deanne, a very strong Christian woman, my plans to leave Phil, she did not try to talk me out of it but only said to me, "Be safe." She was very serious when she gave me those simple, sincere words of advice. She knew Phil and what he was capable of doing. She knew how scared I was of leaving him. I wasn't afraid that I could not make it on my own, but I was afraid of what Phil might do to me or Kati or himself, when I told him.

It was the Fourth of July and Ken wanted to take us out on their older ski boat along with some other friends of theirs. It was a beautiful day to spend on the lake with friends and family. Ken gave his friend, Kati, and me a ride, when Kati decided to water ski. She was a good swimmer and had skied before. She was staying up on the skis even though Ken made some waves for her to jump. He was not doing anything reckless when she went down smoothly. Kati came up from under the water and was crying that her neck hurt. Ken's friend jumped in the lake to get Kati out. He supported her neck and back as much as possible as he lifted her into the boat. I got her flat on the bottom of the boat and held her head as we made a quick dash back to shore. I knew I had to keep her calm so she did not hyperventilate.

Once we got to shore, Phil started questioning me and was going to take over. I told him with words, and backed it up with a look, that he better leave me alone. I had the situation under control and he better back off. Someone called the ambulance, and I rode with Kati in the back while everyone else followed us to the nearest hospital. The hospital took x-rays to make sure nothing was broken in Kati's back or neck. She had severe whiplash and received a neck brace. It was late, and we all headed back to the Koyles. We felt that Kati should take an extra day or two to rest before we drove the nine-hour drive to Minnesota, so we bunked a couple more nights at the Koyles' hotel.

While we were waiting for Kati to feel better, Phil and I drove to St. Louis to pick up Kati's car that the military shipped for us. Kati wanted to drive her car to Minnesota, but was not able to because of her neck. Phil drove the motor home with Kati, and I drove Kati's car to Minnesota, the next state we would call home.

We arrived at my mom's house in Lafayette, Minnesota, and started looking for jobs and a place to live. We both agreed we would look for jobs in Marshall, Minnesota, about ninety miles from Lafayette. Kati was going to play college soccer at Southwest State University, in Marshall, and I didn't want to miss any of her games. Marshall was the home to the Schwan's Food Company, and we thought we could get jobs there. Marshall's population of twelve thousand was located in the southwest corner of Minnesota. Marshall seemed like a clean, friendly town with opportunities for employment. We spent nights at my mom's house, and drove back and forth, with Kati's car, to Marshall for the first couple of weeks while we looked for jobs and a place to live.

While staying at Mom's, she was having trouble with her sewing machine, so I took it apart to clean it. I had it sewing like a new machine, and Mom bragged about me to Phil. She told Phil what a wonderful job I did, and his jealous reply was, "She never does anything for me." He took all the joy I had in my heart from helping my mom and smashed it in my face. I felt like I shouldn't do anything nice for anyone else because Phil would just get jealous and turn it around to hurt me. I could only "do" for Phil, but whatever thoughtful thing I did for him wasn't enough, and it wasn't right.

We decided it was enough driving, after two weeks from Lafayette to Marshall. We drove both the motor home and Kati's car to Camden State Park, twelve miles south of Marshall on Highway 23. It was the middle of July 2000, and Camden State Park was to be our home for the next five weeks.

Living in a twenty-three-foot motor home with nothing to do besides look for jobs, and take long walks through the park, was very relaxing. Phil and I slept on the top bed above the seats, and Kati slept on the couch that opened to a bed. Phil wanted to make love to me with Kati right below us. I thought it was a gross thought to be even thinking about making love with anyone in the room, much less our daughter. I tried to think of what it would be like to be a teenage girl and know your parents were screwing right above your head. I couldn't do, or wouldn't do, it, so once again this caused a lot of tension between Phil and me. I found any excuse I could so I didn't have to be in bed the same time he was. This was hard to do when there were no other rooms to go to.

Phil thought he could get a job at Wal-Mart as a manager because he had done a report in college on Wal-Mart and felt he knew all there was about the company. He went in for an interview and told them how he would run the place. He went in with a know-it-all attitude and was sure he would get the job. It didn't go over very well, and he didn't get the job. This was a little humbling for him.

Phil continued looking for a job. He was not a quitter by any means. Phil found a job at the local Hy-Vee grocery store and started to work rotating shifts. When he worked nights, Kati and I had to find things to do so we didn't go in and out of the motor home while Phil was sleeping during the day.

Phil was working and needed Kati's car every day, so I bought me a used, small, red, four-door Aspire. I continued to look for work.

Kati wanted her boyfriend, Chris from Alaska, who was now living in Florida, to come and spend a few days with us in the motor home. Phil agreed to this and Chris flew in to Sioux Falls, South Dakota, ninety miles southwest of Camden. Kati, her boyfriend, and I took off in my red Aspire for a couple of days to see the Mall of America and the Minnesota Zoo near Minneapolis, three hours northeast of Camden. The three of us spent one night in a motel in the Twin Cities. It felt good to be away. I did not have to worry about getting lost when I was driving because I didn't care if I was lost or not. I had no idea where I was really headed so it was an adventure. I wasn't going to have Phil angry with me for not knowing where I was or where I was going. I could have fun without having to feel I needed to be perfect and have everything planned for the trip.

Kati's boyfriend, Chris, flew back to Florida, and I got serious about looking for a job. I applied at Schwan's Food Company in Marshall, and after contacting them a few times, I was hired. I told them I needed a job that kept me so busy I did not have time to think. I would not start for a couple of weeks, which gave me more time to find a house.

Phil and I were looking at houses to buy. It was the first of August, and I knew I was going to leave Phil soon but still had not told him. I was still hoping he would change. I was always looking for signs the marriage might work out after all. I cried as I walked. I prayed, asking God to forgive me for what I was about to do.

I wanted God to love me, but did not know if he would for breaking my marriage vows, for abandoning one of his needing children. I felt God was counting on me to take care of Phil, and I was not holding up my end of the bargain. I felt my calling in life was to take care of Phil, but I had nothing left to give him. I was tired of living scared and unhappy. If it was my job to make Phil happy, I had not succeeded in the twenty-three years I had lived with him. I felt I was a rotten person and just maybe if I left him, he would be happy.

I was so confused. I was so scared. I just wanted to be loved for who I was. I wanted God to love me even though I had to do leave Phil. I wanted God to give me a sign that I was going to be okay. I wanted a sign that Phil was going to be okay and that this was really the best for both of us. The sign did not come. The only sign I received was a strong feeling in my heart that told me I had to go though with leaving my spouse. I didn't know if the feeling in my heart was enough proof that I was meant to leave the marriage. I wanted God to write me a note saying you have my permission to leave Phil. I wanted it in writing. I wanted a book of directions. I wanted someone to take my hand and lead me out of this. I was scared of the present and scared of the future.

I wanted to find a house Phil liked and could afford payments on without my income. He was getting about $2,000.00 in retirement pay from the military, and with his employment check he could make house payments. I did have hope, the size of a pinhead, that maybe we could work out this marriage thing, so I did keep that in mind when we looked at houses, too. I finally found a house to rent on the outskirts of town.

We moved in the house near the end of August—the same time I started my new job. Kati turned eighteen this August, and moved into the college dorms so she could start soccer practice with the team. Our furniture arrived shortly after we moved in. I took it upon myself to unpack and reorganize all of our stuff. This was just "stuff," and I knew there was nothing in the boxes with magical powers to make me happy. I felt Phil could keep most of everything when I left him. There were a few things that were the kids' or had been in my family that I wanted to keep. There was nothing worth fighting over. I knew Phil would throw most of the things away because he thought most of my stuff was just junk. He placed his caribou head over the couch in the living room, and we made this house a livable place, but I would not have called it a home. It lacked love and caring and a warm feeling. It was a structure of four walls that held up a roof.

Only a week after I started my job at Schwan's, the area I was working in was sold to US Bank. I didn't notice any changes except for the name of the company I was working for. My job was going okay. It was nice having co-workers and a safe place to spend my days. Phil could not get in the building I worked without a card that had to be swiped in order for the door to open. He knew the building where I worked, but did not know where I worked in the building.

Phil had been using the old car I bought or using Kati's car to get to work. We still had the motor home, so if all else failed he could use it. He did need a vehicle of his own, but we never talked about it. I came home from work one day, and he had bought a brand new 2001 black pickup. He was so excited about, and all I could think about was that we did not talk about this ahead of time. I knew it was his money, but we had a daughter in college, a son trying to make it on his own and were still looking at houses to buy. I felt in a healthy marriage couples would talk over major purchases before the purchase was made. I kept my mouth closed and tried my best to look happy for him. That is not what my heart was saying.

After work I came home and walked two miles so I would be tired enough to sleep. During those walks I did a lot of praying. Semi-trucks passed me as I walked, and so many times I was tempted to step out in front of one, just to end all the pain I was in. I fought with God. I wanted to be a good child and do what God wanted me to do. I thought maybe if I ended my life, he would think that was better then leaving Phil. I knew, though, that if I died, Phil would most likely kill himself, too, and our children would be without any parents. I knew my children still needed me, and I needed them. I felt so alone in the world. I felt like the whole world had it together but me. I felt worthless. I felt I was letting God and my kids down. Twenty-some years of being told how dumb I was and that I couldn't do anything right had worked itself deep into my brain. Besides not being able to live up to Phil's standards, I felt I could not live up to God's standards. There was a flicker of hope in my thinking and that is what kept me going. If my parents had not given me the foundation of love they did when I was a child, I would not have felt that maybe, just maybe, I was a lovable person.

September came and, in fewer then two months, I had to find a place to move to. I still had not told Phil I was leaving him and that thought was eating away at me. I knew Phil began drinking again, and I didn't dare say anything to him. He would just deny it anyway and would figure out a way to make me feel bad for accusing him of drinking again. Somehow or other his drinking would end up being my fault. I knew he had been drinking because I found beer spilled on the computer keyboard. This was not like Phil to leave a mess somewhere. To me it was as if he was calling for help, but I felt I could not help him. He needed to get the help by himself. I could not lead him to an AA meeting. I was hoping he would go on his own and then just maybe, just a little maybe, I would not leave him. As I was going to empty some leftovers into a cereal box that was in the garbage, I found a beer can he had hidden in there. This made my heart hurt. I told myself that I was not ever, no never, going to live scared with Phil drinking again. I wanted someone to love me too. I wanted to come home to a secure home. I wanted to know I could share anything with my best friend of a husband, and he would try to understand. I longed for a healthy relationship. I longed to be given the choice about making love. I longed to be held with caring hands that would only nurture me and not hurt me. I longed for words that boosted my self-esteem and not control my thoughts.

I told my sisters I planned on leaving Phil. They were concerned for me. Luann asked if she should be there when I told Phil I was leaving. I did not want anyone there when that day came. I felt I had gotten myself into this situation, and I had to get myself out. I did not want anyone else hurt either, not knowing how Phil would react. I was ready to die if that is what it came down to. I felt I was almost dead anyway. My letter I wrote to my family was still at my sister Luann's house hidden in my dad's army coat. My family would find it someday, if needed.

I knew I needed a place to move into when I left, so I continued to meet with the realtor. I asked her not to call Phil if she found a house, and I ended up confiding in her about my plans. I told Phil I was looking for a house I could use for my embroidery business just in case he saw me looking at houses or if the realtor called. I needed a house I could afford on my own, without any of Phil's retirement money or anything else that was ours. I did not want to hear from Phil how I needed him or that I still had to depend on him. I needed to do this for myself, by myself.

I contacted a lawyer about a divorce. I didn't know if I should just serve Phil papers or if I should talk to him first. I didn't know if Phil would say, "Get out now" or beg me to stay or just shoot me. I was going to be prepared for anything he dished out to me. The first lawyer

I talked to would not listen to anything I had to say about Phil in case I did not use her; she wanted to be available for Phil. The second lawyer I talked to took his time to listen to what was happening in my life and why I wanted out. He told me I was entitled to half of Phil's military retirement and half of the assets we accumulated in the twenty-three years of marriage. I told the lawyer I did not want any of our things, but only wanted to get out of the marriage. He then tried to explain to me that I felt the way I did because of being verbally abused for so many years. The abuse led me to believe I didn't deserve anything. He was right, but I still didn't want any of our assets.

Both lawyers informed me I could not divorce Phil until six months after arriving into the state of Minnesota. Okay, so six months it would be. I could still move out of the building with four walls holding up a roof and move into something else that still had four walls and held up a roof, but would also hold me safe.

November was getting closer and I needed to do something or I knew I never would move out. Once again I set a clear goal for myself and knew I had to meet it. I saw a house for sale in the paper. I called the realtor, and we set up an appointment to meet. Out of all the houses I looked at, this one had character, was livable, and something I could afford on my own. I talked to the bank and explained my situation. They approved me for a loan on my income only. I made a deal with the owners of the house that I could move in the last week of October and rent it until February. I thought it would be easier to tell Phil that I am renting a house than buying a house. Renting seemed to be less permanent, and I felt I had to make telling Phil I was leaving as easy on me as I could. My mom and Armin loaned me the money for the down payment. All I had left to do was tell Phil I was moving out. That was it.

By this time I was numb to life. I was too scared to even think, yet a calm feeling came over me. If Phil decided to shoot me, that would be okay, too. I didn't care. I just had to move on one way or another.

I did tell my co-workers that if I did not show up to work some morning, to call my nephew Dan that lived in town to come and check on me. I left his number in my desk at work. Some of my close co-workers knew what I was about to do.

It was now or never. This was the time to tell Phil I was moving out. Phil was lying on the floor in the living room watching TV when I sat down next to him and informed him we had to talk. Ever so calmly, with a matter-of-fact voice, I told Phil that I found a house and was moving out. I told him I found a house and at this time I was only renting. I was going to move in two weeks. I asked him if he would like me to leave that night. I was prepared to if I had to go. I had clothes in my car and money at my nephew's. Phil said I could stay. That was it. I had said it. No one was at the house with me, and no one was sitting at the end of the street where I needed to flash porch lights to let them know I was okay. I had done this on my own.

Phil was shocked, to say the least. He could not believe what I was telling him. He couldn't believe how calm I acted. I acted as if I had told him I was going to the store to get a loaf of bread. No big deal, I was just moving out. He wanted to know why, and I explained to him I was tired of living the way I was living. I was tired of being scared and of his secret drinking and being put down.

He just could not understand, then he got angry. Not physically angry and not where he called me names, but "put up the shield anger." He said he hadn't known. He didn't know I was that unhappy. He didn't know I was that scared. He didn't know his words were hurting me that bad. And I was thinking, where in the hell have you been for the last twenty-three years? I could not believe he had no idea what was happening in our marriage. I guess he thought I liked to be told how stupid I was and asked "what's the matter with you?" when I didn't see things his way. I guess he thought I liked having him screw me after he looked at a porno site and was turned on by some other female. I guess he thought I liked it when he drank and then become obnoxious with me. I guess he thought I liked all the lies he told me. I guess he thought I liked it when he told me not to question anything he said, but to let him do whatever he wanted. Well, he was wrong. After he realized what was happening was true, one of the first questions he asked me was, "Can we still make love once in a while?"

I could not believe he asked me that question. Was that all our relationship was to him? Was I just his sex toy? Was I just his to use how he wanted? Was I just a piece of meat to him? I guess his question answered my questions.

Phil went to work that night but came home early because he had been crying and was sick to his stomach. I was prepared for this reaction too. I had seen it before, and I knew I would only hate myself if I gave in now and I would despise Phil even more than I did. I also knew Phil would throw these words of mine in my face any chance he got, so once I said the words "I'm leaving," I knew there was no turning back.

Phil called his parents and told them I was leaving. He was so heartbroken. I wanted to hold him in my arms and let him know everything was going to be okay and I would stay. But I couldn't. I just could not do any more. I felt so bad to see him hurting the way he was. I had always taken care of Phil in the past. Now, I felt the best thing for both us was for me to move out. Maybe finally Phil would get help. Maybe a few years down the road, when I could really trust him again, we could get back together.

We talked some more the next day. All Phil could keep saying between sobs was, "I didn't know, I didn't know." I wanted to cry back to him, "Why, why didn't you know? Why didn't you see how unhappy I was? Why didn't you look so we could have made this marriage work? Why didn't you listen to me when I tried to tell you how I was feeling instead of coming with your favorite words 'oh well'? Why didn't you get help with your drinking problem instead of blaming me?" But I didn't say anything. I was just as numb as Phil was.

I was not going to let him get to me. I had built my brick wall very high and very strong and nothing was going to get through that wall—not tears, nor words. Nothing.

Phil went from crying to anger. But, not where he hurt me or even said things that were degrading. He told me I was not going to get any of his retirement pay, and he knew how he could stop me from getting it. [I am sure he was talking about killing himself.] I told him I was not after his retirement.

The only things I wanted when we went our separate ways were a few items that came from my family. I didn't want the house in Missouri that we were renting out. I didn't want any of his IRA or stocks or anything else I was entitled to in a divorce. First of all, I was not divorcing him. I was only moving out at this time. I could have gotten a legal separation, but I didn't feel that was needed. I didn't have the money for one thing, and I didn't think Phil would go out and charge a bunch of stuff and then stick me with the bill. He was not mean like that. He was a liar, but I could basically trust him on this. That is another reason it was difficult to understand Phil.

Phil went to work and came home with a different feeling each day. He was still working nights and I was working days, so we did not sleep with each other. One morning he came home and thanked me for leaving him. He said this was the best thing I could have done for him because now he is getting help. He joined AA and was seeing a counselor. A couple of days later he came home and told me he didn't understand how I could be doing this to him, with me saying I was a Christian and all. Then, again, he came home sicker than a dog and not able to stop crying. He was losing weight and looking awful. He was having nightmares when he did sleep.

Another day, when I came home from work, he was lying on the couch sleeping, and I noticed the caribou head that had caused hard feelings between us was gone. When he woke up, I asked him what he had done with it, and he told me not to worry about it. He said he was having nightmares about it, and he got rid of it. He also said he was selling all of his hunting stuff. He had purchased quite a few things because it was soon hunting season and was now going to practically give them away. It was not my place to say anything to him.

In just a few more days I would be moving out. My niece and nephew, as well as some of my daughter's friends, were going to help me. Phil was going to help also. This must have been the hardest thing he would ever have to do. He came and saw the house before I moved into it. It was an old house that was livable, but needed some work. He was very quiet when he was looking around. I wanted to hold him. I wanted to give him a hug. I wanted everything to be okay between the two of us. I wanted to be a family living in this house. But the damage had been done. There was no putting the pieces back together. Both of us had to get repaired before we could be whole again.

I came home from work to where we still lived and could not find Phil in or around the house. I saw a letter on the table in the kitchen and knew he had left it there for me to read. It was not a real suicide letter, where he actually said he was going to kill himself, but it was a letter indicating suicide. I walked to our closet, with a feeling of my stomach choking the rest of my body, to look at the guns and see if any were missing. I really didn't know how many guns he had, so I couldn't tell if they were all there or not. I walked down to the basement with my heart pounding so hard, not knowing what I was going to find. Phil was not there. I didn't want to go look in the shed in back of the house. I was afraid of what I would find. I looked out the window at the shed and, finally, after several minutes, crept outside to have a look. Phil was not there. I called the local help line to see what I should do. I don't remember what they told me. A few minutes later Phil walked into the house looking like a person that had a vacuum cleaner suck all the life out of him. He was a walking shell. I knew he was crying for help, but he was also playing mind games with me. I hated mind games.

◼ I want to beat the keys on this keyboard. I want this pain to stop. I don't want to think anymore. I want a warm blanket around me and a hot cup of tea in my hand. I want to stop feeling scared. I want to know I am going to be okay. Today, not even a hug is going to help. I have to fight this battle of being frightened that lives within me. I have to win. I have come this far, and I can't quit now. I will finish this story.

That night before I was to move out Phil asked me if we could "make love," or was it "have sex," "screw," or maybe even "f**k each other." I don't remember. I do remember, for the first time, I felt I had a choice. I said yes, and it was the best sex we ever had during our twenty-three years of marriage. It was not because I loved Phil, but because I knew I was going to be free starting the next day. Phil's anger was not going to tell me how to live my life. Phil's silent treatment was not going to control me. I knew I would rather live alone and be lonely than to live with someone and be lonely.

Moving day arrived and Phil and I had not fought over a single piece of furniture. There was nothing in the house that was worth fighting over, except for my mental health. Everyone showed up as planned, and Phil was there to help me move also. He was so devastated. I could see the pain in his face and hurt written all over his body. I had to move out. I had to go on. [Phil, I am so sorry that our marriage didn't work out.]

I spent the first night in the house alone. I was alone with no one to be angry with me for something I did not understand. I don't remember if Phil went to work that night or if Kati spent the night at the house with him. For the next few weeks I unpacked boxes, and Phil kept bringing more boxes of stuff over that he did not want. I had asked him not to throw things away but to please let me go through them first. He was doing that for me.

He stopped by my house at 5:00 or 6:00 a.m. and left the newspaper by my front door. He was just quiet enough to act like he didn't want to wake me, but just loud enough to wake me. He was hurting. I was hurting. Two injured people together only make one big mess and do not heal each other. I didn't want him stopping each morning. I didn't want him calling. I wanted Phil to get healthy and be happy with himself. When he could live by himself, and with himself, then maybe we would be able to work things out. Until that time I knew I had to be strong for both of us and not give in and let him take over my life again.

The week after I moved into my house, Luann, Bruce, Dan, Diane, and their two kids showed up at my door one Saturday to help get the yard into shape. They raked and pulled and carried all kinds of things out of the yard. I couldn't have done that without their help.

Phil drove by as they were in the yard working. I didn't see him drive by, but he told me about it later that night. I asked him why he didn't stop and talk to us, and he replied that he thought he was not welcome. Phil and I had plans for dinner that night, but because of my family helping me with the yard, I felt I needed to take them out to dinner. I met Phil at church and told him what had happened. Anger again. He wanted just the two of us to go out and eat. I tried to explain that I had not planned on them helping me that day, but I felt I needed to thank them for all the work they had done. I invited Phil to join us, but that was not part of his plans. Standing outside the church, Phil started yelling at me and causing a small scene. I told him it was his choice if he joined us or not for pizza. He said he was not going to join us and got in his truck to head to his house.

As I was driving away, I noticed he was following me. I figured he had changed his mind, and he had. When we arrived at the bar that served pizza in the neighboring town, Phil and I went in together. The rest of the family was there, and we all tried to act civil to each other. They were never mean to Phil. They respected him because they loved me. Bruce asked Phil questions about his work and other things, and Phil only gave one- or two-word answers. It was a very cold and tense dinner. I went home exhausted. I was tired of thinking what kind of effect every word that came out of my mouth would have on Phil. I was tired of being a peacekeeper. Phil later complained to me that no one talked to him that night. It was not true. It was Phil that would not talk to anyone.

I told Phil I paid for Kati's first semester of college, and he needed to pay for her second semester. He was making twice the money I was but he felt he could not afford to do this where he was living now. This was the first time Phil had to take care of paying things on his own. This was the first time Phil realized I did without a lot of things so he and the kids could have their fun. This was the first time Phil realized that money did not go very far. I had been too easy on him, but he told me that he makes the money and it was his to do with what he wanted. It was just up to me to make sure he got what he wanted, and I had to figure out a way to make it stretch. He didn't really have all the toys he wanted, but he did have most things in life that he pouted to get.

Thanksgiving was getting close. I didn't want Phil at my mom's, and I didn't want him alone either. I was hoping someone from where he worked would invite him out to their house. Phil agreed it would be wierd for him to be with my family, so he worked that morning and was home in the afternoon. My daughter and I went to my mom's for an awkward day.

Phil wanted Kati to take his truck, so Kati drove us to my mom's house and back. I did not feel comfortable driving anything that was Phil's. We left early and headed back to Phil's to spend the evening with him. He prepared us a meal we consumed with fake smiles. One holiday was over, and we all survived.

Phil wanted me to spend the night, but I would not. The three of us watched a few movies, and I laid on the coach next to Phil. I didn't want to, but I had not become strong enough to say no. I was still afraid of his anger. I still tried to keep peace for the sake of my children. Besides, he was hurting so badly, and I just wanted him to be okay. His hand went in my pants. The feeling of worthlessness crept in me again. Couldn't he understand that I wanted a friend first, and then we could maybe work on our marriage? That is all the further things went that night. I got into my little car and drove back to my old house where the four walls protected me from the outside, but could not protect me from my thoughts.

Phil began searching for help. He was looking for a counselor. He called several churches in the area looking for a pastor to talk to him. He said none of them returned his calls. He said he was feeling lower than dirt. Not even a pastor would talk to him. He found a co-worker that was ordained and he listened to Phil. This man also told Phil of a pastor who had a church in town and would listen to him. Phil called and talked me into going to counseling with him. We met the pastor and he held meetings with us once a week. He asked us the questions he would usually ask people before marriage. If the pastor asked me a question about Phil and I explained my feeling, Phil then took his turn and blamed every one of his actions on me. I felt everything Phil did was because of me. I walked out of the pastor's office feeling hopeless. I knew I was not to blame for everything Phil did. I knew in my heart that I was a good person. I knew I was not out to hurt Phil, but I had to hold up my shield against his words or they would pierce through my body. I was willing to try counseling. Deep down I think I wanted our marriage to work. I knew it would take years to heal the wounds, but we had to start someplace. The wounds were not healing, only growing deeper.

Phil had started seeing Gwen, a local counselor, on his own. He also started going to AA. He was having a difficult time admitting he was an alcoholic. He cried when he talked about it. He said he did not want to be one of them. He received his twenty-four-hour coin for not having a drink in twenty-four hours. He bought the books and started to work the program for the first time in his life. He was struggling. I don't remember hearing any apologies from him. Maybe I was still at fault in his mind.

Phil called and we talked. I was glad I had co-workers and a safe place to spend the weekdays. He called me at work. He called me at home. I always talked and tried to help him as much as I could. I always had to be the strong one, and this was no different. He was depressed and lonely. I thought I could be his friend and help him by giving him words of advice on how to get on with his life. Basically I just listened to what he had to say.

Phil had been coming over and feeling a little too comfortable in my home, where I had striven to stay save. He helped me fix the dryer vent. We had a cup of tea together. He stood by me with sad eyes and the pleading voice of a drowning man and asked if he could move in upstairs. "Hell NO," is what I wanted to shout. My mind raced. I thought now if he moves in, where will I go? This is my house. A panic engulfed my soul like a boa constrictor taking its large body and squeezing its victim. I could feel I was losing myself. I wanted to run, but where? This was supposed to be my safe place, my goal, no one was going to tag me "it" here. I didn't want to play anymore. I still wanted to scream "no, no, no, no, you cannot!" What I did tell Phil was that I could not have him move in. I knew it just would not work out. I explained this to him in a calm voice, like I would use to tell a two-year-old that he couldn't eat fifteen cookies because he would get sick. Phil looked crushed. He tried his best to manipulate me, and it did not work. I did not give in. I had to save me. He left. I cried. Life was not supposed to be so hard. I didn't want to have to be this strong. I didn't like turning my back on someone that was hurting. I was hurting too.

Phil called a couple of days later. There was anger in his voice. He and I had been going to church on Saturday nights, and I no longer felt comfortable going. We got into a discussion on this, and I couldn't, or wouldn't, give him the answer he was looking for about why I wasn't going to church with him any longer, or if I would ever go to church with him again. He told me he knew how he could fix the problem of me making up my mind and hung up. I once again thought this was his way of saying he was going to kill himself. He liked to play mind games with me and, after the last time, I was told by a counselor not to look for him, but to call the police to do a courtesy check instead.

That is just what I did. I called the police and told them what he had said and what I thought his state of mind was like. They went to his house and could not find him there. The police called me and told me he would not answer the door and his truck was not there either. I told them I felt he was out at the state park where we had lived for five weeks. They police drove the five miles to the park and looked for Phil's truck. I felt that if Phil was there he would be on the south side near a bridge, which was really on the outside of the park. They could not find him. I felt Phil knew just what he was doing. He knew I would come looking for him. I didn't, but I sent someone. I was done playing games.

Later that day Phil stopped by again. I knew I needed to tell him I had the police do a welfare check on him before he found out from someone else. While we stood facing each other, he took his hands and placed one on each side of my face, squeezing enough to hold me, but not to hurt, and said sternly, "Don't you ever call the police. I promise you I will not kill myself."

Phil had been living in the rented house by himself for one month. He didn't think he could make those rent payments, truck payments, and college payments with the money he was making, so he tried to find a less expensive apartment to move into. He stopped by and told me about all the awful places he was looking at and that he could not find something suitable to live in. I would not give in. I would not let him move in with me. I would not! The landlord Phil was renting the house from also had apartment buildings and, after some talking, he and Phil agreed Phil could move into one of his apartments and take care of the building for less rent.

Kati and I helped Phil move into his apartment the first of December. There were a few things Phil did not want to move up two flights of stairs, so we brought boxes to my house for storage and placed them either in my attic or in the shed out back. He no longer needed the new washer and dryer we purchased when we moved into the house; those went into my shed. He didn't want to hang most of our good pictures on his walls, so those went into my attic. The apartment had two bedrooms and one of those was to be Kati's. He wanted her to feel welcome in his apartment.

Phil's counselor Gwen had him doing jigsaw puzzles and keeping a journal. Phil also started writing a book for each of our children about his life. He was still going to AA and was losing a lot of weight. He ate TV dinners, soup, and fruit. Kati spent as much time with him as she could. She was trying to make life easier for her dad. She was trying to make him happy. Neither of our children ever told me or asked me to go back to their dad. They knew. They lived the life also. They loved their dad, but they knew how he could be. They knew how he treated me. They knew how he treated them. They saw. They felt. They were our children.

Phil's birthday and our anniversary both come and fall in the first two weeks of December. Kati and I took Phil out to Applebee's for his birthday dinner. Out in the parking lot, as we were leaving, I gave Phil a hug as I had several times before. He embraced me, and we went our separate ways. The only gift I wanted to give Phil, I was not capable of giving. I wanted him to like himself. I wanted him to be happy and be able to live with himself.

Christmas was fast approaching, and Phil and I went shopping together for the kids' presents. We each paid for half and then went over to his apartment to wrap the gifts and get some of them ready for shipping to Lueck in Oregon. It was our anniversary and Phil wanted me to spend the night, but I would not.

■ Something new has happened. I don't remember much from here. I am blank. I don't know if I have forgotten because too much happened in a short period or if it is because my counselor advised me to read my own story. When I asked her if she would recommend anyone read this book, she said, "Yes, you." Me? The thought of me reading this and realizing this is my life is scary. I wrote this one chapter at a time, handling each situation just as I did when it happened. To think that I have to read this whole story knowing this really happened to me puts a panic in me. I am so scared! I did not deserve to live this way. I am a nice person who is very caring. I work hard and try to do my best in life.

I think what really scares me is I don't know if I would do things differently if I had to marry Phil again. I know what I did was sick, but I haven't come to a place in my life where I have told myself I could have done it different. I think it is because I can't change the past and if I think about all the dumb things I did, I would hate myself for not protecting the kids and me.

I will take a deep breath and plunge ahead. I know my memories will come as I write. I have a majestic guardian angel that helps me as I relive each event. I can do this. I can.

Phil was still stopping at my house almost daily and leaving the newspaper at my door. He stopped on his way home from work after working all night. I didn't know how to discourage him without hurting him more than I had already. I was still afraid of his temper. I was still afraid of his hateful words. And worst of all, I was still a caretaker.

My work was going well. I enjoyed my co-workers and was building up my self-esteem. After we completed a special project at work, we all went out to the local bar for drink and food. The company picked up the tab, and I only had one drink. I saw Phil that evening and told him about this outing. I could instantly feel the anger expanding in him. He did not like it that I was in a bar when I would not go to a bar with him. Why would I go to a bar with him? He was an alcoholic, so why in the hell would I want to go to a bar with him and then go home and be abused? I was not against "a" drink, but with Phil "a" drink turned him into a nasty person.

Christmas meant that our schedules were not working out to keep meeting with the pastor who was counseling us. Phil was still seeing Gwen and asked me to see her with him. I went to a meeting in her office and there Phil laid into me once again. He only had anger in his voice. I believe he was hurting, but that is not what I heard.

Once again, I heard what I rotten person I was. I heard how I hurt Phil. How I never did anything right. How I didn't support him. How my kids did not like me. I heard the hatred in his voice. I saw the disappointment in his eyes. I curled up as much as I could while sitting on the couch next to Phil when he was telling Gwen all about me. I was feeling lower than a spit wad. I didn't fight back. I knew it wouldn't do any good anyway. I would only receive his anger twice as hard if I said anything. But what I couldn't figure out is, if he hated me so badly, why did he still want to be married to me? If he thought I was such an evil person, why was he fighting to get me back in his life? Why could he not just let me go? I walked out of her office feeling like I should not be living. But, at the same time, I was relieved someone else saw the side of Phil I had been living with for so many years. I was thinking maybe Gwen could help Phil. Maybe I wasn't crazy. At last, maybe someone else saw the side of Phil I was afraid of living with.

Christmas came and we survived. Kati and I went to my niece Cammie's home to spend the day with the rest of my family on Christmas Eve day. We spent the night there, and the next morning we went to Phil's apartment to spend the day with him. We watched movies and ate lots of food and opened gifts. Phil gave me his class ring. I'm not sure why he gave me his class ring. I said, "thank you," because once again I did not want to cause a scene in front of our daughter. I didn't want Phil getting mad. I don't remember what else I got, and I don't remember what I gave Phil except for a picture I had enlarged and placed in a special frame of our kids when they were little. It was hard to know what to get him to let him know I cared about him, but did not love him.

Phil wanted us to spend the night. I didn't want to leave Kati alone with Phil, having to deal with a depressed dad, so I spent the night also. If Kati had come home with me instead of staying with her dad, then she would have had to deal with the guilt of leaving her dad alone and depressed. I didn't want her to have to deal with that also. This was Christmas, and she deserved a happy day. I would do anything for my children. That is one reason I stayed married to their dad. I would do almost anything not to have a fight. I did sleep in the same bed with Phil. I can't explain why I did it except to keep peace and I didn't have the strength to see him so sad. I don't remember if we touched each other or not, but I do know we did not have sex. I am sure this gave Phil mixed messages. I didn't initiate going to bed with him or asking to spend the night. I was still the caretaker of my family.

Phil had his work Christmas party in the middle of January 2001, and he invited me to attend with him. After the meal we stayed for a very short time, then he wanted to leave. I had him drop me off at my home instead of going to his place. There was not any fighting or evil words exchanged that night. We both were becoming numb.

■ My body is itching just thinking about being in bed with Phil. My hands, my feet, and my head are feeling like they did when I was feeling trapped in the marriage.

I don't remember what we did New Year's Eve. I think Phil worked, but I am not sure.

Phil asked me to go back and start seeing the pastor with him again. I told him I was not getting anything out of it at this time and would prefer not to go back until we both got the help we needed as individual people. He did not like this idea, and he suggested I also start seeing Gwen on my own. I agreed. I could not afford to see her on my own at this time. I was still trying to figure out my living expenses. Phil was making more money than I. Gwen didn't accept insurance, and she charged about a third compared to most counselors. I did not like the idea of him paying anything for me. I did not want to owe him anything. I felt that any time he did something for me, he expected something in return, which he did if it was nothing more than being worshiped for being a wonderful person. Plus, it was easier to do what Phil wanted than to argue with him some more. I had to pick my battles and I didn't feel this was worth fighting about.

Phil dropped off a book for me to read. It was a book he had gotten through some church that stated how families should live and work together. Phil underlined many things in there I had done wrong in the marriage. He said there were things he did wrong, but made sure I saw what I had done wrong also. I think one of the things he made a comment about was supporting him as head of the household. I don't know how much more I could have done to support him. I had mixed emotions about reading this book. First of all, I did not read the whole book, but only looked at the remarks Phil had written. I felt I was being manipulated into going back with him. His comments also worked in reinforcing the doubts in my mind whether I was a good person or not. Maybe I really was that terrible person he said I was, and just maybe I deserved every wicked word I received from him. Maybe Phil was too good to me, and I was not giving enough in the marriage. Maybe?

I started reading a book my sister recommended. It was *Journey* by Danielle Steele. It was about a young lady who was being physically abused by her husband in a southern state. They were poor and were presented as white trash. A rich man from a northeastern state discovered this lady and rescued her. He ended up mentally abusing her, and I don't remember how it ended. I do remember this book made a huge impact in my decisions to say to Phil, no more touching, no more kissing, and no more stopping at my house in the morning. No more. I wrote him a letter explaining my feeling the best I could.

Near the end of January I started a journal. I was told by many people, including Gwen, writing in a journal would be a good way to heal my emotional wounds. My first entry in this journal was January 24. It read:

"It has now almost been three months since I left Phil. Tonight is a really hard night. "The Hymn of Promise," my favorite song, is what is keeping me going. Part of me (my heart) just wants to crawl in Phil's arms and let him know everything is okay and part of me (my head) says don't be a fool, it won't work, he'll just hurt you again and next time, Chris, you won't make it.

Oh, twenty-four years is a long time to live with someone and not miss or love some part of him. Oh, God, please hold Phil in your hands and let him know you love him. Let him know he is okay. Oh, I'm so sorry for everything, but I just can't go back. I just can't.

About five minutes ago I got a call saying I got a part in the play *Odd Couple* as Cecile. This should be fun. I can do it. Dad and my little girl, I love you! Sorry, God, if I'm not doing the right thing. I'm so sorry. I tried to love him, and I do, but not in the right way. God, please me love me, please!

I just want to run away, but wherever I go, there I am, right, Dad?

I need to go get some work done. I'll be okay. Chris"

It was the end of January, and I was closing on the purchase of my own house. I thought I needed to have Phil sign the papers giving up his right to homestead. I got the loan on my own without any of our money or Phil's income, including his retirement. Again, I did not want to owe Phil anything. This would just give him an excuse to control me. I was determined to do this on my own. I went to work early that morning so I could get a little extra time at lunch to sign the papers for the house. After arriving at work, I got a call from Phil. I was not at my desk when he called, so he left a message on my phone. He sounded awful, like he was dying. He said he was dizzy and could not see and thought he was having a heart attack. I asked my supervisor if I could take off and go and check on him.

When I arrived at his apartment he was lying on his bed with one shoe on and half dressed. He looked awful, but I had seen him this way before. I asked him if I should call 911, and he said I shouldn't and that he could make it down the two flights of stairs if I would drive him to the emergency room. As I helped him get dressed, I looked around his room. He always had everything neat. I noticed the shot gun that was resting in the set of deer antlers hanging on the wall near the foot his bed. The gun was open with two red shells sticking out of the back, ready for action. I did not say anything to Phil. What would I say? He had promised me would not kill himself. He would only make some rude comment back to me if I said anything. It gave me a strange feeling, but I had lost so many mind games that I did not want to play any more games.

The hospital ran all kinds of tests on Phil to make sure he was not having a heart attack. They could not find anything wrong except for maybe an inner ear infection. They sent him home after writing out a prescription. We stopped at Hy-Vee and got his medicine, and I took him back to his apartment. He did not want me to help him upstairs, but I did anyway. I left him to sleep, and I went back to work.

■ God, hold me. I am so sorry.

At work I let my one co-worker listen to the message Phil left that morning. She also stated how pitiful he sounded. I left work at lunch to pick up Phil so he could go with me to sign the papers. He said he would go, even though I told him he did not need to go. I picked him up because he was still pretty sick. He sat in the office as we went through the signing of my house mortgage. I knew in my heart this was why he was sick. The thought of me buying a house on my own was more than he could handle, but I had to do it. He didn't need to sign anything after all. I took him back to his apartment where, in a cold voice, he said, "Congratulations," and he shook my hand. This time he would not let me help him upstairs.

The next day I went and checked on Phil to make sure he was doing okay. He was lying on the couch when I entered his place. He basically told me to leave. Anytime I talked to him he seemed so depressed. I wanted him to be happy. I wanted a miracle. I wanted him to be glad to see me. Well, maybe not so glad to see, but I didn't want him to hate me. Why I cared, I don't know. Maybe I will figure it out years from now. But I was tired of acting happy when I saw him. I thought if I brought some smiles to him, maybe he would smile back. I was still trying to make him happy, but, looking back, maybe this made things worse. Maybe he thought I really was happy about the situation we were in. I was not. I was just as miserable as he was, only I didn't take time to think about my feelings. I was hurting, but was so used to trying to be the super woman that would try to take everyone else's pain away that I could not show my own pain.

My birthday was just around the corner, and Phil said he was going to go and see his parents because his mom called and said his dad was really sick and probably wouldn't be around much longer. [I heard this many times before.] He bought me a small tape recorder and gave it to me in case he was not back in time for my birthday. He flew out to see his family without saying good-bye to his daughter. This really upset Kati when she found out he left and did not even tell her he was going. She was also having some very personal problems besides her parents. She needed help, but didn't feel she could turn to us because we were not handling our own problems very well. That Saturday she called crying and telling me she had just tried to kill herself by slitting her wrists with a shaving razor. She left some marks on her wrists. It was not deep enough to get any medical attention, but she needed mental attention.

I did not have much energy left. I loved my daughter. She was crying for help. She was crying for attention. She came over to my house with a soccer friend of hers and explained to me what was going on. I felt she was not real serious or she would have found a different way of trying to kill her self. I was glad she didn't succeed. She had so much to give the world. I did not want to handle any more problems, though. I put on my blinders and said she was going to be okay. Her friend was going to stay with her that night in the dorm. I did not call Phil to let him know. I felt that was up to Kati to call him. I knew if I called him he would fly back here at that moment, and there was nothing he could do for her. He had enough of his own problems. He was coming back in a day or two anyway. The second night I stayed in the dorm with her. She was mad at me for not trusting her to be alone. I loved her too much to take any chances that she might try to kill herself again. I would do anything not to lose my daughter.

Phil flew back, and Kati talked to him. I do not know what his response was. I don't think he said much to her. She was still hurting. He was hurting. She had also starting drinking and shouting for help. Phil was still sick and was shouting for help. Phil was angry with me for not calling him and letting him know about Kati. I explained to him that if I thought she was going to try it again, or if she had seriously hurt herself, I would have called him.

While Phil was seeing his parents, he also went to see his high school friends Cory and Rachel and Cory's family. He didn't talk much about his trip. He said his dad was really sick and that he was glad that he had gone to see him.

On my forty-third birthday, Kati and I met with Phil where he worked for my birthday dinner. We talked and I could smell the booze on Phil's breath. Kati could smell it too, but we both knew not to say anything. We would be wrong in accusing him of something he would not do. We would be dumb to even think he would be drinking.

Two more days passed, and it was Valentine's Day. Phil called me at work and told me he loved me. I could not repeat those words back to him. I wanted to let him know I was thinking of him. I went to the local department store to look for a card for him. I found one that basically said I was thinking of him. It did not mention anything about love or being special. I went to his work and handed him the card and left.

The next day I got a call from him and, again, he was angry with me. He wondered how long it took me to find a card that said nothing or if I just ran in and bought the first card I found. I could not win. If I had given him nothing, I would have been evil, and if I had given him something about love, he wouldn't have believed it and accused me of playing games with him. I still did not love him, and I was not going to pretend that I did. I did care about him. I didn't like to see him suffer. I didn't like to see anyone suffer. I felt guilty about leaving him, and I wanted him to be okay so I could ease my own guilt. Twenty-four years of being blamed for most things that went wrong does not go away overnight. I believed I was responsible for Phil's problems. I shouldn't have felt guilty, because I didn't do anything on purpose to hurt him. I was only saving myself by leaving him.

It was Friday, two days after I gave Phil the card. He took Kati out to lunch that day and called and talked to his mom. Phil called and asked if we could go out that night. I suggested that maybe I could go over to his place and we could eat. He reminded me that I stated in my letter to him that I did not want to be alone with him. I was not going to argue with him and decided we would go to a local restaurant.

When he came to pick me up, I was on the phone with my niece. I had a good day at work and thought I could handle anything Phil would dish out that night. Before I got off the phone, my niece said she loved me. I replied back to her that I love her too. Phil heard this, and I thought I could feel the tension in him grow. I felt I knew Phil so well I could tell what he was thinking. I felt he was upset that I could tell everyone else I loved them but could not say those words to him. He was right and wrong. I did love him, but not as he wanted me to. I felt if I said those words of love to him, it would not help either of us. I was still afraid to say anything to him.

We went to the local restaurant where I tried to carry on a cheerful conversation with him. I told him about the movies I had seen that day at work about making the work place a fun place to work. I told him about moving the cheese, where people have to change their old ways in order to keep up with the world. I was hoping he was listening to me. Then he asked me if I was happier when he was with his parents. I told him I was not happier, but more relaxed. I knew his parents were taking care of him. I did not explain anything more to him because, at that time, he reached into his inside coat pocket to get something. My first thought was he had a gun and was going to shoot me. I was calm. I was ready for all this pain to stop. He pulled out his checkbook. That was my clue the meal and conversation was over. I quickly took a couple more spoons of my soup. I had lost my appetite anyway. I had all the life sucked out of me within ten minutes of being around Phil.

Phil had a couple of movies with him, and I asked if he wanted to come in and watch them. He made some comment on how I would not put up with him that long as we were getting out of his truck. I just shrugged my shoulders and did a little laugh, thinking that I cannot win with anything I say. It was a little laugh of "here we go again." Phil was angry. He accused me of laughing at him. He said I was enjoying playing mind games with him. I was not laughing at him, and I wasn't trying to play any kind of games with him. He came in my house while I looked for some pictures he wanted to use to finish the books he was writing for his children about his life. I found a few pictures of him and Lueck together and gave them to him. He went to his apartment and worked on the memory book for Lueck.

After he left I was so mentally exhausted. I was glad I did not have to go to work the next day. I sat down and wrote in my journal.

As he came in my house that night he yelled at me and asked me what he had to be happy about, I told him to choose something to be happy about. I told him I did not like being around him because he was always sad.

You know, I really wanted to love Phil. I really wanted to be happily married. Maybe this is why I pretended so long. He just has a way of taking all the air out of my balloons and then tearing the balloons apart. I feel sorry for Phil because it must be so terrible being mad all the time. I feel sorry for Kati. She tried to kill herself last Thursday. That is what happens when you live in a sick home.

I finished writing, then I went to bed. I could not think anymore. I cried. I felt so hopeless. I felt drained. I did not know how to stop everyone else's pain, including mine.

It was about 9:30 p.m., and I had almost cried myself to sleep when the phone rang. It was Phil. He wanted to talk. I was tired. I wanted to sleep. He was mad. He told me what a rotten mom I was, how our kids hated me. He told me what a rotten wife I was. He asked me if I was going to divorce him or not. I told him no. I was not ready to divorce him. I still was hoping that down the road we could work things out. I knew he was not mentally ready for me to make anything final. I was not ready to make anything final. Again he told me I had to make up my mind about our marriage. Something told me not to let him get to me and say something I would regret. He said he had to know. I asked him what he was going to do. He replied he was tired of people asking him that question. I was getting angry with him. I was tired, and I just wanted to go to sleep. We were not getting anywhere in the conversation, and I just wanted it to end. I was not hearing anything he said. My ears were going numb, just like after being in a loud concert and sitting in front of the booming speakers. Again he told me I needed to make up my mind about our marriage. Again I told him I was not ready to get a divorce. I calmed down, and I told him I had enough of this conversation and was going back to bed. I had nothing left in me. I was an empty shell. I said good night and started to hang up the phone when I heard the noise of a gun going off, or a door slamming. I was still. He wouldn't have. He couldn't have. He did.

CHAPTER 12

ONWARD

Luann and Bruce left their house as soon as Dan called them and told them about Phil. They arrived at my house ninety minutes, and eighty miles, after Dan called them. Dan and his dad, Bruce, went to Kati's dorm to see if they could find her. She has just arrived there and was drunk. They brought her to my house where I proceeded to tell her dad just died. She collapsed on to the floor in a pile of sobs. I held her and both of us cried. Family tried to comfort us, but this was our own hell we had to face.

Now what? I just wanted to sleep. I just wanted this nightmare to stop. He shot himself while I was on the phone with him. I stayed with him, putting up with hell so the kids would have a dad—for nothing. He only thought about himself. It was so like him. He didn't think of anyone but himself. His children will need his love, and his grandchildren will need a hug. All he thought about was how he could get even with me for me leaving him. He wanted me to suffer for the rest of my life. I knew if I told him I was going to divorce him while on the phone that night, he would have pulled the trigger then. His action was evil. I felt he hated it when I was happy. He liked to control me. He didn't want me to go back to college when I did. He didn't like me to succeed in the career I had. He didn't like that he was losing his control over me. He couldn't even control himself. He couldn't stop drinking. He couldn't control his temper. I was now determined, more than ever, to get control over my own life. His actions were not going to make me feel like a worthless person ever again. It would take a while, but I was going to be a whole person with a real smile.

In the mist of tragedy an angel looked over us. If I had not heard the shot, then Kati or I would have found Phil the next day. If Kati found her dad, I am afraid I would not have a daughter today. She was at a party in the apartment across the parking lot from where Phil lived. She heard the sirens. I'm sure she saw the police cars at her dad's apartment when she left the party, which was close to two hours after Phil shot himself. But, she never went there to see what was going on.

That night, after Luann arrived at my house and Kati sobered up some, we sat around the dining room table talking about what we had to do next. Kati asked if we could still go to her soccer banquet the next day. I couldn't think of any reason why we couldn't. Life was going to go on and if Kati wanted me to go, I would go with her. I don't know how many of her teammates knew what had happen. We were so used to putting on our smiling mask that one more day of looking like everything was okay was no big deal to us.

Lueck and Kyle came the next day. They flew into Minneapolis, from Portland, Oregon, and my niece and family picked them up and drove them to my house. Lueck had not shed a tear. He was angry with his dad. All my family were now with me in Marshall except for Linda and her husband, Doug, who were living in Africa. Most of my nieces and nephews were staying at Dan's house, a few blocks away. The funeral was going to be held in two days.

I called Phil's folks to let them know what day the funeral was going to be and to see if they could make it there that day. If the day of the funeral was too soon for his parents to get here, I would change the date. Neither of Phil's parents worked, so I thought they would come for their son's funeral. I was not prepared for the cold question they shot at me when I told them about the date. Donna wanted to know what I had done to Phil. What *I* had done? What about what Phil had done to me, is what I was thinking. But I was not going to argue with her. Her words hurt very badly. I had not done a thing to Phil, but protect myself. Anyway, they were not coming. I said I would pay for them to come if it was the money they were worried about. No, they were not coming. Donna wanted no part of me. I understood through the short answers and the cold voice that pierced my heart that she thought I was at fault for Phil pulling the trigger.

I called Phil's good friends Cory and Rachel in California, the ones he had just seen a week earlier, to let them know about Phil. Donna had already called them, and I was not ready for their response either. The first thing they asked me was, "What did you do?" They weren't coming either. No one from Phil's side of the family came for his funeral—no one. They blamed me for not caring about Phil. If they hated me so badly, they still could have come for our children. I received one card from a cousin of Phil's that we had not seen in years. Donna had twelve brothers and sisters, and Jim had at least two sisters still living, plus all the cousins, and only one person sent a card. Donna had control over the entire family and if Donna didn't like someone, no one else better like them either.

After talking to Donna and Cory, I wondered what Phil told them about me when he was there the week before. Couldn't they see he had gone there to say good-bye to them? He knew what he was doing. Phil had this planned. This was not a whim. Phil shot himself with his grandpa Ross' gun on the anniversary of his grandpa's death.

We had Phil's body cremated, but before it was, Lueck wanted to see his dad. A pillowcase with some stuffing was placed over Phil's face. The undertaker dressed Phil is some clothes he had around his office and laid Phil on a table for Lueck to say his good-byes. Kati did not want to see her dad this way. Phil had lost a lot of weight since the last time Lueck saw him. I don't remember if Lueck cried, but I don't think so. He touched his dad's arm with the eagle tattoo. This was about the only way Lueck knew it was his dad, because of the pillowcase over his head and all the weight Phil lost in the previous seven months since Lueck had seen him.

The next day was the funeral. For only living in Marshall seven months, there were a lot of people there for us. My co-workers were there from US Bank, Kati's soccer team, Phil's co-workers from Hy-Vee, and friends and family. Before the service started, my children and I were looking at all the flowers that were sent. Cory and Rachel sent flowers, but made sure they were addressed to Lueck and Kati only. When I read the card, I was hurt and angry at the same time. Tears of confusion flooded my face. Lueck saw my reaction and gave me a huge hug. How could they be so spiteful at a time like this? The funeral was very simple. The three of us were in one of the front rows and just let our tears flow. Lueck was crying for the first time. They were tears of relief that we would no longer be abused, tears of sorrow that we will miss the side of Phil that was kind, and tears of anger for all the pain we were feeling. I was so thankful for family and friends who had helped comfort us.

After the service, the Veterans of Foreign War did the twenty-one gun salute. If this had not been such a serious event, it would have been funny. These old men were doing their best, but one dropped all his shells while trying to load his gun. They couldn't figure out where to stand and kept switching places and the "Taps" played on a tape recorder. If I had known they didn't have a real bugle player, I would have found one. After the twenty-one gun salute, they handed us the empty shells. Think about this. This funeral was for a man who had just blown his head off, and the VFW just handed us empty shells.

That day, when we arrived home from the funeral, there was a message on my answering machine from Cory and Rachel. They wanted their shirts back that Phil had brought to me to embroider. They said they would pay for the shipping if I could only send them back. My sisters thought I should embroider "a--hole" on the shirts and send the shirts back to them. I thought about it, but that would only give them a reason to hate me. I didn't do anything to them. Why were they judging me? When they came to visit us in Alaska, less than a year before, they couldn't wait to leave our house because of bad words they and Phil had. They even booked an earlier flight than planned. If they would have only known the lies Phil told me about them.

I told the story many times those first few days after Phil killed himself, of how Phil called his mom the day he shot himself, how he took Kati out to lunch, and me out to dinner. Lueck was there when I told the story. He was really hurting. His dad had not tried to get a hold of him to say good-bye. But Phil really had said good-bye to Lueck by finishing his memory book for him the night he shot himself. Lueck wanted more. He wanted to hear his dad's words that told him he loved him.

We had to clean out Phil's apartment. I didn't want to go over there. The owners of the apartment wouldn't let us go in until they had the mess cleaned up. Luann, Lueck, and I went over the apartment to see if we could find any clues to Phil's thinking. We could see in the living room where they patched the two quarter-size holes in the wall. The carpet was cleaned or replaced, and they had thrown away the couch and a lamp. We could see where they tried to clean the ceiling. It was an eerie feeling walking into his place.

In Phil's apartment, Lueck searched for something, anything, that maybe his dad left him. He said he was searching to make sure Phil didn't leave anything that could hurt his sister, but both Luann and I knew Lueck was searching for something for himself. Lueck took apart pictures and frames, looked in holes in the walls where the electrical wires had been, searched drawers and inside books. Anger and hurt was taking a toll on Lueck's body. Just like any child, all he wanted was his parents to love him. He did not feel his dad's love. Phil loved him the best he could. I don't think Phil knew how to love a son. Phil thought he was never good enough for his parents, so how could his son be good enough for him?

Lueck never did find any answers that day in his dad's apartment. He is going to have to find them in his own heart. We did find a suicide letter Phil had written on January 21, almost four weeks before he shot himself. It was in an envelope, in a drawer, addressed to me. The return address said "nobody." I didn't read it. I had Luann read it to see if there was anything I needed to know. I knew Phil was good at lying and turning the truth around to his benefit. I couldn't handle any more mind games. Luann said I would be better off not reading it at this time, if ever.

We continued looking around Phil's place, and I could tell by the pillowcase on his bed that there had been something square and heavy that had been on the pillow. I would guess it was the box of shells. Phil had written in his address book, on the date I had gone with my co-workers to the bar for a celebration drink, "Gambler, Chris's bar." I had been there for one drink, one time, and it had become my bar in Phil's mine.

Dan and Bruce helped clean out Phil's apartment. I didn't want to go back over there. It was not a good feeling to be in there. I could feel the depression hanging on the walls, in the carpet, and on the ceiling.

A couple of days after the funeral, my good friends Jody and her daughter Jessica flew in from Maine to be with us. Lueck and Kyle had to head back to Oregon a couple of days after Jody arrived, so I got them a ticket for the train. It was great having friends here. Jessica was good for Kati with her zest for life. They knew Phil very well because we spent a great deal of time with them in Maine. Jody and Phil had searched for pinecones at the edge of the dark woods to use for wreaths to sell for the church choir. Jody was good at making Phil laugh. Jody also understood what it was like to be afraid of someone and to love them at the same time. She had a brother who was a lot like Phil, where he was crazy one minute and your best friend the next.

After a week, Jody and Jessica left for Maine. I went back to work at US Bank. At work, I sat at my desk and let the silent tears wash my face. They were tears of sorrow for something I so much wanted. I wanted a good marriage, a caring husband, and a family my children could be proud of. I cried for the pain Phil must have felt. I cried for my children who had to battle this in their own way. I cried because I no longer had to worry about phone calls from Phil and wondering what he was going to say or do next. When my co-worker looked over at me, I wiped my tears and placed the smile back on my face.

Kati confessed to me that she planned on killing herself that Saturday after her dad killed himself. That was before he died. She planned on taking that same gun he used and going to Camden State Park and shooting herself, but once her dad was dead she no longer wanted to kill herself. She felt he saved her life. She saw how final death was. She no longer had to try to make him happy. I found a note she had given to him a few days before he shot himself. The outside of the note said "#1 Dad."

Dad,

I just want you to know how PROUD of you I am. I am really noticing a difference in you. You are becoming a positive person, and that is how you need to look at life. I know I am only eighteen, but I have learned a lot about life in those eighteen years. Life is tough; you need to wake up saying, "I am going to make it though this day."

Take a negative situation and turn it positive. Don't put your head down, Dad! Keep your chin up high. Keep up the intensity you have. And, Dad, don't forget I am always here for you, also, the Lord is a good person to talk to. I know he listens. I love you, Dad, and I am extremely proud of you for going to AA and counseling. Keep it up.

Love Always, Katherine Lee"

Things were getting back to a routine. I made it though the winter by going though boxes of stuff and painting the inside of my house. It was nearly the end of summer, and I was learning to live alone. Kati had moved into a small house by herself just a few blocks from me. Phil's mom had only called or written a couple of times during those six months. She never asked if I needed anything or how I was doing. She wanted Phil's ashes and the suicide letter. I can't remember how she found out about the letter. I think one of my children told her. They hadn't read the letter either. It was in my dresser drawer just in case I wanted to read it, but I didn't want to read it. I knew he would try to make me feel guilty for what he chose to do.

The day I got the letter from Donna requesting a copy of Phil's suicide letter really upset me. Why would I send her a letter I hadn't even read myself? I walked into my bedroom and pulled out the letter from my dresser drawer and read the letter for the first time. I was so angry with both Phil and his mom. I was angry with Phil for playing mind games with me and for Donna for asking for something that wasn't hers. If Phil wanted her to see the letter he would have sent her a copy. If I sent her a copy it would just give her more fuel to hate me. I don't think she could hate me anymore then she already did, but then again, maybe she could.

On the top of the letter it says...

Nobody 01-21-01 and Sorry, Mom.

Chris, I cannot do this anymore, so I am taking the coward's way out. If you never acknowledge this, you will be set for life as well as our children.

I am sorry for being the terrible person you have made me in your mind. I am sorry I talked you into marrying me. You are right in everything you think about me. I'm an abusive, perverted alcoholic, who could not support you or our kids, who did nothing right by you or Lueck or Kati; you are and always were right, and I was always wrong.

I cannot stand that you hate me when I am so in love with you. Sorry that you cannot understand that I love making love to you. That is who I am.

I wish you had been stronger. I wish I didn't lie or drink. I especially wish you had not lied to me the last couple of weeks allowing me to touch and kiss and you reacting so lovingly and kind and gentle. When you laid in bed with me and we enjoyed each other and you laid your head next to mine and instructed me what to do, it was precious. You told me on the phone today you wouldn't do those things with a friend—yet you just want to be my friend—yet we are married—yet you said you did not enjoy it—yet you instructed me and came with pleasure—yet you didn't want to be doing it and were again lying next to me and hiding your true feelings—yet you talked to Gwen and hate the things I did or you believe I did—yet now, you think you might be mad and even hate me.

I am sorry I let you know any of this confuses or bothers me. I am sorry I forgot it is all about you—well, honey, now it is.

I hope you get everything you want in life—and since you weren't making love to me as you say for the last twenty-four years—what were you doing to me?

Remember this was my choice and had nothing to do with you—enjoy your new life, and I hope you can love the next guy you just want to be friends with for twenty-four years.

> Love always,
> Your long lost love,
> Phil
>
> To be a Christian is to forgive and move on.
> Something you taught me—so I am moving on so you can."

I read the letter that day, and I was right about playing mind games. I could hear his voice in the letter that killed my spirit so many times. After reading the letter I went for a "power" walk. I took off walking like I had to get somewhere before I died. I walked fast and hard. I walked with all the energy I had. I walked into a new sub-division not far from where Kati lived. There I saw fresh mud. This urge to be a kid again and the anger I was feeling led me into the mud. I took off my shoes and let the mud gosh through my toes. The mud coated my feet like shoes. I loved the feeling. I didn't care who was watching me or what they were thinking. I was doing something I wanted, just because I could. It felt so good. I had the power to do something I wanted, and no one was going to tell me how dumb I was again. I let the cool mud soothe my pain. As I walked over to Kati's house with my shoes in my hand and my feet so covered in mud that I couldn't see them, a young girl rode up to me on her bike and asked me why by feet were covered in mud. I replied to her "because I can." She couldn't believe an old lady like me was having fun with mud. As I knocked on Kati's door, I felt younger and lighter. I hoped she had a hose, so I could wash my feet, and I walk the rest of the way home with my shoes on. We both had a good laugh. We were both healing, one giggle at a time.

I didn't know what to do with Phil's ashes. I had a marker placed in Lafayette's cemetery for Phil. I debated if I should have the marker in the military cemetery in St. Paul, Minnesota, or in Fresno, California, near his parents, or in the cemetery in my hometown. I didn't want the marker in my family plot, so I had it placed near our plot. I didn't know if I would ever want to be buried next to Phil or not, but the options are there if I choose or if my children choose to. I know I didn't want his ashes in my house. My mom had strong feelings that I should bury the ashes at the marker and my children didn't really care. I gave a lot of thought to why I wanted to keep the ashes. I came to the conclusion that it was only a power trip I had over Donna. The ashes were still at the funeral home, and I talked with the director of the home and he arranged to have the ashes mailed to Donna. What I found so ironic was that they didn't, and I didn't, want Phil when he was alive, but we both wanted his ashes. I didn't really want his ashes; I just didn't want Donna to have them. I never did send her a copy of the suicide letter. I suppose she will have to buy this book in order to read the letter.

EPILOGUE

A few months after Phil died, I walked by an office full of people at work. There was a man in there who looked like Phil. An instant panic came over me. I was instantly afraid. I had forgotten that feeling. The other incident that caused me to panic was whenever I saw a black pickup truck like the one Phil bought. The anger Phil had towards the kids and me was not easy to shake. I talked to a friend about this and all he did was listen. All I needed was to talk about it, and the next day, when I saw a black pickup truck, I wanted to give the driver "the finger." I was not going to let Phil hurt me any longer, dead or alive. I was going to be strong and happy. I deserved to be happy. I was going to be happy if it killed me.

Each day that passed held fewer and fewer tears of anger and grief. I felt confused. I didn't want to live with Phil, but I didn't want him dead either. I grieved the marriage I wanted and never had and wasn't ever going to be able to have now. On the other hand, I was much more relaxed knowing that Phil would not be at my door at 6:00 a.m. anymore; that he would not be calling, crying that he can't live without me; that I didn't have to hear any more lies. Before long I went a whole day without crying. I began healing from twenty-four years of abuse. I continued to go to counseling, and just last week went to my last session with Gwen, after four years of counseling. She helped me deal with guilt by having me examine what I really wanted. I didn't want Phil to die. I just wanted the pain to stop. I feel the main lessons I learned were I am not a wonder woman, I don't have any special powers to make anyone happy, and I am not an angel. I also learned I can't control how people feel, I can't make anyone change, and I am only an ordinary person. The only person I can control, change, or make happy is me. That doesn't mean I have to hurt people to get what I want, but I also don't have be hurt to give people what they want.

One of the best things I did for myself was go to a divorced and widowed group called Beginning Experiences. There I learned to care again. I learned I was not alone in my pain. I learned to receive and give hugs. I learned I was an okay person. I started to grow a circle of friends. I was very determined to be the best person I could be. I was not going to let Phil control the rest of my life. I was going to be in control of me once and for all. I reached out to friends and let myself make mistakes and learn from them. I depended on friends when I was down. I called family when I had bad, or good, thoughts to share. Everyone listened, and I continued to learn I was an okay person.

One of the things I did in Beginning Experiences was attend a weekend retreat. There I had to write a good-bye letter to Phil.

February 3, 2002

Dear Phil,

I have my water bottle and my tissues next to me as I write you this letter to replenish my tears as I wipe them from my cheeks.

Philip Mark Harris, first of all I'm sorry I was not stronger for you. I'm sorry I could not save you from the treacherous waters, the burning building, or the cliff's edge you were hanging on to.

I was going down with you, and if I entered the water, I would have drowned, and if I came in to save you from the fire, I would have been lost because of the smoke. Your hand was slipping from mine as I heard you scream going over the cliff. All the tools were there, Phil, to save yourself, but you wanted me to do it for you, and I couldn't without giving up my own life. The life jacket was there, Phil; you just had to go the to AA meetings. The fire alarm was next to your hand when the fire started; you just needed to see a counselor and tell her you need help. Pull that alarm, Phil. Really, Phil, that cliff was not as tall as you thought. You could have landed safely, but you convinced yourself it was too high to survive. Philip, you could have made it though this life if you would have seen life for what it was.

You exaggerated most things. When you told me something, I could usually divide it in half or double it and come closer to the truth. I'm not sure why you thought you always had to lie. How could I love you when I never got to know you?

You know, Phil, I think we both wanted the same thing in life and that was to have a good family life. We just came from two totally different worlds that we crashed trying to land on the same target.

For some things I did, I'm truly sorry. The thing I'm most sorry for is the kids and I were not there when you returned from war. Please forgive me. You must have been so lonely. I'm sorry! I'm sorry that I didn't stand up to you. You were so good at putting me down and changing the blame when I asked you to not do something. I was afraid of you. Even when it seemed we were having a good time, I never knew for sure when the kids or I would do something to make you mad. That look of yours that said "I hate you" hurt so badly. The head shaking, when I said or did something you didn't like, told me I was worthless. Not speaking for days was driving me crazy. I tried to act like it didn't bother me for the kids' sakes, but it wore me down. When I asked you why you were mad, you just answered, "you should know, figure it out." I really didn't know what I had said or did. I couldn't read your mind. I was spending so much time trying to figure out what you were thinking and feeling that I forgot about me. You were telling me when I could be mad, when I was sorry or not, and that I couldn't disagree with you at all. I was feeling like a doll under a glass case. I could be looked at, dusted, but I had to look pretty and say the right things when you pulled my string. Your drinking hurt. Your lies were awful. You were so scared you were going to lose me that you nearly killed me. I felt you were a small child, scared of the world, when a small tender bunny came into your life. You were so glad to have something warm and soft in your life that did not hurt you, but loved you, that you held that bunny so tight trying to love it that it almost died. The bunny bit you, trying to get free, and you couldn't understand that you needed to learn to hold gently so the bunny could grow and live. You thought if that sweet bunny doesn't love me, then no one will love me. That was not true. You need to love yourself first so others could love you. You needed to hold gently.

I get angry when I think of what we could have been. You did your best, and I did my best, and someday, when we meet again, I hope we can laugh and hug together. Damn it, Phil, you took our kids' dad away from them. You better be watching over them. You better help me make sure they're okay.

You won't be here to hold your grandchild. Damn you, Phil! In Beginning Experience, I hear other people's stories, and they were no worse off than you. If you weren't so angry with me, you could have gotten help. I'm bound and determined to be happy. You really wanted me to suffer the rest of my life by blowing your head off when you thought you could get me to say I would divorce you. What you didn't understand was that I cared about you. I hoped so badly you could find inner peace. I hope you have found it now. I pray God is holding you tight, giving you all that love you so desperately needed. I pray for your parents that someday they can get rid of their anger towards me. They don't ever have to like me, but the anger is not healthy.

Okay, Phil, I'm going to close the door now. I'm not going to slam it, but close it gently to show you that once and for all, I cared. Please don't enter my dreams anymore unless you feel I need to understand something. Give my dad and our daughter a hug from me. Give yourself a hug too. I forgive you for all the pain you have caused me. I will be happy. I've learned a lot because of you. I will take those lessons and help others. A kiss on the forehead and a twinkle in my eyes, be at peace Phil. We will be okay.

Love,
Chris

I would describe emotional or verbal abuse like a bed sore. A bed sore starts from the inside and works out. By the time anyone sees the infected sore, it is too late. That is the same with verbal abuse. Words are not stuck to someone's face nor leave black-and-blue marks on the body. The words eat away at the inside, and soon the body and the soul become infected with pus, and the person withers away.

In the suicide letter, Phil states we would be set for life if I never acknowledged the letter. I am not sure what he was talking about. We had three life insurance policies. One was in my name only, one was in both the children's and my name, and one was in the children's names only. We each got less than sixty-five thousand. That does not buy a house and barely pays a four-year college degree. He shot himself, and he thought people wouldn't know he committed suicide? The house in Missouri, that I didn't care if I got or not, was now mine. I sold it and put the money away. I didn't get his military retirement, but I am now entitled to other funds. I work full time and love having a career. In 2005, I earned a master degree in business administration. I am not dumb after all.

As I write this, four and a half years after Phil's death, I am feeling so much lighter. I don't have someone mad at me all the time. I don't have to worry about what I say. I now laugh from the stomach, and the glow in my eyes is real. My only real concern is for my children. Because their dad left them insurance money, they have not yet learned what their talents really are. They are still hurting from years of physical and mental abuse, but think they can handle this on their own. I would say they are surviving, but not living. Lueck received more verbal abuse than Kati. I am not sure if her dad or any of the relatives ever sexually assaulted Kati. I don't think she knows. I want to take my kids' pain away, but I can't. They have to work through this, just as I have to work through this. They are going to be okay too. They are both very strong people.

Lueck became a dad to a cute little guy in February 2004. Lueck was looking for love and acceptance in the wrong places. I think he could make a good dad. His biggest problems are he does not trust anyone with his real feelings and thinks he can solve all his problems on his own.

Lueck is working on his life journey, and I know God has very special plans for him. He has a very large giving heart, which sometimes gets him in trouble.

Kati has struggled through college, but she did not quit. She is going to be a caring teacher and will protect all kids from abuse any way she can. I feel Kati does now want to love another man because she didn't always love her dad, and now she feels she is a lesbian. I believe she feels guilty when she thinks she loves another male because her dad was a very jealous man. I will always love my daughter even though I don't understand her desire to be with women. We have become the best of friends over the last few years.

By the way, Phil's dad is still living, or should I say, still dying, as I write this. He is on oxygen because of his failing lungs. He is living at home, and Donna is still taking care of him. My children don't have much to do with them. Kati used to call her Grandma on a regular basis, but Donna made her depressed by talking about Phil and how sad he was and how sad they were. She has decided on her own not to call and talk to them except for maybe every other month. I am sure Donna is blaming me for Kati not calling them anymore, but I didn't have a thing to do with Kati's decision. Lueck is not angry with them. He just doesn't call and talk to anyone too often.

One of the things I have done for me was get a small tattoo of a balloon on my upper chest, to remind me no one is going to ever hold me down from being me and fulfilling my life with my thoughts and dreams. I hope someday I will meet a special person who will want to sail the skies with me, instead of holding me back. My balloon is once again on the rise.

Since Phil's death, my experiences of dating have been a learning process. I thought I was ready for dating six months after Phil died, but God knew better than I did. It was at least one year after Phil's death that I had a relationship with a man who looked a lot like Phil. This relationship lasted nearly six months, until I saw the jealousy he had when I talked to other people.

Another one of the few men I have dated had some of Phil's personality. No matter what happened to this male, he was usually the victim. He could not see what his actions and words were doing to others. He could only see what others were doing to him. We dated for over a year when I noticed I was losing my self-esteem by the comments he made to me. I was becoming very scared I was going to lose all my own thoughts and emotions again. I even started to even think about the flowers I planted in my own garden and wondered if he was going to like them or not, instead of whether I liked them or not. It was remarks like, "Why are you planting those weeds?" that I heard that caused me to start second-guessing my own thoughts and feelings again. Perhaps, most people wouldn't let those words bother them, but I was still not strong enough to let words of unnecessary criticism bounce off of me without them leaving some sort of dent.

I am not sure who the men will be, if any, that I might have relationships with in the future. I need to accept living alone and being okay with who I am before I can move forward. I do hope I learn and grow with each person that comes into my life. I know both of these men have played an important part in my healing. They both helped me learn to trust myself a little more. They were both placed in my life when I needed someone to help me get though some tough times. God knows what he was doing, and I have to trust him to see the bigger picture. I have learned that I don't need a male in my life to feel good about myself. If a man is going to be that special person, he will be in my life because I want him to be there, not because I need him to be there.

I now have a list of qualities I am looking for in a man before I will get involved. He must have faith in God, be honest, know how to listen as well as to talk to me, be kind to everyone, do things on the spur of the moment, laugh, know how to give as well as how to take. He must also love my children, love his children, support my dreams, and be very patient. He can't be an alcoholic, smoke, tell me how to think or feel, nor ever say a hateful word to me. We don't have to agree on everything, because that would be boring, but he must know how to disagree respectfully. The frosting on the cake would be that he knows how to dance and that he is taller than me. It would nice if he has some meat on his bones, has a kind voice, and can support himself financially and still have enough money left over to take me out to some place fancy once in awhile.

I know I can't go back and change anything. If I could, I would have left Phil the night I tried to talk him out of getting married, except then I wouldn't have my children. I feel that whenever I would have left Phil, he would have tried to kill himself. I think about what would have caused less damage to the kids—if I had left Phil when they were younger, he might have tried to kill our children when he had them with him. I don't know. I only know what I did, and I did the best I could at the time. If someone was in this same situation and they asked me for advice, I would tell them to get out of the marriage. It is not worth hurting yourself and hurting your children. You are also not helping your spouse by letting them control you.

I am now healing. When I first started this book three years ago, I wanted to title it *I Understand*, Meaning that I understood why people stayed in abusive relationships. After reading my story again, and stepping back and seeing what really happened in my crazy life, I am titling this book, *What the Hell was I Thinking?* If you see yourself in this book, please be safe and get help if you need it.